Broke'n'English:
Learning to live in Sri Lanka

Jerry Smith

"I feel as if I were playing the buffoon in a vast comic opera."
Leonard Woolf, District Commissioner in Ceylon and later husband of Virginia

2

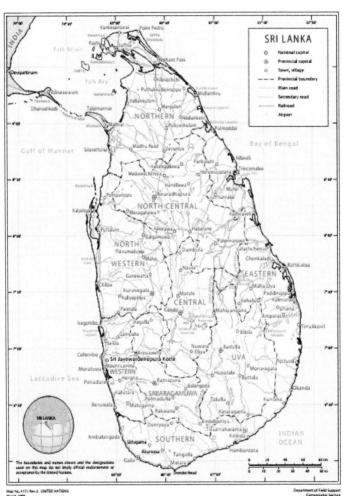

One

Home

On a June morning in 1971 a thirteen year old girl stood with her parents at the end of the long pier stretching out an accusing finger from Talaimannar towards India. Behind them were a Mini Moke and an Austin 1300, both stuffed with possessions and essential supplies for the journey that lay ahead. In front the old twin-deck ferry across the Palk Strait to India was preparing for boarding. The Martin family were about to leave Ceylon for the last time, after almost a century.

Five months later, after an epic journey through India, the Khyber Pass, Afghanistan, Iran, Turkey, Greece, Yugoslavia and the Alps they made it home to England. "Home?" said Sally to her parents. "It might be your home. It's certainly not mine! Grey buildings, grey people, grey skies. This isn't home".

For twenty seven years Sally had never been back to the land of her birth, the place she still thought of as home. Lack of money, and lack of interest on the part of her previous partner. At the end of 1997 I surprised her on her fortieth birthday with three return air tickets to Colombo for the following February. One for her, one for me and one for our eight-year-old daughter Jemima; the older kids had by then left home. In February we set off to Manchester airport for the Emirates flight to Colombo via Dubai.

Ding Dong.

"There will be a slight delay in boarding due to a minor technical problem. Further information in 15 minutes." ...

"Further information at 1.30." ...
"Further information at 2 o'clock." ...
"Would passengers booked on Emirates Flight 036 to Dubai please make their way to the departure lounge where they will be served with light refreshments and drinks. Further information at 6 o'clock."

They plied us with burgers and Coke, and we settled down for a long wait: "Would passengers Martin, Smith (and various others) please report immediately to the British Airways desk." Grabbing hand luggage and duty frees, scooping up the burgers and drinks, to discover that we and fifteen others had been booked onto an internal BA flight to Heathrow and onwards to Colombo with Sri Lankan Airlines. The Emirates plane had irretrievably broken down. But we were all booked on one ticket, a big happy family of eighteen strangers, which meant we had to stay together. Anyone getting separated from the group wouldn't be leaving Manchester Airport any time soon. There followed a guided trek through the byways of the airport with frequent stops for head-counts, then a plane to Heathrow where another shepherdess ("*Please* try to stick together, no loitering") guided us through their undercroft to Terminal 4 and the night flight to Colombo.

The blast of heat on leaving the plane and walking across the tarmac to what was then a tiny terminal building was anticipated but still somehow came as a shock, as did the surprisingly small scale of the airport. Inside the terminal Sally turned to me and said: "You know, I had to resist an almost uncontrollable urge to kneel down and kiss the tarmac when we got out of that plane, the way the Pope does."
"Good thing you didn't. It would have been mortally embarrassing."

Sally was back in the land she has always called home, although when she lived there it called itself Ceylon. I'd made an uncertain landfall in the country that was to become my home too.

A Ceylon childhood

Sally's links with Ceylon had begun when her great grandfather, Henry Thomas Martin, moved there in the 1880s to become a tea planter on Luccombe Estate, in the heart of the hill country near Maskeliya. He died young, at the age of thirty seven, as did so many of the early white settlers, but his eldest son Edward Harry decided after a conventional English public school education, to follow his father's footsteps and return to the country of his birth. Not as a planter, though, but as a civil engineer designing roads for the Public Works Board. His son, Sally's father Tony, returned to the planter life, to which he brought his young wife Pamela in 1946. Pamela produced five sons which impressed the locals enormously but left her yearning for a daughter and eventually Sally obliged, being born at the end of 1957. The staff commiserated with their *locu nona* (great lady) for her terrible misfortune at having borne a girl; Pamela was naturally delighted and finally gave up procreation having maintained her hourglass figure despite having smoked and drunk her way through six pregnancies with no obvious ill effects on the health or intelligence of her children.

Tony graduated from planter to various management jobs in import/export firms and eventually became a Visiting Agent, a kind of tea estate inspector. The family moved from the hills down to the sought-after suburb of Cinnamon Gardens, Colombo 7. The house in Bullers Lane into which Sally was born is now an ice cream parlour. The other posh homes have been divided into apartments or let out as offices or consulates. The Colombo smart set now live either in luxury apartments or further out of town. But late 1950s Ceylon, though it had been independent for a decade, was still a place where the former colonial masters continued to enjoy privileges and comforts and to run most of the upper reaches of the economy. Especially in their clubs. Tony and Pamela's favourite haunt was the Colombo Swimming Club on Galle Road opposite the President's Colombo residence, Temple Trees, and at the time next to the British High Commission. Tony and Pamela were life members of what was at the time a foreigners-only club. After her ballet lessons Sally would be taken by her nanny over to the club where the children swam, chatted on the wall by the fountain, taught one another their versions of the facts of life and devoured Coke floats on Daddy's credit bill while their parents talked business or got drunk. Or both. David Wilkie, the British Olympic gold medallist was one of the other child regulars. Sally once beat him in a race. He was very ill at the time.

So progressed a post-colonial Colombo childhood of ballet, swimming, parties, foreigners-only schools, foreigners-only clubs, English food and nannies. And uncles. Pamela had film-star good looks and enjoyed the company of plenty of male admirers who liked to indulge Sally either altruistically or as a route to her mother's affections. Rides in fancy cars, gifts of chocolates which even as a girl she didn't much care for, and on one occasion, aged just five, a glamorous night out going around Colombo's night clubs with one of her 'uncles', equipped with corsage and drinking what would now be called mocktails. To her 'uncle's' consternation Sally was fascinated by the luxurious ladies' loos and spent the majority of her time in each club they visited checking them out, leaving him, a handsome forty-year-old man, knocking plaintively on the doors of a succession of ladies' lavatories calling "Sally, are you in there? Please come out!" to the ill-concealed disgust of the respectable matrons present.

The family never stayed long in one place. Everywhere was rented and tied to Tony's current job, and he changed jobs a lot. For a while they lived in Bauer's Flats, a pre-war apartment block in the historic Fort area close to the harbour. While there Pamela acquired another admirer who lived in a small lighthouse at the far end of the long port jetty. Sally doesn't recall whether he was the lighthouse keeper, or just some guy who liked living in a lighthouse. She and her Mum visited the lighthouse once a week, often braving monsoon waves crashing above head height over the jetty, to play Scrabble.

Five of the world's seven turtle species live in the waters around Sri Lanka. When Sally was a child and people knew little about conservation, and even the sainted David Attenborough was making his TV name collecting animals for zoos, she and her brother used their pocket money to buy a baby turtle a youth was selling on the beach down the coast at Hikkaduwa and smuggled it back in a tobacco tin full of sea water. She's yet to explain how she came to be in possession of a tobacco tin at such an early age but let that pass. Her mother was not best pleased but too kind-hearted to deny the turtle's right to life. So the creature – called Myrtle or Bertle as its gender was indeterminate – lived in a tank in their seaside flat and was fed bits of minced up meat. The servants ran to the sea with buckets to keep it supplied with sea water. It grew, and grew, eventually requiring a very large tank and very large pieces of meat, to request which it had learned to ring a bell attached to the side of the tank. Finally her Mum's patience ran out and the turtle was handed over to Dehiwela Zoo where the staff decided it would be interesting to see if they could adapt it to less saline water. As a result it died. "Why didn't they just put it back in the sea?" I hear you ask. Because it was so used to humans as a food source it would have swum up to the nearest fishing boat and rapidly ended as curry, that's why.

Not content with sending her five-year-old daughter on a tour of Colombo's nightspots Pamela dressed up the by now eleven-year-old Sally, stick thin and with long shapely legs, in the skimpiest of mini-skirts adorned with paper flowers and entered her in the BOAC Ball's fancy dress competition 1969 as 'Flower Power'. She won not only first prize but the mind-boggled attention of the local press photographers. The photograph, in which Sally wears a nervous 'what am I doing here?' smile, still adorns our wall. For younger readers, by the way, BOAC stands for British Overseas Airways Corporation – one of the forerunners of British Airways. Their annual Ball was held in the Grand Oriental Hotel overlooking the harbour and the passenger terminal. You can still sit in the lounge on the upper floor and look out over the deserted passenger terminal, imagining Union Castle and Bibby liners discharging men in solar topees and women with parasols.

Times changed, slowly at first. While the British continued their lives of privilege and running the economy, the politics was firmly in Sri Lankan hands and the majority Sinhalese were bent on reversing the powers and rewards the British had given to Tamils (who were regarded as more loyal, trustworthy and hard-working) and developing a kind of majoritarian national socialism which Hitler would have felt comfortable with. Indeed the Sinhalese are Aryans, a fact that Hitler was apparently a mite uncomfortable with. Waves of riots and violent conflict swept the country, and Colombo was particularly affected. It was time to move out. Some years previously, when Sally was a baby, the family had lived briefly on a tea estate called Meenawatte, near Kandy, and in 1969 found the lease on the house was again available, so they decided to leave the capital for the hills once more. Tony's job already involved him visiting and inspecting estates all over the hill country. It was normal for these visits to take place at weekends so the whole family would go and spend the weekend with the family who ran the estate. This was especially useful for the planters' children, and indeed their wives, who led a pretty lonely and isolated, if comfortable and privileged life. So Sally already knew several planter children, who tended to be either very young or girls. Boys were inevitably sent to boarding schools in England as were Sally's own brothers.

Meenawatte had been uninhabited for years and the termites had had a field day, breaking through the floors and building their high-rise blocks in every room. It took several months to make the house habitable but Sally felt immediately at home, happy to trade her Colombo social life for the delights of being in the country and surrounded by animals all of whom, she decided, required her urgent care and attention. At the age of eleven she also traded schooling for what passed as home tutoring but in reality consisted mainly of being taught how to arrange flowers, embroider, manage a household of servants, having the occasional Shakespeare or Austen thrust into her hands and learning how to bluff her way through various topics of social conversation. All designed, naturally, to prepare her for finding Mister Right. Who would certainly be English with a serious pedigree and probably a planter of some description. She never did return to school and ended her British career as the director of an arts centre where she was the only one of forty staff who was not a graduate.

There were dogs, of course. Several of them to all of which Sally was devoted. Her days were spent on long jungle walks with one or more dogs, finding pools and waterfalls and getting covered in leeches, swollen like bunches of black grapes around her legs. Then returning before dusk to wash, de-leech and get into her evening wear. Dressing for dinner, even when there were only Sally and her parents at table, was considered de rigueur. When her brothers were home from their English schools in the summer holidays they had to stand when she entered the room. Making ones older brothers bounce up and down like jacks-in-the-box was of course a great source of amusement until she was told in no uncertain terms to stop abusing her gender.

Reepicheep was Sally's palm squirrel which lived in her abundant curly hair. Excellent nesting material. "Sally, you're not going out like that!" "Like what, Mummy?" "With that animal on your head. Take it out at once and brush your hair." "Oh, Mummy, do I have to?" Sadly for Reepicheep he fatally mistimed a jump out of her hair and was swallowed by one of the dogs who fancied a snack. Hearing Sally's screams her Dad came in and, realising what had happened, started beating the dog, which only made Sally worse. "But it's not his fault. He's only being a dog" she managed to blurt out between sobs. Quite right, too. Ballypooches fared better against dogs, being armour-plated. Like giant woodlice they roll into a marble-sized ball when threatened and Sally, when she'd done with rolling them around, stuffed her pockets with them and forgot about them until her mother admonished her at lunch, not being particularly enamoured of the sight of her daughter with large creepy-crawlies emerging to clamber up her blouse. Put her right off her food, it did.

All pet mongooses are called Rikki or Tikki or Tavi (or some combination) thanks to the efforts of Mr Kipling, who also bakes exceedingly good cakes. Rikki was Sally's mongoose and for a mongoose was a moderately talented artist. One day when Sally was painting with pots of poster paint he climbed up on the table, put one paw tentatively in the red pot and walked across the paper.

Looking back at his handiwork he decided that the picture required a little blue to be complete so returned, put another paw in the blue paint pot and repeated the exercise. There are those who would say they'd seen worse at the Tate Modern. All mongooses also love eggs. The reason they take on deadly snakes is not because they have heroic tendencies or even because they hate snakes but because the snake stands between the mongoose and its lunch, viz the snake's eggs. Rikki, being a mongoose of superior brain power, quickly found out that much bigger eggs are to be found in houses, totally unprotected by snakes. The only snag was that these super-eggs were kept in the kerosene-powered fridge so it was necessary to find a hiding place, maintain a close watch until someone opened the fridge door, then insinuate oneself silently into a forgotten corner of the fridge while no-one was looking. A couple of hours would pass before the fridge door was again opened revealing a pile of eggshells and a very plump, shivering mongoose.

Sally's fame as an animal lover spread to the kids in the lines, as the tea estate workers' houses are called, and they brought her a succession of injured or orphaned baby creatures, mostly beyond help. But she did succeed with a nest of baby parakeets whose parents had probably been predated by a larger bird. She looked up how baby birds were raised and the answer was that their parents fed them with chewed-up insects. Chewing up and spitting out insects was a step too far even for Sally but she compromised by grinding insects in Mum's mortar and pestle and spitting into the mixture before feeding it with tweezers to the baby birds. All of them fledged and took up residence on the curtain rail from which they shat voluminously down Pamela's curtains. Until one day a flock of parakeets flew by and as one they followed out through the French windows and joined their older raggle-taggle brothers and sisters.

We always want what we don't have. In Sally's privileged childhood it was what her brothers had. They got Scalextric sets, bikes, even guns for their birthdays while Sally was given dolls. And a year's supply of antheriums to practice her flower-arranging. She was not much given to flower-arranging, but she held a particular hatred for dolls and used to take them down to the lines to give to the estate workers' children. Her nanny felt obliged each night to go and re-possess them only for the whole charade to be repeated at the next opportunity. When she finally tired of trying to give her dolls away she hit on playing fantasy games with them. Now that's pretty normal – all girls play princesses and queens with their dolls don't they? Well, most, anyway. But Sally's fantasy was Beggars and Prisoners. Her dolls clothes were ripped into rags, and makeshift prisons constructed to house the miscreants.

As with dolls, so with food. Pamela and Tony employed a Sri Lankan cook well trained in western cuisine. Rice and curry was reserved for Sundays only – an interesting volte-face when one considers that this is staple Sri Lankan fare but regarded by the British as 'Sunday best' food while really expensive and exotic stuff is laid before them every day. "Oh, not lobster thermidor again" Sally once famously complained. After making a token stab at her parents' choice of dinner she'd sneak away on the pretence of going to bed, hop out of the window and leg it across to the servants' kitchen to share their tasty, spicy food and learn the technique of eating rice and curry with her fingers, a skill which has stood her in good stead to this day.

But even a country house and a neo-colonial lifestyle are not immune to the wider world. In the south of the country the JVP – Janatha Vimukthi Peramuna – had begun an armed uprising which rapidly spread. The JVP claimed to be both Marxist and Buddhist and Sinhala nationalist. Its supporters were disenfranchised and poor Sinhalese people not at all content with what they saw as a transfer of power not to the Sinhalese majority but to the Sinhalese elite. When the uprising took place Sally was with a friend and her family on a short holiday near Trincomalee; her parents were in Colombo on business. The JVP blew up all the main road bridges as well as the railway lines so both Sally and her parents had to find their way via back roads with lots of wrong turns and dead ends. The parents eventually made it to Kandy but were naturally in a state of panic about where Sally was. In 1971 there was no means of mobile communication. They headed for the Queens Hotel, the colonial watering-hole in the centre of Kandy, as it was too dangerous to head home to Meenawatte. And there they waited.

Meanwhile Sally's friends were trying to get to Kandy from Trincomalee via small country roads and tracks when they were stopped by some JVP cadres. Guns were poked through the car windows and everyone was ordered – most politely – to get out. The spokesman apologised for the inconvenience: "Very sorry madam and sir, we needing this car. We will take out your bags and no harm to you and missies." And they were left by these well-mannered insurgents standing by the roadside with their bags, in the middle of nowhere with no idea what to do next. Very soon a tractor and trailer turned up and they and their bags were taken to a nearby village. Presumably the JVP had arranged this. After a wait of several hours, up came a police jeep to take them safely on to Kandy. The Queens being at the time the obvious place for a rendezvous there they headed, and so to Sally's mortification her screaming and tearful parents greeted her in the hotel's lobby, in full view of all the mystified guests and staff.

The rising tide of Sinhalese nationalism had, by the end of the 1960s, turned its attention to all foreigners. Sri Lanka for the Sinhalese, it was argued logically, was not just about keeping down the Tamil and Muslim minorities. It was also about getting rid of foreign residents and confiscating their property. Massive duties were imposed on imported goods. Punitive rates of tax laid on foreigners working in Sri Lanka. Fierce exchange controls prevented what money they retained from being sent abroad. Property ownership laws were changed to minimise foreign land holdings. Pamela tried to keep the leaky ship afloat by writing scripts for D C Thompson's illustrated romances – she wrote the content of the speech bubbles and the 'stage directions' describing the scenes the artist needed to draw. This brought in enough British money to pay her sons' school fees direct. But it was clear that the future for foreigners in Sri Lanka was becoming bleak and when Tony lost his job that was the end of the road. Or rather the end of the road was the ferry waiting at the pier in Talaimannar. "If we have to go back to England" Pamela told Tony "We're going to have the journey of a lifetime. We're going to do it overland." And do it they did: Pamela, Tony, Sally and a young Englishman who'd arrived via the hippy trail through India and took up their offer of a lift home in return for doing a share of the driving. The vehicles, as I've said, were an Austin 1300 (a small family saloon car) and a Mini-Moke (akin to a set of motorised roller skates). 'LONDON OR BUST' was written on the fronts of both vehicles. The route included the Khyber Pass, the deserts of Afghanistan and pre-revolutionary Iran, Turkey, Greece and the former Yugoslavia with an accidental side-trip into the USSR. But that is a tale for another time.

A match made in Yorkshire

Early in 1986 I'd just moved with my thirteen year old daughter Jo, from suburban Nottingham to a two-bedroomed cottage near Hebden Bridge in rural Yorkshire. A small house with a large garden, as befits my priorities. "Jerry's just bought a garden with a house attached" one friend commented. On my final visit before moving in the couple I was buying the house from told me about my new neighbours. They included, two doors down, a composer, Julian, and his partner, Sally.

"I'm afraid there's been some terrible news about Sally", they said. "She was in a bad car accident and she's in hospital. She'll never be able to walk again." That winter was exceptionally severe and just above my house the road was blocked by an eight foot snowdrift on the March day I moved in. As I was supervising and helping with unpacking the furniture van an ambulance drew up two doors down and Sally was carried out on a stretcher and into their house. I'd just clapped eyes on my eventual lifetime partner for the first time.

I was too preoccupied with settling in and in any case visiting the sick always makes me nervous so I made no attempt to introduce myself to my new neighbours. It was a month later that I answered a knock on the door and came face to face with a tall skinny man in a Homburg who introduced himself as Julian and invited me and Jo to a Sunday lunchtime get-together with all the neighbours. Sally had by then graduated to a zimmer frame and the dire prognostications I'd heard were clearly exaggerated. As the homebrew flowed and the April Pennine snow flurries hurtled past the windows Julian, Sally and I all started to get along superbly. Jo also began what turned out to be a lifetime friendship with a girl her own age from a house on the other side of us.

I wasn't suited to be a single Dad; hadn't thought it through. Especially the father of a teenager who'd previously been living with her Mum but was feeling displaced – as teenagers are wont to do – by her Mum's new partner and even newer baby. The Yorkshire grass was greener, or so she thought. But my job involved frequent overnights away from home and she was left to her own devices far too much. And that means trouble. Even out in the sticks teenagers can sniff out a house unattended by adults at several miles' distance and converge on it with cheap cider, skunk and who knows what else. Sally came to the rescue; without being asked she took on the job of checking up on the goings-on in my house whenever I was absent, but in a way that endeared Jo to her, offering support rather than authority. I never really appreciated it at the time. There was still the occasional wrecked sofa or table to deal with on my return, but Sally was holding my life just about together without my realising it.

Julian and Sally also managed a rock string quartet of classically trained musicians who remain, for my money, the best unknown band that ever existed. The *Acrobats of Desire*, since you don't ask. They lived too far away from one another to function as a regular band, but on one autumn day I came home from work to find them playing in my front room (I've never been one for locking doors). "It's Sally's birthday tomorrow", they explained. "We're rehearsing a late Beethoven quartet for her". Op59 no1, I remember well. Still one of our favourite pieces of music of any genre. Another time I returned from an overnight away and Jo told me she'd spent the previous evening and overnight at Julian and Sally's. "Julian asked if I could help polish some metal bars", she told me. "They're for some kind of musical instruments, you wouldn't believe how many there are, though. It took all night."

That was the start of what became the country's first, and as far as I know only, community gamelan orchestra. Based very loosely on Balinese gamelans the orchestra was more than forty strong with the players' ages ranging from seven to seventy and musical abilities ranging from people who couldn't read a note and had never played anything in their lives through to professional musicians. I sat somewhere in the middle, as a pretty poor keyboard player who could at least sight read a score. Julian was the musical director, Sally and I kept the social, logistical and administrative side of things running smoothly. For several years we performed all over the country including week-long residencies when we camped on municipal playing fields or played folk festivals.

Jo left home at seventeen to live in a farm caravan with her then boyfriend. I spent more and more of my free evenings at Sally and Julian's house with their growing family. Originally there was just Merigen, a ten-year-old with unfeasibly red hair when I first met him. Born when Sally was just eighteen and married to her first husband, his unusual name was garnered from Sweet's Anglo-Saxon Reader and means 'of the dawn' since Sally's labour began one dawn and ended the next and she was understandably reluctant to name her son Dawn. When he checked a few years back the only other Merigen with an on-line presence was a female Filipino advertising herself for sex. Then Julian and Sally long-term fostered a brother and sister, Daniel and Angela. Sally had wanted more children but had been told she would be unable to conceive and IVF, then in its early years, had not succeeded. So long-term fostering was an obvious choice. And months after Daniel and Angela arrived Sally confounded medical science by getting pregnant. Professor Robert Winston, who had been her consultant before he became famous, had the good grace to admit he'd been wrong to rule out her chances of conceiving naturally. Jemima was born in 1989. And the three of us became closer and closer, our lives and those of Sally's four children increasingly intertwined.

Just before Christmas 1991 I'd returned from two months' solo travelling around Australia with a final week in Bali on a personal gamelan pilgrimage and threw myself with gusto into the festive season spent, inevitably, mostly at Julian and Sally's house with tides of friends ebbing and flowing. Tides of alcohol, likewise. Julian, who enjoyed a drink in those days, sometimes nodded off and was persuaded up to bed by Sally. One night she started telling me how unhappy she was.

"He sometimes leaves me feeling abandoned and uncared-for. For one thing there's his love affair with his music – he can spend whole days locked in his room composing, sometimes not even coming down for family meals and taking no interest in me and the kids – except Jemima who he dotes on. Fruit of his loins, see? Then there's the affairs. Well, I can't prove anything but I have my suspicions. He's always had the occasional fling and frankly I've turned a blind eye. If he needs that much sex and I can't provide it, then that's no problem provided he still loves me. But I'm no longer sure he does. And recently he's been trying it on with a couple of my friends and that's going beyond the limits. They told me about it, of course – that's what friends are for." "Flings ain't what they used to be, then" I joked pathetically. "Look, I'm trying to be serious, Jerry. Do you want to know about this stuff or don't you?"

Frankly, I wasn't sure I did. Julian had become a close friend and I didn't want to hear bad things about him. I didn't want to have to take sides. "I do" I half lied. "But I just find this so hard to believe. I've always thought of you two as the perfect couple – unconventional, for sure, but completely suited to one another". I almost added "That's why I feel safe being here alone with you" but thought better of it.

"OK then, I'd better let you in on the worst bit", Sally continued. "Julian's always been against marriage, but he did say that if there was ever a really good reason to get married he'd reconsider. Well I found a good reason but he won't have any of it".

"What's that, then?" "Angela and Daniel. I want to adopt them, and give them some security and stability and so does he – or at least he says he does. But Social

Services told us that the law says we have to get married if we're to have any chance of adoption. And he won't. Not even for the kids! That might just be the last straw for me. If he won't marry me, even to secure the kids' future, I'm not sure I can forgive that. I don't want to force him so maybe I'll have to leave and try to find another way forward."

A week or so later In the early hours of New Year's Day 1992 after everyone had finally left after seeing in the New Year, Julian had again crawled off to bed and Sally and I remained, slumped at the kitchen table, cuddling as one does with close friends when drunk and declaring how wonderful each other was. And I still hadn't seen it coming....she looked at me, suddenly alert "But for me it's become more than that, more than just friendship. I think I'm in love with you. Don't even know what you feel …. Shit! I wish this wasn't happening. I never meant it to happen. I really didn't."
Time… I needed time. But what do you say when there is no time and you're not the sharpest thinker on the planet? "Sally, love, I don't know what to say. We're both pissed. Maybe we shouldn't be having this conversation." Pathetic. So she kissed me and it felt very special indeed. Not sexy special, deep special. Life-changing special. "What do we do?" I asked plaintively once I'd regained the power of speech.

Cooling off was what we tried to do. We agreed not to see each other alone for three months and I stopped visiting Julian and Sally's house. Predictably it didn't work and things in Sally and Julian's relationship deteriorated further, and in April Sally took the heart-stopping decision to leave him and rent a place of her own with Merigen, by now fourteen. Two-year-old Jemima would spend half time with her and half with Julian. Angela and Daniel's Mum grabbed the opportunity she'd been waiting for, to go to court and challenge the fostering arrangement, and won the return of her children. I meanwhile stayed put and tried to avoid Julian. Neither Sally nor I wanted us to live together so soon. It was a testing time and I was helped a lot by Jo's total enthusiasm for my new relationship; her Dad was in love with her favourite woman (her Mum excepted, of course). It buoyed me up through the periods of doubt and sudden attacks of 'What the hell have I done?'

A friend had an unmodernised cottage for rent up a dirt track in the woods the other side of Hebden Bridge and offered it to Sally with apologies for its condition but furnished after a fashion, at a cheap rent and available immediately, the previous tenant having selfishly died there without giving due notice to quit, and the house was full of the paraphernalia of a recently deceased old man. Threadbare suits hanging in wardrobes, dentures lurking in drawers, that kind of thing. A garden gloomy with overgrown rhododendrons and a patch of shaggy grass that had once been a lawn. It made sense for me to visit Sally rather than the other way around, given my proximity to Julian. I had a good job and a pleasant if small house; Sally had no job, no money and lived in a festering cottage where youngling earthworms often came out of the taps and the furniture had alarming tendencies to break. She did of necessity have a car –an ancient Opel – whose flooring was rotting and threatening a Flintstones impression. We once found a live frog in the well of the rear seats.

"Can't I help you out? Maybe buy you some furniture, get a load of coal for the fire?" I asked. "Thanks, but no. I got myself into this situation and I'm going to get myself through it and out the other side without anyone's help. I know you mean well and I'm truly grateful, but No." "So I have to join you in shivering in front of a fire of gathered sticks, sitting on rickety chairs, drinking cheap coffee and tap water with worms in it, do I?" The point was taken and my self-interest and Sally's feminism met half way. I would be permitted to bring bags of coal and bottles of wine – as well as Merigen's favourite Fanta – and also to tackle the overgrown garden at weekends. But no more. No money, no new furniture.

After a year of this we decided it was time to live together. I put my house on the market as it was too small for the four of us, especially as Angela and Dan had begun to stay most weekends – it suited their Mum to dump them back on Sally while she went out for a good time. I've never been good with the fluctuations of the housing market, always having timed the starts and endings of relationships to fit perfectly with having to buy at the top of the curve and sell at the bottom. The house wouldn't sell for anything like what we needed to put down a deposit on somewhere big enough for all of us. Renting was the only option in the short term. A young couple we knew through the gamelan had recently moved to the area and rented a four bedroomed cottage called Stonesheygate; they'd now found a place to buy and told us their tenancy was ending and we might be interested in taking it over, so we went to have a look.

With Stonesheygate Cottage it was love at first sight. Dating from the eighteenth century it overlooked the National Trust-owned ravine of Hardcastle Crags with the high Pennine moorland beyond. Built of smoke-blackened stone, with a collection of semi-derelict outbuildings and a small patch of garden, it was a warren of dark rooms inside. The only heating was an open fire in the living room and antique electric storage heaters in three of the four bedrooms. Water came from a spring on nearby Popples Common – 'popples' being an old and beautifully onomatopoeic Yorkshire word for springs. Sewage ended up in a septic tank. There was no gas supply. Originally two small cottages knocked into one a long time back, part of the ground floor of one cottage served as a woodshed, coal shed and store.

Merigen begged to differ. "Mum, it's way too far out of town. None of my friends is going to come right out here, I'll have no social life. Can't we find somewhere in Hebden?" He had a point. But there was nowhere affordable in town. So we set out to make Stonesheygate Cottage a go-to venue for teenage boys. And succeeded perhaps too well. Within a few months every spare bed and every sofa was taken by Merigen's friends ranging from overnighters with perfectly good homes to return to, to waifs and strays who became more or less permanent residents. One of them – who's still a friend of ours – lived in Merigen's walk-in cupboard for a year. "You can't get Mat in there" we told Merigen when he first asked whether it would be OK for him to move in. "Yes we can. Mat's six foot three and the cupboard's six foot five, I've measured it." Game over.

The route to a teenage boy's heart lies through his stomach and an endless supply of tasty home-made food was the key to the success of our informal youth centre. We also didn't mind much what they got up to in Merigen's increasingly crowded bedroom, including a mural wall covered with stoned meanderings, since papered over for some future occupant to find. Sally went in one evening to find them all smoking weed and listening to Bob Dylan. "Come on guys!" she exclaimed in mock indignation "That's not on! That's what our generation did. You need to find something different to do!" They weren't sure whether she was being serious. Autumn brought enthusiastic teenage ramblings across the nearby fields, searching for psilocybin mushrooms. The crop being duly delivered to our kitchen it was Sally's parental responsibility to sort out which were likely to provide psychedelic experiences and which were likely to result in serious stomach cramps or worse.

Angela and Dan also came back to live with us, though this time there was no official fostering arrangement or payments. On more than one occasion they'd escaped from their bedroom in the middle of the night, found a phone box and asked us to pick them up as their Mum had again gone out for the evening leaving them locked in their room shoeless to prevent escape. Once it was snowing and they had made their way to the phone box in bare feet. I drove the hour each way to the council estate where they lived, picked them up and we informed the Social Services. Sometimes their Mum with her current boyfriend would come and pick them up, other times they stayed for days. Eventually Mum went off to live in Gran Canaria. When they asked her what would happen to them she said "Oh, you can go and live with Sally and Jerry. They'll be fine about it." And of course we were. Both eventually went to university – the first graduates ever in their family's history – and both are now successful professional people and great parents. We like to think that we broke a cycle of bad parenting, worklessness and poverty for two children at least, and both Angela and Daniel remain very much a part of our family.

We married in 1995. We did it officially at the local register office but then properly in a pagan-inspired ceremony on Popples Common that evening. It was an unseasonably hot early May evening as a procession left Stonesheygate headed by a four-person-operated fabric dragon (created for one of the gamelan's street theatre performances) and followed by an eighteen piece street band put together that afternoon by a musically talented neighbour and friend. Then came two decorated drays provided by the theatre company, *Horse and Bamboo Theatre*, that Sally was by then working for on which we and our children, Sally's Mum and a couple of brothers were precariously perched, decked out in fantasy costumes created by yet more talented friends. On the common stood a forty foot fire sculpture, a 'wicker man' built by another friend. The ceremony began, based on the stages of the alchemic process as a metaphor for our marriage. The officiating 'priest' was the husband of my ex-wife – I do like to keep things nice and neat – who remains a close friend and who, when not advising social enterprises and workers' co-operatives on their constitutions and legal affairs, studies the old religions. Children and teenagers danced in formation as the sun set; the ritual words were spoken and we were handed flaming brands and led off, tied at the wrists by red and green strings and faces daubed with red and green paints, to set light to the wicker man. As the flames reached his groin a Catherine wheel spun into action; higher up and a firework heart blazed; at the top of his head a crown of Roman candles finished the job off. The image of the burning man was later appropriated by a Manchester band for the cover of their first album. We would have appreciated an acknowledgement.

Five hundred people came to the common, only just over half of whom we'd invited. The others heard on the grapevine that something good was afoot in a public place.
We'd informed the police and the fire service as well as arranging for the St John Ambulance to attend in return for a collection. So we were a bit surprised to hear the siren and see the flashing blue lights of a fire tender hurtling up the road towards the common. Turned out that although we'd informed the West Yorkshire Fire Service on whose turf we were, the blaze had been spotted from over the hills and far away by the Greater Manchester Fire Service in Rochdale who had not been forewarned. The fire crew were very jolly about it all, though. 'Hundreds flock to alchemy wedding' was the headline in the following week's Hebden Bridge Times, setting off a month-long debate in the letters columns between the

local pagans and Christians, which we wisely stayed right out of.

The following day a reception and twelve-hour non-stop cabaret at *Square Chapel Centre for the Arts* in Halifax ended the proceedings. Sally was at the time a Trustee of the centre and later its Director until we moved to Sri Lanka. All the performers played for free and acts ranged from Appalachian clog dancing to Rolf Harris impersonations (it was OK to impersonate Mr Harris in those days) to free jazz to poetry to classical piano and flute recitals. And of course the gamelan. I sang a couple of self-penned humorous ditties which were misprinted in the programme as *Jerry Smith: Cosmic songs*. The wedding cake was baked, all four tiers of it, by Sally's ex-husband (Merigen's Dad) who was at the time a professional baker. Like I said, we keep things nice and neat. The whole weekend cost two thousand quid, far less than the cost of an average wedding in 1995. It's amazing what you can achieve when you have large numbers of talented and creative friends.

M's Gems

Doing a solo trip around Australia had belatedly given me a taste for travel. And Sally was desperate to revisit Sri Lanka. It was just a matter of time, and saving up the money, before we did. I never met her Dad, Tony. He'd died in his early sixties long before Sally and I knew one another. One of our mutual regrets is that we never got to know each other's fathers; both of us know for sure they'd have got on like a house on fire. But Sally's Mum, Pamela, known to all as M, was still very much around and delighted that I was planning to take her daughter back to the land of her birth.

A family coat of arms, featuring – appropriately – some legless birds, and a family tree dating back to the time of the Plantagenets come from Sally's father's side. One ancestor had been Richmond Herald, not as you might suppose a local newspaper but a position granted to him by his good friend George V. They were mates largely because Sally's ancestor was one of the few other people in the land who knew the rules of Real (Royal) Tennis. The Richmond Herald's job was to award coats of arms to the deserving rich. "And have one for yourself while you're at it" the good King suggested. Another relative was among the founders of the Fabian Society and was close to George Bernard Shaw and H G Wells. A third was the first actress to perform Ibsen's then outrageous *A Dolls' House* on the London stage. And a fourth captained the liner SS London and went down courageously with his ship when it sank in the Bay of Biscay – though it seems the disaster was also at least partly down to his rash seamanship which rather takes the gloss off things.

Sally's Mum, though, is an enigmatic figure. She claimed to have been born in the Isle of Wight but internet searches and a visit to the island's registry office have failed to find anyone of any similar name within several years of what must have been her birth date. She had no siblings, and we'll probably never find out more about her. She died in 2002. On the Mexican Day of the Dead to be precise – she was never a woman to do things by halves. Among her many achievements she was Radio Ceylon's first disc jockey in which capacity she brought risqué calypso music to a bewildered Asian island: "Oh, Sir! Don't touch me tomato! You can touch me on me pumpkin potato" being a particularly choice example. She was also the station's agony aunt which required her to solve problems such as advising a man who phoned in a plaintive voice: "Please help me! My wife has shabby buttocks. What to do?", and another who posed the culturally perplexing question of "What is the use of knife and fork for eating fish and chips when bread and butter is served?" She met and escorted Vivien Leigh and other luminaries during the filming of *Bridge on the River Kwai.* She was friends with the Bawa brothers, Geoffrey and Bevis, among the most illustrious non-political sons of Sri Lanka, as well as with Barbara Sansoni, founder of Barefoot, the most prestigious shop in the island. And as I've said she had a host of male admirers – Sally's 'uncles' – whose company she clearly adored though whether any of these relationships were full-blown affairs is a matter of pure conjecture.

One of Pamela's admirers, known to Sally as 'Uncle Ray', owned a gem mine near Ratnapura. He also owned a plane, a Tiger Moth, and was generally a dashing sort. Ray died shortly afterwards when he was piloting his Tiger Moth in to land at Ratmalana, the original airport for Colombo. He got caught in the slipstream of a jet. The little biplane bucked, buckled and fell to the tarmac. And so, via his will, a collection of gems came into Pamela's hands.

Gems, of the semi-precious variety, are commonly found in Sri Lanka and remain one of the country's most important exports. But if your images of Sri Lankan gem mining involve such things as pithead gear, or trucks on rails being pulled by sweaty men or beasts, or dynamite, or huge opencast craters you're way off beam, I'm afraid. Gem mining is a small-scale operation, still carried on in much the same way as it was in Uncle Ray's time. It is centred around Ratnapura, a place I've only visited once. We stopped off in town to have a look at the Gemmology Museum. It was closed – apparently never to reopen though as usual I may be wrong on that one. On we went, mildly disappointed until our driver Dhanushka suggested we take a look at a working mine. "Is that allowed?" I asked incredulously, thinking in British health and safety terms. I'd left my hard hat at home, for a start. "Yes, Sir. Not a problem. Anyone can go."

In a paddy field in Pelmadulla a few miles beyond Ratnapura, stood an unprepossessing wooden shelter with a palm-thatched roof. Dhanushka pulled the van over and led us on a muddy footpath through the paddy and explained to the knot of men hanging around that we wanted to take a look at their mine. With the help of Dhanushka's translation we learned that the miners receive food and shelter only, and any cash they earn is based on what they dig out of the sodden earth and soft rocks many feet below the surface. Below the thatched roof a deep and unlit shaft had been dug with a rope wound around a wooden drum on a metal spindle. The rope descended into the inky depths and guys clung to it and were wound up and down in their human wishing-well by the surface crew. Rough-hewn and un-shored galleries led off the shaft at intervals and the miners crawled along these in search of semi-precious stones. Some days they would find nothing, and receive no pay. Other days were better. But these were poor men, no doubt. Sally recalled Uncle Ray's mine, and others she had visited, as being much shallower, wider pits accessed by home-made rope and timber ladders so perhaps things have changed. But not for the better. Two smartly-dressed men materialised from nowhere – gem dealers in the hope of making a sale. How they sniffed us out I have no idea. We didn't buy, but we did give some cash to the workers.

From a life of colonial comfort M had gradually fallen on hard times and in 1998 was living on a minimum state pension in a council tower block in Fulham, though she maintained a decent drinks trolley to the end. Her politics had also changed, from high Tory to Labour and she helped run the local tenants' association. She sometimes used her background, cut glass accent and former beliefs to detain unwitting Tory party canvassers at election time, plying them with gin and tonics to keep them off the streets and trying to convert them to socialism. But while not dirt-poor, she could certainly do with a bit of cash to liven her remaining years – she had recently turned eighty.

Sally recalled playing as a child with Uncle Ray's boxes of gems and a set of jeweller's scales with tweezers. Where other children might weigh out sweets and sort Smarties into their various colours she was nonchalantly handling semi-precious stones cross-legged on the nursery floor. She knew that Pamela had had to leave them behind in Sri Lanka in 1971. "Wouldn't it be great if we could find Mummy's gems when we go to Sri Lanka?" she piped up one day. I knew Sally well enough by now to realise that this was not actually a question, it was a statement of intent.

"Mummy", she asked down the phone a month before our trip, "You remember those gems Uncle Ray gave you, the ones that I used to play with? Any idea where they are now? I'd like to see if we can find them and bring them back for you." "Sally, you're such a romantic. I've no idea where they are. No doubt stolen by someone or other. There's no point looking for them, they'll be long gone. You know the Bandaranaike government wouldn't let us take anything out of the country when we left so I had to leave them behind." "But I still want to try. Where did you leave them?" "I'm not sure. I expect I left them with our bank. The Chartered Bank. But I doubt even that exists these days." "Where was the bank? Have you got a receipt or anything?" "It's in Fort – don't you remember it? We used to have to go there a lot." (Indeed Sally did recall it immediately). "But there's no paperwork I can remember seeing, must have lost that years ago."

Ten days later, another phone call. "Sal, darling, you remember we were talking about Uncle Ray's jewels you used to play with? Well, by chance when I was looking for something else I just came across a Chartered Bank statement with our current account number on it. But that's all. Might it be of any use?" Well, it was a start. It did prove she had an account there and maybe the account number could identify the location of something she had left for safe-keeping all those years ago. Slim chance, though. Jemima had been brought up on Enid Blyton-type quests and a real-life one got her extremely excited. Faced with a romantic wife and an eight-year-old stepdaughter wound up like a spring in anticipation of a great adventure resistance was futile. I shelved my rationalist objections (this sounded like a great way of boring ourselves silly, spoiling our holiday and achieving precisely nothing was what I felt but wisely chose not to say). We were headed for Sri Lanka, Sally was going home. And we were on a mission.

Two

Colombo Swimming Club

Few tourists visited the (allegedly) war-torn island in 1998. We had expected to be plagued by airport touts offering taxis but the arrivals hall was deserted. These days it's thronged with drivers carrying name-cards. We wandered around with our baggage trolley looking lost until a gun-toting khaki-clad guy came up to us and I assumed we'd already inadvertently transgressed some law. "Can I help you please?" "Erm, we wanted to know where we can find a taxi."

He spun around without a word and marched off. A few paces away he turned, beckoning us to follow, which we did, not knowing whether our destination would be a cab stand or the detention suite. A few barked orders, a "Wait here please" and a cab appeared. There were soldiers and police everywhere. On the long road into Colombo cyclists carried sofas upside down on their heads, lorries were painted like gypsy caravans, roadside advertisements offered products long forgotten in the west (Rinso, for heaven's sake!). Tiny shanty factories with impressive sounding names usually involving some combination of the words 'Nippon', 'aerospace' and 'technology' lined the road. Roadside stalls professed to accept all major credit cards. Roadblocks popped up every couple of miles, often sponsored by corporations in the way businesses sponsor roundabouts on UK roads. Not for the first time I was left pondering the ingenuity and sheer brass-neck of capitalism. The all-pervading tropic smell of diesel, incense, fish and rotting fruit percolated through the car. AC in cars was a rarity back then.

We had nowhere to stay. Our destination was the Colombo Swimming Club, where Sally's family had been life members. We had tried many times to contact the club by phone and e-mail from England to see if it would be possible to take out temporary membership and stay there. Nobody picked up the phone or it cut off. E-mails all went unanswered. Finally we wrote a letter but received no reply, so we decided to trust to luck and just turn up.

The club stands on the sea side of Galle Road, confronting the ocean across the no-man's land of the coastal railway line. On the opposite side of Galle Road is Temple Trees, the President's official residence. Sally knew this, of course, but we hadn't drawn the obvious conclusion – that security would be skin-tight across the road from the President's hangout in a war situation. Our taxi was duly stopped at the road block at the end of Galle Road. "Sir, not possible to go to Colombo Swimming Club. Road is block."

Another group of soldiers in fatigues (I had by now realised that the khaki guys were police) came to surround the car and I assumed we were in for a gruelling search-and-possibly-destroy event. At the very least we'd have to trudge the final quarter mile or so in the sticky heat with heavy baggage. Sally had other ideas. "Leave this to me" she said and got out of the car with Jemima to begin an animated conversation with the soldiers, whose AK47s swung around Jemima's head. What on earth was she doing? I wondered, from a cowering position in the rear seat. She's normally so protective of Mima, why is she offering her up as a child sacrifice to this scary lot? Soon Sally returned to the car with a beaming grin and we were waved through and down Galle Road to the club. Sally had simply shown them her passport showing *birthplace: Colombo*, chatted about the old times and Jemima had added her child's blonde charm. The road block melted as ice cream in a Swimming Club Coke float.

"Yes, Madam and Sir, we have your room ready", said the man on the reception desk. This was an excellent surprise given the difficulties we'd had in communicating from the UK. Lesson one – just because Sri Lankans don't reply doesn't mean they don't care or do anything. They just don't seem to have our western need for communication, confirmation and reassurance. Our temporary membership would be sorted out tomorrow, the helpful receptionist continued, "Today Poya Day" he explained. Poya Days are Buddhist public holidays held every four weeks, on the full moon. We hadn't thought to check this in advance, the main (and for us weary travellers drastic) implication being that no alcohol was available anywhere. Damn and blast! Jemima headed straight for the pool and hung on in there until she was fished out. Sally and I nursed our jet-lag and tiredness in the more adult manner – desultory conversation, occasional pool forays, non-alcoholic drinks. Sally was at times lost in remembrance of things past. So little, it seemed, had changed since 1971, except that half the forecourt and one of the twin imposing gates had been sold off to a hotel development, and the high diving board had gone. "Too danger madam" was the response when we enquired as to its fate. I read, wandered around with my camera, watched the immensely long and ancient trains roll by and the sun going down over the Indian Ocean. We managed to stay up to a respectable hour then fell into bed.

Sally had set the agenda before we left England. There being no apologies for absence to record it went like this:
1. Stay at the Swimming Club (check)
2. Meet up with Peggy, her former nanny with whom she was still in touch.
3. Go with Peggy up to Meenawatte and find which of the former family servants are still around.
4. Find Great Grandfather's and Grandfather's graves and pay due homage to them

5. Revisit the family's holiday haunts in Wilpattu National Park and the Sea Anglers Club near Trincomalee.

6. Liberate Mummy's gems from the Chartered Bank. Any other business? Oh, and maybe look at the odd tourist attraction if time permitted.

I formed an immediate attachment to the Swimming Club despite my aversion to swimming. There appeared to be as many staff as customers. A team of six was apparently needed to run the accounts department alone – roughly the same as the entire finance section in the local council I worked in at the time. The system operated on three basic principles: first, the maximisation of paperwork; second, a fine-grained job demarcation system related to social status; third, a management regime that required at least two, and preferably four, people to look on wearing serious expressions while someone else worked. This last rule applies throughout the island, and to digging holes in the road equally as to working on a desktop. Hence when we foolishly locked our room one night with the key inside it took four people to solve the problem. We gazed on in wonderment as first a guy came to assess the situation and refer it to a superior who could take a management decision as to the best course of action, after which a third went off to get a ladder which for some reason he was unable, incompetent or not allowed to climb, and finally a fourth guy came along and climbed in through the window and let us back in. There was, of course, just the one key – no master and no spares.

At breakfast a voice behind us boomed "Good God! You must be Tony Martin's daughter! Look just like him – except female of course." Tony Horsfall was one of the handful of planters who had never left Ceylon. He had worked with Sally's father and even filled in bits of his career before she was born that Sally was unaware of.

He'd also worked on Luccombe Estate, once managed by Sally's great grandfather.

"The Martins of Ceylon – you're a well-known family here, you realise?" he continued. "Or at least you were at the time." "Daddy's dead now", said Sally, "but Mummy's still very much with us. Did you know her?" "Not really. I wasn't one for the ladies."

Tony has since had the bar at the CSC named after him – a tribute to any drinking man and one that stirs envy in the loins. The only other ancient denizen of Sri Lanka to be feted in this way by the club is Arthur C Clarke after whom the dining area is called 'Arthur's Space'. Some years later we did spot Sri Lanka's most famous expat, by then extremely frail, being gently lowered into the pool by two attendants, after which he fairly shot off down a length. Tony was also very old and, like Arthur, is no longer with us. He died a few years later following an accident which was related to us by a Swimming Club waiter as: "Madam, Sir, Mr Tony Horsfall Sir falls off the ceiling." We assume he somehow fell from a roof and never recovered. At least he didn't fall from a horse.

Early on our second morning a knock on the door. I was up and dressed, Sally and Jemima still in bed. "Someone to see you", the man from the Swimming Club announced. "Mrs Perry." Not knowing a Mrs Perry, or indeed anyone in Sri Lanka, I said it must be a mistake but he insisted so I followed him. At the foot of the staircase stood the diminutive figure of Peggy, Sally's former nanny, unmistakeable from the photographs. She'd been given a few hours off work to come to Colombo and see us. 'Work' consisted of looking after the children of an American family who were in Sri Lanka for an extended holiday, though she looked frail as though she should have retired long ago. This, she explained, meant that she would not be able to accompany us to visit Meenawatte. But she would contact the Banda family, the former Martin household servants, to tell them to expect us. We all had breakfast together and made plans to spend time with her at the end of our holiday. Meanwhile we had things to do, people to see and places to go.

Up country

The two 'crack express trains' (average speed maybe 30kph) from Colombo up to the hill country are the *Uderata Menike ("Upcountry Maiden")* and its younger sister the *Podi Menike ("Little Maiden")*. Puts a new slant on Virgin Rail. I've always loved trains, the creakier the better. And the ride up from Colombo via Kandy to Ella and the terminus at Badulla has to rank as one of the world's most scenic rail journeys. Not much has changed on Sri Lanka's sleepy railway system since Sally's childhood. Steam gave way to diesel eventually, and some of the oldest rolling stock has been replaced by second-hand Indian and Chinese train sets, themselves already looking tired and worn. But the former teenage train-spotter in me would feel completely at home among the semaphore signals, ancient trackwork and station paraphernalia of retiring rooms, lamp stores, Chief Engineer's Offices and the like. We have on our shelves a book written in the 1980s called *"Sri Lanka by Rail"* which includes an island-wide timetable. The timetable remains the same today, but now you can look it up online, no need to buy the book. Progress. All routes go to or from Colombo and outside the Colombo travel to work area trains are few and far between. One line snakes its way across the Royal Colombo Golf Club's course – are there any other golf courses in the world where play has to be halted to let an ancient train crawl past? Up at the railway town of Kadugannawa, at the top of the relentless climb to reach Kandy, is the national railway museum but only an expert could tell the difference between the trains on display there and the ones rolling past, still doing their duty in the twenty first century. Fares are ridiculously cheap and the advance booking system has taken me years to understand – I won't attempt to describe it here, just don't try it yourself without professional support and possibly counselling.

In 1998, though, it was easy to buy first class tickets to travel in the observation car on selected trains. So we took our seats in the rear view windows of the *Uderate Menike* as it crawled out of Colombo at eight thirty in the morning past sidings already being taken over by jungle, abandoned carriages covered in lianas, shanty neighbourhoods, derelict factories, river crossings, intriguing first glimpses of rural life, egrets studding the paddies, the venerable tradition of waving to trains still being carried on. Scores of villagers using the railway tracks as a footpath. The sight of distant mountains. After an hour or so of jolting around on unmaintained tracks speed slowed to a crawl and the long ascent to the hill country began. Bare rock tunnels, vertiginous views into canyons where sandbanks entwine rivers far below, always the solid block of Bible Rock in the distance. Subtleties and depths of green. So green.

Until you reach Kandy, anyway. Our first experience of Kandy was not good; it was the station toilets. They are slightly better these days and there are separate facilities for foreigners and, this being Kandy, the island's cultural and religious centre of gravity, a third special one for monks. But bladder control is still the best strategy. Also 'improved' these days is the walk into town. In 1998 it was a marvellous souk where you ran the gauntlet of hundreds of stallholders selling short eats (spicy snacks), fruits and vegetables, and tourist paraphernalia. Now it's a soulless pedestrian way as far as the chaotic clock tower bus station and from there you're on your own, taking your chances with the traffic. As our home town Kandy features a lot in this book but it was also Sally's home town for part of her childhood when, after moving from Colombo, the family lived on the Meenawatte estate, on the lower slopes of the pointy-topped Hunasgiriya mountain a little north of Kandy.

So we took the meandering and extensively potholed road up to Meenawatte estate, past rice paddies, through the town of Wattegama, a left turn, a right up a tinier road still and then we looked out for a building site. Yes, there it was, a great excavation of the red earth on the right. Peggy had indeed contacted the Banda family who still lived nearby, and arranged a prominent place on the road where we could meet Kalu Banda who had been Second Servant, responsible for the cleaning and maintenance work in the house. Sally's parents by that stage had had a mere six staff, having fallen into straitened circumstances. At an earlier stage of her childhood there had been one whose sole job was polishing.

We stopped and asked one of the workmen: "Where Kalu Banda?" "Here Kalu Banda" – pointing to a youth who turned out to be Kalu Banda's son and who, grinning broadly, greeted us and hopped into the tuk-tuk for the short ride on to milepost eleven where KB himself and various members of his family were waiting. Sally stayed calm and controlled despite obviously wanting to do more than greet him with the appropriate handshake, since so much as a hug would be, if not downright improper, at least hard for him to handle. "Kalu Banda! *Ayubowan!*" she began before introducing us: "*Mage mathia*, Jerry; *mage duwa*, Jemima." His eyes lit up. "*Sinhala katakarannuwa?*" (you speak Sinhala?) "Ah, *tikkak, tikkak*" (very little). "English *katakarranuwa?*" "*Ne*". In the almost thirty years since they'd last met Sally had forgotten her Sinhala and he his English. We were reliant on our driver to interpret for the rest of our visit, and his English wasn't too great either.

Kalu Banda's house was perched in jungle high above the road, accessed by rough steps cut into the sheer hillside.

One of his daughters, whom Sally had known as a babe in arms, carried Jemima up while Sally and I struggled to the top. The two daughters had babies of their own with them. Both their husbands were away, one at work, the other in the army fighting the Tamil Tigers at Batticaloa. KB's younger brother Gori Banda was also away in the army. He is a little younger than Sally; she once 'employed' him with her pocket money as gravedigger for her pets' cemetery. Also present were the paterfamilias Ram Banda himself, now in his seventies, and his wife. But KB's wife, Aslin, was working in Jordan. A lot of Sri Lankans, especially women, work in the Middle East to supplement meagre family incomes back home. Ram Banda at first refused to sit down in his own house in the presence of white people, and specifically Sally. This was more than embarrassing and hurried negotiations via our driver produced a compromise – he would sit *behind* Sally.

Jemima was made a great fuss of. She in turn fussed over the two naked babies, which responded by urinating all over her. We were ushered into the garden at the front of the small house, from which plastic-covered sofas and chairs were produced. 'Cool drinks' i.e. tepid Coke and Fanta, and bananas and sickly-sweet cakes and biscuits appeared, which had probably cost a week's wages. Kalu Banda and one of his daughters disappeared into the kitchen and rustled up a meal in shades of pink and yellow "with no chilli" (which means only slightly spicy). The pink bits turned out to be curried tinned salmon, the thinking going presumably along the lines of 'food is curry, English people eat salmon, therefore we should make salmon curry for our English guests,. As sustenance it was let us say different, though we've since learned that Sri Lankans curry prodigious quantities of tinned mackerel and only the better-off curry fresh fish. To curry tinned salmon, then, would represent a special occasion and as an occasion it was utterly delightful.

I felt stupidly but distinctly privileged to have been welcomed into the home of a poor, rural Sri Lankan family. The house itself was basic but carefully looked after despite having to accommodate so many people in such a tiny space; the living room contained shelves of religious pictures and family photographs. A very tacky shrine in the corner including a gold-painted plastic Buddha still wrapped in his transparent plastic packing accompanied by a giant ghetto-blaster. A rogues' gallery of Martin family photographs was pasted around the walls. And we learned that a soldier in Batticaloa was going around with a picture in his pocket of Merigen as a young boy (but we did not learn why). We had brought with us a picture of Stonesheygate, our home in the Pennines, which everyone duly admired in an uncomprehending way. Then it was time to go, onwards and upwards to nearby Meenawatte.

Photographs diminish reality rather than record it (really good ones erect something different in its place). Candid freeze-frames capture uncharacteristic expressions. Posed pictures fail to illuminate either individuals or relationships. With pictures of houses it is even worse. A photograph cannot demonstrate to a stranger what it is that makes a place home, what is comforting, what is disturbing. Interiors can only hint at the spatial relationships of rooms and exteriors rarely do more than suggest the setting, the environmental context of the place. So although I had seen photos of Meenawatte I was entirely unprepared for the experience of seeing Sally's old home in the flesh. Meenawatte looked, above all, old. Grown out of and into its surroundings. It also looked, from the long approach track, quite small though inside it appeared far larger, a veritable Tardis of a house. The rooms were high, wide, airy and cool, the width of the open connecting doors generous, there were large areas of what in box-house Britain would be thought of as wasted space. Only part of the house was in use and glimpses into adjoining rooms and spaces lent an air of mystery. In the hallway sunlight fell in stripes across the floor and net curtains wafted in the breeze.

Both house and garden were even more neglected than I had expected, though the current owners had looked after the part of the house they used. Floors were clean though not polished, furniture of a basic kind set out neatly. From what we could gather, the owners were using the house as a base camp when working on the estate but lived elsewhere. KB summoned up two men to let us in, one of whom we understood to be the owner's brother who lived nearby. The main cash crops were spices, mainly cloves and pepper. We were given a kilo of cloves to add to those presented to us earlier by Kalu Banda so we now had accumulated enough to supply the whole of Yorkshire for at least a year. When we told them how much this amount of cloves would cost in England we were met by looks of utter stupefaction.

Parts of the house, including Sally's old room, were locked up for the use of the owners when they stayed. The former nursery had become a gloomy hole not even used for storage. I tried in vain to visualise the neat vegetable garden which had formerly occupied the patch of jungle Sally was indicating behind the house. Nor could I imagine how the interior would have been furnished and decorated. But in the imagined background were the strains of a big, noisy family living here long ago, and the screams and laughter of a happy, daredevil little girl and the barking of her dogs. Views are (almost) timeless. Although the heat haze obscured the last six of the ten ranges of hills visible from the terrace I was not disappointed. Trees formerly lopped had grown up again, partly obscuring the 270 degree vista. The photographs I took would not, I knew, do it or the house justice.

Over breakfast the next morning we learned that the owner of the Lake Inn where we were staying in Kandy had himself been a tea planter, taking over an estate from its Scottish owner when he returned to Britain around the time Sally's parents left Sri Lanka. The estate had been next door to Luccombe in Maskeliya where Sally's grandfather was born and which was managed by her great-grandfather whose grave we would soon be seeking. Following his retirement from the tea trade he'd moved nearer to Kandy where he had run a cattle farm near Wattegama.

"Where near Wattegama?" "On Elkaduwa Road, near to Hunas Falls". "That's near to where I lived! Do you know Meenawatte estate? Do you know the Banda family? They used to work for us." "Yes, I know it very well. Also all the Banda people. We have a girl here who comes from Meenawatte. She works in kitchen – I talk to her."

Instantly he was back to report that yes, she did remember Sally's parents and her time at Meenawatte. Before anything more could be said we noticed a woman of around forty standing shyly in the shadowed doorway behind him, looking out at us. Then she exploded into a broad grin and exclaimed *"Bunnis Nona! Bunnis Nona!"*.

After weekly trips to the Silva Bakery in Wattegama Sally used to return with buns for the children of the lines to eat. *'Bunnis nona'* was the estate children's name for Sally at the time –'lady who brings buns'). Although she spoke no English the delight on both her and Sally's faces was worth more than words.

We have revisited the Bandas a few times. In 2001 we had Merigen and Lucy with us and various members of the clan were present including the now very frail Ram Banda. Kalu Banda was out at work on a local building site. Gori Banda was again away from home somewhere or other. There had been some mix-up in the message from Peggy and they had expected us all the previous day so he'd taken the wrong day off. Aslin, who had been working in the Middle East last time we visited, was there and quite overcome at seeing Sally again after thirty years. The two babies from the last visit were now four-year-olds. On a more recent visit we took Sally's brother Jeremy who they had last seen as a small boy known to them as 'Ba Master' for some reason lost in time. Sally emerged from the van first and excitedly announced "Ba Master here with us". The family peered into the van: "Where Ba Master?" they asked. "Here! I am Ba Master" said Jeremy and they did a double-take having expected, it seems, to find a miraculously preserved six-year-old boy rather than a middle-aged man.

Kandy stands at a mere two thousand feet. The mortal remains of Sally's ancestors lie much higher up, in the real hill country, so it was back on the train once more. At Peradeniya Junction the *Uderata Menike* was waiting when we arrived, on time for once, and it was heaving with bodies. We discovered that February was the height of the Sri Pada (Adam's Peak) pilgrimage season and for the journey to Hatton it would be standing room only. The pilgrims were all bent on climbing the sacred mountain through the night in an endless shuffle up the steps to the top where a fortunate few might see a spectacular sunrise – if it wasn't cloudy. Then shuffling back down again, wrecking one's knees. Never really appealed to me, that one. Puts the 'grim' in 'pilgrim' as far as I'm concerned. We did manage to find a bit of floor space in the so-called 'restaurant car', enough for three of us to sit on our baggage while the fourth stood on a rota basis. Itinerant food-sellers barged past with trays and baskets, crying their wares in staccato monotones. "*Vade!, Vade!*" Cockroaches scurried over our feet.

We'd tried to book seats earlier but all were taken. Despite the crowds, one set of seats in second class was vacant. A sign warned us off: *"THESE SEATS ARE RESERVED FOR CLERGY AND PREGNANT MOTHS".* Entry to the observation saloon meant getting past the train guard, his splendid uniform being about the only remaining vestige of the former grandeur of the island's railway system. He told us firmly that there was no room in the observation car, though several vacant seats were visible through the door, then with a smile as wide as the Mahaweli Ganga he invited us to avail ourselves of the comforts of the guard's compartment; bench seats, lots of room, a private toilet and looking fairly clean. The only other occupants were a couple of backpackers; the woman, who was Swiss, was a self-righteous and opinionated politically-correct character bent on showing off her limited command of Sinhala at every station stop, though she shut up when she realised we could also speak a bit of the language. Her companion remained very quiet – sensible man.

In between swigs from a flat half of arrack the guard pointed out sights and photo opportunities and chatted amiably in the way most Sri Lankans do. At one point he invited us to travel in the locomotive's cab but as it became clear he wasn't going to facilitate this personally and as we were at the other end of a long train it seemed a risky project, much as the boy in me would have relished it. The scenery was spectacular as the train wound slowly uphill on hairpin loops through tea estates, clinging to the sides of precipitous drops, Sri Pada appearing first on one side then on the other.

Hatton was the nearest train station to Maskeliya, Sally's great-grandfather's last resting place. The hotel we stayed in was pretty dire. Dirty, no sheets, only rough blankets. As a result Sally was plagued with bed bug bites to go with her previously acquired swollen knee and ankles. Small creatures love her but don't much care for me, thankfully. Except for leeches which have no taste or discrimination. Jemima had problems with her faulty cooling system which gave her headaches and made her listless. I slept badly and awoke with a pounding headache. First, a group of guys insisted on talking until two in the morning on a balcony the other side of a paper-thin wall. I slept briefly until around five when the cocks started up, setting off the local dogs. At six the Germans across the landing decided to have a noisy breakfast outside our door. At six thirty the disembodied, electronically amplified voice of some imam called the faithful to prayer for half an hour, seemingly right above my head. At seven the first train of the day hooted and clanked its mournful way out of Hatton station and over the crossing by the hotel to add to the fiendish symphony and I got up and went to sit on the balcony and read. The experience put me off Hatton permanently and I've never been back, only through. You can keep your Hatton.

The drive up to Maskeliya was spectacular. Tea bushes in neat rows clinging to every hillside, packed so close it seemed you could set yourself on a board at the top of the hill and sledge over them to the bottom. Waterfalls threw themselves over sheer cliff faces, exotically sculpted mountains clamoured for attention. Dark green lakes dotted with bright green islands. Actually man-made reservoirs, but things of great beauty nonetheless. Unfortunately it seemed that Sally's great grandfather lay at the bottom of one. Maskeliya is a small town which was well off the tourist track at that time, before the invention of the 'tea trails' concept. White people were a rarity. As we passed children would clutch one another and point at us: "*Sudu! Sudu!*" – "White! White!" Even with our driver's help we failed to find anyone who had heard of All Saints Church. Since one of the last people we spoke to was a nun, we concluded that the search was to be fruitless. "Are you sure we've got the right town?" I asked Sally.

"Well, All Saints, Maskeliya is where everyone said he was buried". "But have you ever seen the grave, when you were a kid?" "Not that I remember. And you'd expect a nun to know the names of Christian churches, wouldn't you?" Sally recalled that when the reservoir was constructed in the early twentieth century, much of the then town was drowned and people were relocated further up the hillside. The most likely conclusion was that the church was among the drowned buildings. Likely but, as it turned out, wrong. Anyhow, Sally doesn't give up that easily and resolved to continue the quest the following day. But we found somewhere much nicer to stay than a flea-pit in Hatton.

Upper Glencairn is a former planter's bungalow, about a century old, now used as a guest house. It had once been the home of the eminent Victorian photographer Julia Margaret Cameron. Sally was critical of how standards of décor and polishing had slipped since her time but I found the place wonderfully atmospheric, full of ancient heavy furniture, wooden floors and carved wood ceilings; spacious rooms with antique but clean bathrooms attached. An immaculately-tended garden overlooked Castlereagh Reservoir, dotted with islands, and the hills beyond with fleeting glimpses of the summit of Sri Pada as the clouds parted from time to time. The whole area is full of Scottish connections - a lot of expatriate Scots decided to plant tea in Ceylon - and looking up the lake, with clouds spilling off the mountain-tops, it was easy to imagine oneself in the Highlands. We soon spotted a church on our left and went to investigate its well-kept graveyard. As anticipated, no sign of Henry Thomas in there but the minister noticed us and introduced himself and we told him of our quest. "I am not long here, but Jonathan, maybe he can tell you." He then brought over a frail and bent 90-year old who had been a servant of the kirk for 65 years but who nonetheless could not recollect the grave of a Henry Thomas Martin anywhere in the area. "Is there a church called All Saints?" we asked. "Ah yes, All Saints Church. The Minister of this church, he is inside. He is coming on visit to me".

Back in the van, now accompanied by the Minister of All Saints, we made a brief stop in Maskeliya to pick up the church keys. Then on, about a kilometre along Upcot Road to where All Saints Church nestled in a valley on the left. If you half-closed your eyes the scenery was reminiscent of Exmoor. Once in the churchyard it was an easy matter to find the headstone which we duly cleaned, stripped weeds from the grave and took photographs. The inscription was simple in the extreme:
"HENRY THOMAS MARTIN, OF LUCCOMBE, DEPARTED INTO REST
30TH AUGUST 1895 IN THE 37TH YEAR OF HIS AGE. GOD IS LOVE".

No mention of widow or children. No mention of cause of death so no means of resolving the conflicting views of Sally's mother and great aunts. Sally's mother's version was that he was a drunkard who took his horse and gig too fast round a corner one night and fell out. The great aunts were united in their view that he was returning late from a charitable mission to the local poor when he met with an unfortunate accident. Later we were told he'd died more prosaically of fever; the least interesting version is probably the correct one. I prefer to think that he was feverish, had drunk way too much and then set out on a mission to the poor.

Dying young was the fate of most of the nineteenth century settlers. My favourite place in the centre of Kandy is the Garrison Cemetery, behind the Temple of the Tooth and not much frequented by tourists. The ancient tombstones (made from Wiltshire stone brought out as ballast in the empty tea clippers – smart!) record numerous childhood fatalities – usually cholera – and a fair range of accidental deaths. On my first visit I was shown around by the young and enthusiastic guide who indicated one stone marking the demise of a chap who leapt from his horse and impaled himself on a stake. Careless. My guide continued by relating that he had shown Prince Charles around the site when he'd sloped off from the Commonwealth Heads of Government Conference or some such. "Very nice man, Sir. But very big ears, no?"

In the well-kept if plain All Saints church the minister astonished us by adding that only three months earlier some other relatives - an Irish branch of the Martin family - had visited the grave. At the time we had no idea who these people, might be. We have since met one of them, a wonderful lady called Priscilla who lives in Edinburgh and is Henry Thomas's granddaughter. Her own mother was but a foetus when Henry Thomas died and his widow moved back to England with her three young children including Edward – Sally's grandfather.

Back on the train, we headed for the terminus at Badulla where Edward Harry is buried, but first we stopped off to explore Ella. In the unlikely event of my ever becoming a celebrity and having to complete one of those questionnaires for some magazine which asks "Where and when were you happiest?" I'd answer "1998, in Ella" – being careful to point out that Ella is a place not a person. We found rooms in a former planters' bungalow, full of character. The food was excellent and the manager and staff were friendly, eager to please and attentive. We were enjoying the last of the light and the first of the pre-dinner alcohol when the sky suddenly darkened, like the onset of an eclipse. Lightning began flashing across the horizon and scattered heavy drops of warm rain fell - the kind of rain where you can identify precisely where on your body each single drop makes contact. The power went off and we sat outside in the lightning-punctuated darkness on a balcony surrounded by warm swirling mists with cicadas providing the wallpaper music. Fireflies coursed erratically through the gloom. The headlights of vehicles crawling up the pass through Ella Gap below us and the crunching of gear changes provided the counterpoint to the storm sounds. In the distance a forest fire burned. Earlier still, in the late afternoon sun, we had sat on rattan planters' chairs on the terrace of Ella Rest House sipping beer, writing postcards home and marvelling at the view down Ella Gap – distant blue hills fringed in the foreground by the precipitous sides of the valley at whose head Ella stands. Flame trees, temple flowers, English roses and dahlias bloomed all around. The Rest House has since been completely rebuilt in modern, trans-national hotel style - no more drinks in planters' chairs on the terrace – and inevitably re-christened with a new naff name. The stupendous view, of course, remains intact.

The dining room was dominated by two outsize portraits, juxtaposed; the Lord Buddha partnering the Queen. Just before dinner a stick-like figure shuffled into the room clad in a headscarf, threadbare pullover and plain white sarong, After bidding us good evening he introduced himself as the mayor of the district and the judge. Indicating an old photograph on the wall he explained that this was of himself at the age of twenty and asked us to guess his age now. "Sixty?" we ventured politely.
"No, I am born nineteen thirteen. This my house. I learn English Bishop's College" "Bishop's College in Colombo?" ventured Sally, who had been there herself, aged about five. "No, Bishop's College Matara. England very good country. England people bring laws to Sri Lanka. Laws and justice. Very fair. King George fifth he is like my father, very kind to me. He is very good man, no?"

We had no answer to that one, our own acquaintance with the monarch concerned being pretty much nonexistent, and it would have proved too challenging to have explained about Sally's ancestor, Real Tennis and the Richmond Herald. So he continued in the tape-loop manner of a very old man whose mental faculties are fading. "I learn English Bishop's College. Bishop's College Matara. England very good". "Sri Lanka government no good. Corrupt. I want England come back to Sri Lanka, then all fair". "Everyone come to me for judge disputes in Ella. I am judge. Also I am mayor". He indicated a sign in Sinhala over the front door which apparently attested to this. "I learn English Bishop's College. Bishop's College Matara. England very good, very fair people. Sri Lanka government no good..."

We had been helped in our quest to find Sally's grandfather's grave by Kishan, the owner of the Ella guest house where we were staying. We'd asked his opinion on the best way to uncover any records that might exist. He took up the challenge with the enthusiasm we were already coming to expect from so many Sri Lankans: "Ah, the problem is it is now Friday and all offices will be closed soon for the weekend. But I will see what I can do." It was by then around 4pm. A couple of hours later he reported that he'd phoned a friend in Badulla. "This man has checked with the records office but there is nothing about your grandfather. But he is asking many people and I will talk to him again in the morning". We were thankful but not encouraged. In the morning there was no further news but Kishan asked whether Sally's grandfather would have been Catholic, Church of England or some other denomination. Sally said C of E on the basis that there were no Catholics in her family and on the assumption that Anglicanism represented the default setting for non-religious Englishmen of her grandfather's generation. We were advised to find the Anglican church in Badulla and enquire there.

The short train journey from Ella to the terminus at Badulla crosses Demodara nine arch viaduct. This picturesque but not especially striking piece of engineering is hugely celebrated by the Sri Lankans and has its own website containing the following impenetrable description:

Built by the British in the early 20th century, the station and the Nine Arcs bridge were engineering marvels of the day. This name is used since the bridge contains of 9 arches. It is also known as "Ahas Nawaya Palama" (9 Skies Bridge) and this bridge is 300 feet long and 25 feet wide. Located almost 3100 feet above the sea level. The bridge connects with two high lands and has been made of large cubic stones. This single piece of steel. The bridge was finally commissioned in 1921. One and only railway station trains travels same horizontal level in place is Demodara Railway station. It's amazing point of Sri Lanka. Inventor of this technology is person who looks after cattle. There is a railway tunnel downside of the Demodara Railway station. The train comes through the tunnel and after travel about 400m gap which round way then comes to Station.

Make of that what you will. As a feat of engineering it's moderately impressive but doesn't stand comparison with the ancient tanks (reservoirs), the great ruined cities or the Sigiriya rock fortress. There are many grander viaducts across Europe. Maybe the celebration is just because it's British built. In that case I say let's organise a Sri Lankan visit to Ribblehead. Now that would blow their socks off. If they wore any. Which in Ribblehead they'd need to.

Badulla –the terminus of the railway and the last resting place of Sally's road-building grandfather, Edward Harry Martin, master of the adverse camber which he deliberately built into roads to deter speeding, presumably reasoning that a few injuries and fatalities incurred for the greater good – *pour encourager les autres* – represented sound engineering practice. Edward Harry had also died young and unnecessarily. He had been in Trincomalee and heading back to Colombo when he experienced severe abdominal pains. His driver wanted to take him to hospital in Kandy, which by then they were approaching, but Edward Harry believed the medical facilities in Colombo to be far superior to those in Kandy and insisted the driver continue to the capital. He was right about the medical facilities but wrong about risk assessment where appendicitis is concerned. On the way to Colombo his appendix burst and he died what must have been an agonising death.

St Mark's church wasn't hard to find and as we pulled up a small group of men gathered round to greet us. Most were officers of the church of some description, the other was Kishan's friend, an older man who also spoke excellent English. He told us that he had discovered from the church records that the grave of Edward Harry Martin did indeed lie somewhere in the churchyard and had phoned our guest house but had just missed us so had come down to the church to wait for us. This willingness to go the extra mile for complete strangers and with no reward is so typically Sri Lankan.

Great news, but we now had the task of finding the grave. The church stood in the centre of a large cemetery. The more recent graves lay on the near side of the church but the older ones were beyond, in what we soon discovered was an area fast returning to jungle. In the heat of the day, oblivious to the possibility of snakes and scorpions in the dry undergrowth, clouds of yellow and white butterflies swirling about our heads, the three of us assisted by Kishan's friend and two of the local churchwardens, vergers or whatever they are called out here took up sticks and billhooks and began to thrash through the mass of vines, brambles, bushes, small trees and tall reedy grasses which had obscured the majority of the headstones. Several graves had no headstone and no inscription. Other headstones had toppled forwards with the inscription face down and too heavy to budge. On others the writing was eroded beyond legibility – Jemima used her fingertips to 'read' one of them and found the date of death to be eighteen something.

I take a boyish delight in announcing that it was I who found the grave. The man I'd been working next to and checking, on the suspicion that he probably could not read English, called me over excitedly, pointing to a headstone. It was indeed the grave of someone who had died in the mid 1940s, around the same time we believed Sally's grandfather had died, but the name was nothing like. My suspicions were proved correct in that while he could read numerals he could not read letters. I praised his observation, explained that it was someone else and turned away when the single word 'Luccombe' caught my eye, written faintly on a nearby headstone. Scraping away the moss and pushing aside the undergrowth the grave was revealed as that of Edward Harry Martin. I called everyone over and Jemima and I set about scraping away the moss with stones, gradually revealing the inscription:
IN LOVING MEMORY OF
EDWARD HARRY MARTIN
OF BEDFORD, ENGLAND
SON OF HENRY THOMAS MARTIN
OF LUCCOMBE ESTATE
MASKELIYA, CEYLON
BORN 31ST JULY 1892
LIEUTENANT, R.A. 1914-1918
DIED ON SERVICE AS
SUPERINTENDENT ENGINEER, P.W.D.
11TH JUNE 1945

Sally stood by the graveside in a state of mild shock. The little working party set to clear the grave of thorny vegetation while rags, cleaning agent and hot water appeared unbidden from the church to smarten up the headstone. Many photographs were taken. Sally wondered if we could buy flowers in Badulla town and come back with them – no need, someone had already been sent to pick some and soon returned with a huge bunch set in a rusty tin can. More photographs. Mutual congratulations. Jemima placed five of her precious bangles on the headstone as a personal tribute. Then we finally left, there being nothing more to do.

Business with the bank

We were making good progress through Sally's agenda but were soon stopped abruptly. Both Wilpattu National Park and the town of Trincomalee were strictly off limits due to the war. Wilpattu was now in the territory held by the LTTE (Liberation Tigers of Tamil Eelam – more commonly known as the Tamil Tigers). They were using it as a training area and had slaughtered most of the park's larger animals for food – having first slaughtered the park wardens. Trincomalee was currently in government hands but still hotly contested and too dangerous to visit. In 1998 the war was at one of its peaks. Even in normally safe Kandy the famous Temple of the Tooth, supposed to house one of the Buddha's incisors, had been bombed by the LTTE just before we arrived. The remains of the suicide bomber's van could still be seen by a wall; roof tiles were still scattered around; lamp-posts leaned at crazy angles; the Queens Hotel opposite, one of Sally's old haunts where we'd planned to stay, had had all its windows blown out and was closed. So it was back down to Colombo to see if we could find Sally's mother's lost gems.

The Chartered Bank was exactly where Sally had remembered it and externally hadn't changed a bit, other than the signboard. It had merged, as banks do, with the Standard Bank to form the originally-named Standard

Chartered Bank, housed in an imposing colonial era building in Fort, the heartland of colonial Colombo. We had made an initial visit, explaining what we were looking for and handing over a copy of the bank statement. We were told that to take things further would require a letter of authority from Sally's Mum. After several attempts at using the Byzantine phone system we did manage to contact her and set this up.

When we called in on our return to Colombo two weeks later, the letter had indeed arrived at the bank and to our surprise, the bank had unearthed not one but two deposited 'packets', one in Pamela's name and the other, which Sally was unaware of, in Tony's name. Sally's letter of authority from her Mum clearly authorised her to do as she pleased with any item in either Pamela's or Tony's name. Nalum, the official assigned to our case, pored over it then, wordlessly, took it backstage. She emerged with a more senior official: "Madam, this letter not enough. You need Power of Attorney."

This, as we learned over the years, is a classic tactic of Sri Lankan officialdom, suggesting the powers that be have read a little too much Kafka. State a requirement the customer must fulfil in order that you can deal with his request. When he has fulfilled it, state a further requirement. And so on until either someone with half a brain and a position of authority intervenes, or the customer gives up, or a violent incident takes place. The good news was, we were told, that once the Power of Attorney had been granted we could do anything we wanted including taking the boxes back to England with us. But we had less than a fortnight of our holiday remaining – could it be done in time? "What is in these 'packets'?" "We do not know, Madam." "Well, can you tell us how big they are?" "No, Madam." It transpired that 'packet' is used as a generic term and could have been something as small as an envelope or as large as a tea chest. Their existence had been confirmed merely by means of a computer search and no-one had been to the vault and actually set eyes on them.

Arranging the Power of Attorney (or, as Jemima appropriately misheard it, 'power of
eternity') took up the entire afternoon, mercifully in a fiercely air-conditioned building.
We could now do nothing for several days until we had confirmation that the bank had received the relevant documents. Then we could make an appointment to
look at what they had. Other than the gems, we assumed the contents were just papers, but on the other hand Sally's brother Simon had visited Sri Lanka a few years previously and left with a cache of small arms belonging to the Martin family which he took back with him to Hong Kong. Lord only knew what we might find.

So off we went for a jaunt down the coast to Galle, from where the treasure hunt continued remotely. Phone and fax lines were zinging as pressure mounted to beat the deadline imposed by our flight. Will the intrepid trio find Queen Pamela's lost jewels and return them to her in her fairy tower in Fulham? Sally got through to the Standard Chartered Bank and the British High Commission with depressing results. The bank had received no communication from London and the person she spoke to denied any knowledge of their own UK head office in Park Lane which Pamela had visited a few days earlier. It later emerged that the papers had been sent not to the bank in Fort but to the bank's Sri Lanka head office elsewhere in Colombo and were still stuck in the bank's internal mail system. The woman at the British High Commission was no help regarding customs duties. "There are strict regulations on tourists taking valuables out of the country, Madam." "But these are our family possessions." "No, you cannot buy jewels and take them out of Sri Lanka without paying the proper duties." "Listen, we're not talking about buying gems. These are my mother's from when we lived here many years ago. Do I still have to pay duty to take them back to her in England?" "Ah, Madam, that I do not know. It is a matter for UK Customs and Excise." "Yes, and you're the British High Commission, so could you please find out for me?" "Sorry, Madam, not possible."

Meanwhile the bank, firmly committed to its Kafkaesque strategy of making up the rules as it went along, now told us that the Power of Attorney may not be enough to release Sally's father's package on the grounds that since he is deceased they would require the additional written authority of each of her five brothers. "But the only reason you know I have five brothers is because I told you so", countered Sally. A quizzical smile was all she got in return. Back up to Colombo. We now had two days before our return flight took off.

We girded our loins for another hard day at the Standard Chartered Bank, arriving as the doors opened at 9.30am. By midday we had made precisely no progress. Nalum was trying her best but being stymied by their legal department who remained insistent that nothing could be done without the written consent of each of Sally's brothers. The log-jam began to shift once Sally had succeeded in getting the legal eagles down from their lofty perch for a face-to-face discussion. By chance, the Chief Executive, an Englishman, happened by and earwigged the conversation. He asked the legal team to meet him in his office. The brief sound of a raised, magisterial voice then the shutting of the office door. The Chief Exec later told us he had explained to his legal 'experts' just what Power of Attorney means and instructed them to stop putting obstacles in our way. We could see the two packets but it would be an hour or so before this could be arranged so we took a lunch break in the Pagoda Tearooms nearby. We chose a selection of cheap short eats, too many for us to polish off though we were happy to pay for them. But no – the system was that the items had been counted out before being brought to our table, our leftovers were then subtracted and we only had to pay for the balance. Jolly good as far as value for money was concerned but one wondered how many times and through how many pairs of hands the food had been recycled in this way.

Back at the bank we were invited backstage to view the two boxes, both of them locked metal chests, one weighing around fifteen pounds and the other perhaps twice that. Certainly enough to blow our baggage allowance, leaving aside the physical difficulty of transporting them to the airport. "You have brought the keys?" they asked innocently. The bank did not have a set of keys. Presumably Sally's parents must have taken the keys back to England and they had long since vanished. Our case had by now been passed for the personal attention of the Director of Operations, a friendly chain-smoking Scot whom we shall call Robert McNeish, who obviously regarded the whole thing as highly entertaining but was also full of profuse and sincere apologies for the way the bank had treated us hitherto. He had the boxes, and us, brought to his office and arranged for someone to come with a hammer and chisel to smash the locks. Then looked on in bemused and indulgent pleasure while we went through the contents.

Pamela's chest, the smaller of the two, contained the twenty flat blue velvet-covered jewel cases Sally remembered playing with plus assorted paper packets stuffed into a large envelope. Many hundreds of cut gems including aquamarines, white and yellow topaz, citrines, star sapphires, yellow sapphires, an unusual red-brown sapphire and a rare green sapphire, quartz crystal, onyx, garnets and zircons. Wildly impressive to look at, and some of the stones very large indeed, but what were they worth? It also contained her grandfather's gold false teeth.

Robert tried to get hold of a contact at the Central Bank who deals with exchange control issues – the only person there prepared to talk sense, as he put it – to find out what we had to do in order to get them out of the country. It was going to be tough. His contact had left for the day. But Robert did manage to speak to a friend of his wife's who was a jeweller. Though she would not be able to supply an official valuation she would be able to give us a rough idea of what the gems were worth.

Margritte (not her real name) was at the bank in less than half an hour with her magnifying glass and set to work studying the gems, literally leaving no stone unturned. Her eventual verdict was that the vast majority were of little worth, being flawed by impurities and imperfections. However a few stones were of significant value – several hundred pounds each at UK prices, maybe more. And a few others were extremely interesting (especially a very large but imperfect sapphire) but impossible to value as they didn't have a conventional market. A serious collector might pay a great deal but only for their collectability, not their potential value as jewellery. And we'd have to locate that collector, which without in-depth experience of the trade would be a nigh-impossible task. Several more stones would be worth getting re-cut to increase their value but only if this were done in Sri Lanka as the costs of re-cutting in the UK would not be worth the increase in value. The collection as a whole, she said, was interesting but unbalanced (too many sapphires and citrines). She estimated that at UK prices the whole lot might be worth between £5,000 and £10,000. She suggested a friend, let's call him Sajid, based nearby, who could be trusted to value the collection and provide an official valuation to use when dealing with the Central Bank and UK Customs. She and I went round to arrange this with him, which he confirmed he would be able to do first thing the next morning.

And what of the contents of the other, larger chest deposited by Sally's father? This contained an antique dagger in a rotting leather sheath and an assortment of ancient surveying instruments which had presumably belonged to Sally's grandfather Edward Harry, the road builder. The rest of the space was taken up by photographs, cans of undeveloped film, stacks of papers and, to Robert's consternation, several boxes of shotgun cartridges of various calibres. Having confirmed that we had no intention of taking the ammo back to the UK with us, he phoned the police to arrange for their collection. Most of the papers were technical records of tea planting, notebooks on amateur radio or Uncle Ray's business accounts written inexplicably in Sally's father's hand. The planting notes at least would probably have been of great interest to scholars and museums. Other papers in envelopes were marked 'personal' and Pamela had forewarned us of this and asked us to bring them home to her without reading them. There was no way we could carry all this stuff home, other than the personal papers, and we learned that the bank would, now that the owner had come forward, levy a charge if anything were re-deposited. So reluctantly all the rest of the papers went into the shredder and we relinquished possession of the dagger, false teeth, film cans and most of the surveying instruments.

Our last day in Sri Lanka dawned. We set off for the bank at opening time where we had arranged to meet Margritte to get the gems valued. Soon after all three of us were round the corner at Sajid's premises on Chatham Street with the entire haul. Sajid said he'd need a couple of hours to sort and value the collection and until then there was little we could do. We tried to take a walk around Fort so Sally could show us where she'd lived as a child but at every corner we were turned back by the army or navy.

Sajid valued the collection more highly than Margritte had suspected – about £10,000 at Sri Lankan prices and up to three times that much in the UK, though he repeated what Margritte had said about the difficulty of realising this sum as much of the collection would be of interest only to specialists. Although the suspected green sapphire turned out not to be so, among the 'topaz' collection was a large yellow sapphire worth about £3,000. A huge garnet was also valuable despite its flaws and two of the star sapphires were particularly good examples. No way could we afford to pay the duty on £10,000 worth of stones. We decided to remove the four valuable ones and 'lose' them – bury them in our luggage and not declare them either to the Central Bank or UK Customs and asked Sajid to make out a valuation form for the remainder of the collection valued at around £6,000. We would either be able to return the four really valuable stones to Sally's Mum whatever happened with the Central Bank or spend our homecoming in Strangeways rather than Stonesheygate. Sajid accordingly made out a valuation form for the remaining stones, we paid his fee and hurried back to the bank with our rucksack full of jewels, being accosted several times on the way by gem-dealers anxious to sell us their wares. It was hard to keep a straight face.

A near-miracle then occurred. Robert finally made contact with Douglas Silva at the Central Bank's exchange control section, explained the story and the valuation, and asked whether it would be possible for us to take the gems out with us the same night. To everyone's amazement, including Robert's, he saw no problem. It was simply a matter of filling out the requisite form in triplicate, taking it to exchange control down the street and getting it stamped. Slightly too good to be true, of course. A search of the bank revealed that they had no copies of the form in question so a runner was sent to the Central Bank to get some. He returned at 2.45pm; exchange control was due to close at 3.30. The forms were completed and typed up and at 3.15 we arrived in Douglas Silva's office with the forms, the valuation certificate, the Power of Attorney and a letter of confirmation from the bank. Douglas passed the documents to a minion for checking and proceeded to engage us in leisurely conversation about tropical fruit. The papers were returned and stamped and we were free to take the gems out of the country. What might confront us at the UK end was another matter.

We returned to the Swimming Club for the last lazy hours of our holiday before our 4am flight. The helpful manager not only arranged for a van to take us to the airport at midnight but also commandeered two members of staff to help carry our bags up the road to the checkpoint and the waiting van, Galle Road being closed at nightfall due to the security situation. Even then Sri Lanka had one last incident in store for us. Halfway to the airport the van broke down spectacularly. The lights went out and all power, including the brakes, failed. Our driver swerved to avoid a parked car, we clipped a passing lorry and finally came to rest at the roadside. A knot of men gathered around offering help and solutions but despite everyone's endeavours the van could not be re-started. A tuk-tuk was hailed and somehow the three of us and all our luggage were crammed in for an extremely uncomfortable ride of another 45 minutes or so to the airport. On the airport approach road the tiny vehicle gave up the unequal struggle and burst a tyre but our driver continued magnificently and bumpily on the remaining two good wheels on his wagon and dropped us right outside the entrance.

Katanaiyaka Airport in the middle of the night was a scene of chaos, with locals barging in front of patiently queuing tourists, tempers and nerves frayed to breaking point, and plenty of form-filling to do. The flight was already boarding by the time we made it into the departure lounge. Sixteen hours later we touched down in Manchester and headed, hearts in mouths, for the red channel. The young guy behind the counter awoke from a little nap. He seemed pleased to have someone to talk to and was amused by our story. The only payment due, he told us, was VAT based on the Sri Lankan valuation which I achieved, just, by taking my credit card to its limit. Sally's Mum had already agreed to repay this by selling some of the gems. Our bags weren't searched and the two star sapphires in Sally's bum bag and the yellow sapphire and large ruby wrapped in Jemima's Winnie the Pooh flannel in the wash-bag remained undiscovered. Our neighbour Maria had offered to meet us and drive us home from the airport and she was waiting as we emerged. She asked whether we wanted to go for a coffee and we replied, in the best gangster fashion: "No, let's get out of here quick. Just drive!" In the car we told her the story. Jemima, who hadn't been let in on the secret contents of her wash-bag, feigned (or maybe didn't) offence.

The proceeds from the sale of most of the gems gave Sally's mother two foreign holidays: an African safari and the chance to visit her eldest son in the Philippines, together with a few creature comforts to eke out her state pension through her final years. After her funeral, at the wake in her Fulham tower block her sons got the family armaments out and waved them around a lot, to my consternation. We all had far too much to drink, as is the custom on such occasions. She left Sally the remaining gems which we still have. They make a cameo appearance towards the end of this book.

My first experience of Sri Lanka would stay with me forever. I'd returned Sally to the place she called home, and it wasn't long before I too was thinking of the country in terms of a possible future home. We'd covered a lot of ground in that first month-long trip as well as spending way too much time in a bank: ancient cities, beaches, mountains. Colombo and Kandy. Birds and animals, to some extent. Jemima's head teacher had been reluctant to allow her so much time off school but later had the humility to agree the experience had done her more good than four weeks schooling. From being a bit of a loner, and a bit bullied, she'd come back telling tales of scrubbing elephants in rivers, strange abandoned cities and tuk-tuk rides; as a result she'd become the most popular girl in class, as well as having gained a world perspective denied to most kids her age. Of course, this was in the days when head teachers were allowed to run their schools and would never be permitted today.

I was keen to come back and learn more. So we did, time after time, and ten years later we had built our home there, though it took seven years more before we could afford to quit the rat race and live in it. During that time I slowly began to understand – in the imperfect way strangers do – this curious, enigmatic, frustrating and inspiring island.

Three

Seven up

Sally was in tears as the plane lifted off from Colombo at the end of that first trip. "Promise me we'll be back". "Absolutely promise. I just love the place. As soon as we can afford it we'll be back". "And we'll take Merigen as well?" "If he wants to come, yes". He did want to come. So did his partner Lucy and his friend Gabriel. And our friend and neighbour Dean. Seven of us. It was another three years before we could pull the fares together but in summer 2001 we were on our way – Dean, who was a teacher with end of term commitments, following a week later. No missions. No quests. Just a grand tour, a monster four week holiday. Which, as it happened, turned out to be a six week holiday thanks to the Tamil Tigers ably assisted by Emirates Airlines.

The Swimming Club, our first port of call again, had changed more in three years than it had in the previous twenty seven. The simple covered area known to Sally as the cowsheds had been converted into a kitchen and restaurant, the former kitchen block was being refurbished with an upper storey as extra rooms, the bar was getting a makeover, a waterslide had been installed – though this too had disappeared by the time we next visited three years later. "Too danger, madam" was once again the explanation. The bureaucracy, however, was timeless. On arrival we had the job of completing various forms to achieve our temporary membership status, causing great consternation among the staff who found it hard enough to deal with the prospect of an unmarried couple (Merigen and Lucy) let alone a married couple with different surnames and a 'nephew' (Merigen's friend Gabriel - we had to call him something) with yet another surname. Jemima they could at least understand. We didn't mention the seventh person, Dean, who would be with us when we returned in a couple of weeks - it would have been the final straw. We'd deal with that situation when it arose. "Hey! Mima! Do you realise that when we come here again, with Dean as well, we'll be the S Club 7?" I quipped. (Yawn. Groan).

Jet-lag duly dealt with we headed up the coast to Negombo. We stayed at the Ice Bear, a lovely beachside place with sandy, shady gardens with ducks, hens and a pet monkey. A gate from the garden opened onto an unkempt beach. We spent the rest of the afternoon doing very little then, as the day cooled, walked up the road and found a beach cafe. Excellent food, with Gabriel and Jemima particularly in gastro-heaven tucking into lobster thermidor and chicken cordon bleu respectively. Spelt 'Gordon Blue', inevitably. Saturday night festivities on the beach with disco music, kite-flying and hot snacks stands provided the contrast. Eventually the sea turned the kind of naff pink one associates with cheap prints, fringed with frilly lace from the breakers, and the sky traded oranges and blues, the whole scene finally exhausting itself in star-studded indigo.

Next morning we strolled off to observe the large-scale fish-drying operations on the beach. This was a surreal sight with fish sorted into different species laid neatly in rectangles on the sand in an area the size of a couple of football pitches. Indescribable stink. Then on the advice of the owner of our guest house we set forth in the afternoon for a boat trip on the backwaters of a river north of Negombo. We hired a van for the ride up to the river, about 10km away, armed with directions to the house of a 'Mr Babu' who ran the boats, and a hand-drawn map of sorts. Having got somewhere near, the driver stopped various locals to ask "Where Mister Babu house?" No-one, it seemed, had heard of the mysterious Babu or his boat trips. However boats were also advertised from the swish-looking Dolphin Hotel nearby so we made our way there. They redirected us to a more down-market restaurant just along the road. It took some persuasion to encourage a teenager called Peter to take us out in an old plastic six-seater outboard with one seat missing. Jemima had to perch on the prow.

The two-hour trip was billed as 'romantic'. It was many things but romantic was not among them. The boat's motor had its own ideas of when to start and stop and the fuel line became detached from time to time. Merigen, who at the time travelled everywhere with a water pistol for protection, rashly demonstrated its use and handed it to the youth to try, after which it never left his hands. Peter, little more than a kid, was more interested in squirting us than identifying birds or water life or indeed piloting his craft. Eventually he turned over the management of the boat to Merigen, assisted by Jemima, while Lucy and Gabriel bore their soakings and Peter's manic laughter with British stoicism. As an older generation, deserving of at least some respect, Sally and I were subjected only to the occasional squirt. The early part of the trip took in bits of riverbank cottage industry, namely an illegal arrack still in a jungle clearing and, a little further on, the chance to see a family of toddy-tappers working in a grove of coconut palms connected by high-level ropes. The arrack was damned good stuff – though Sally can't abide it. Too sweet. The best that could be said for the toddy was that its taste was less unpleasant than its smell. Jemima doled out sweets to the toddy toddlers and we were on our way once more. The languid river finally exhausted itself at a spit of sand separating it from the ocean, lacking the energy to break through. We turned around and headed back to Negombo.

On to Anaradhapura by way of Padeniya and Yapu Hua, two of the less visited ancient sites. In each place we were virtually the only tourists and certainly the only white people, though the downside was that none of the information boards was in English so we could only learn something of the history of these fascinating places from the accounts in the *Lonely Planet*, from our driver Norman and from conversations with people on the site. Padeniya is a medieval Buddhist temple complex with some exquisite wood carvings and Buddha images. Yapa Hua is the 'mini Sigiriya', a hundred metre high rock rising sheer out of the plain with steps up to the ruins of a citadel about halfway up. Apparently there are the ruins of other buildings on the summit, as in Sigiriya, but unlike Sigiriya the summit was inaccessible to all but experienced and properly equipped rock-climbers. From the platform ruins we took a path skirting the side of the rock face and heard the distant growling of a sloth bear. Sloth bears are so-called not because of their lazy habits (on the contrary, they are fast and dangerous) but because of their long clawed toes. They blend aggression with stupidity, a combination not to be messed with. So we found discretion to be the better part of valour and returned the way we had come. A monk opened up a rock-cave temple at the foot of the hill by the entrance with a gigantic rusty key; its walls and roof were covered in lovely ancient frescoes.

Close to Anaradhapura is Mihintale. The climb to the main temple, via a series of ruined buildings, involves nearly two thousand, admittedly shallow, steps. The trees provide shade most of the way up while the sun is still low. The stairs were lined with delightful wayside stalls selling fruit, trinkets and religious icons. The sun was high as we made our way slowly back down from the summit temple and the nearby Cobra Pool. We heard screaming behind us and turned to look. A young girl had started to run down the steps and was now going so fast she was out of control and heading straight for Jemima. A mango-seller standing nearby moved across and managed to stop both of them as the girl cannoned headlong into Jemima, hurting his shoulder in the process but with nothing more than a bad shock for both kids. This act of heroism, Sally judged, was worth not only a bit of cash but a *"bohoma stuti"*, remembered Sinhala for "thank you very much" and only used when someone has done something extra special. Like saving your daughter's life.

Having his own little platoon suited our Anaradhapura guide perfectly. 'Police Banda' was not as old as Anaradhapura but pretty ancient nonetheless. 'Banda' was his family name. 'Police' was his way of reminding the world that before becoming an Anaradhapura guide he'd been a policeman, all of twenty three years previously. And we weren't going to forget it. His knowledge was encyclopaedic, his English excellent and his manner didactic and military. Gabriel in particular was repeatedly instructed to "pay attention. This important," as Police Banda marched us from site to site according to a precise schedule held in his head, tut-tutting whenever Merigen and Lucy whose relationship was then in first blush broke ranks to canoodle or to explore something they'd noticed on the way. That there was an element of self-deprecating jest in all this only gradually became apparent at the end of the tour, when he organised us into singing a variety of marching songs. Having thus been well entertained we gave him a decent tip. He must have been in his eighties but boy, could he set a cracking pace in the heat of the day. Luckily, Anaradhapura is set exquisitely in sparse woodland and there is plenty of shade to be had.

The next day a rash of new roadblocks appeared in the city. Norman, our driver, explained cryptically that this was because of a big anti-government demonstration in Colombo, some 200km away. Anaradhapura was the closest we'd come to the war zone, with Tamil Tiger territory only a few miles up the road and road blocks and checkpoints sprang up with alarming frequency. Four hundred people were slaughtered here in 1985, at about the same time the Tigers closed Wilpattu National Park by massacring all the park rangers. As a result, driving around the area was like being a piece in a board game played by the gods, who alone knew the rules and moves. I tried following where we were on a map and kept finding we were two or three kilometres away from where I'd calculated our position to be. The overhead sun in the middle of the day gave little help in direction-finding.

Next stop Sigiriya. I'm not usually a fan of tourist hotspots. I wouldn't advise a first time visitor to London to see the Tower at all costs, or a visitor to Rome to see the Coliseum. *Chacun a son gout.* Do and see what appeals to you rather than what the guide books tell you is important. But I make an exception for Sigiriya. Even if you're only in Sri Lanka for a week, try to see it. Yes, it's prominently displayed on virtually every tourism website. Yes, the entrance charges for foreigners are as steep as the rock face. Yes, it's plagued by touts and scammers. Yes, you'll probably have to make the final stretch of the climb to the top as part of an endless crocodile of people, including these days coachloads of Chinese folk sporting selfie sticks. All of which would normally put me off. But Sigiriya is really something special. Though first you have to find it. Not difficult, one would think. It's a damn great volcanic plug rising sheer out of a flat plain, tantalisingly visible in snatches between stretches of scrub jungle as you approach. As a UNESCO protected site a lot of money had been invested by well-meaning NGOs in signage. Nice, clear big metal signs. Which provided ideal roofing material for the local population. And employment for a series of native guides who offer to show tourists how to get into the place, in the absence of the signage which they and their neighbours had appropriated. So tickets were obtained from an isolated hut a mile up a dirt track off the road and nowhere near the rock. From there the track directly towards the rock had been closed for some reason, necessitating a lengthy detour back via the road and up another long dirt track to the car park which was a further ten minutes' walk away from the entrance. There we found the main ticket office, which was closed. Jemima needed to use the nearby toilets which were guarded by an unsavoury-looking man so Sally went with her. As they left the extremely smelly facility the man attempted to charge them fifty rupees for the experience. Sally offered ten, which he refused, so she took the note back and in turn refused to pay anything. Ten rupees is what you pay even now for well-maintained toilets in oases such as the Kandy City Centre building. Off we went again in search of an alternative entrance in the maze of dirt roads around Sigiriya, finally succumbing to the need to take on board a local guide to get us through the last mile or two, for a suitable fee, of course.

Once inside we were immediately surrounded with a new horde of 'guides', one of whom gestured dramatically behind him: "The rock! See, the rock!" and held out his hand for payment. Well I never! Hadn't spotted it, mate, thanks for pointing it out. The rock fortress is approached via extensive formal water gardens, which were (and are still) being excavated and revealed. In Sally's childhood all of this lay buried under jungle. The archaeological techniques are very un-British in that they involve partial reconstructions following excavation, using original materials found nearby. I have to admit I prefer this style. It may be anathema to the intellectually rigorous archaeologist but is a darned sight more informative and meaningful to the visitor than the practice of leaving everything uncovered as it was found, then carting the interesting bits off to some museum.

In the water gardens we saw our second cobra of the day. The first had slid across the road in front of our car earlier. This one was resting on the grass only twenty yards or so from the main drag. So I strode off towards it, camera in hand – being that kind of a stupid git. The cobra decided on this occasion to show mercy and slid away rapidly – too rapidly for me to photograph it. Instead I got a venomous tongue-lashing from Sally for putting myself in unnecessary danger: "If that cobra had felt threatened you'd probably have been bitten." "But I was only trying to photograph it, not chase it!" "I suggest you tell that to the snake. At some point you'd have been entering its territory which you'd find was not neatly marked by a garden fence. Once over that line it could have turned on you and bye-bye Jerry."

Beyond the water gardens the climb starts in earnest, through the boulder gardens (a boulder being on average around the size of a small house) and up marble stairways onto the rock. Sections of the climb involve metal ladders with handrails, alternating with horizontal stretches on platforms hanging dizzily over the void below. Sally defied her vertigo magnificently but took a breather while the rest of us did the detour up a spiral staircase to see the gallery of tenth century frescoes in a cave – beautifully painted, amazingly preserved and mildly titillating depictions of half-clad women with unfeasible waists and breasts. The frescoes are covered with ancient inscriptions which were at first assumed to be religious in nature but, when deciphered, were more along the lines of "Cor! Look at the knockers on that one!"

At a gentle pace we continued the climb up to the Lion's Paws, about two thirds of the way up and all that remains of what was once an immense brick lion's head through whose jaws lay the onward path on rock-cut steps to the palace at the summit. Some large black blotches up on the rock were pointed out to me by Sally, who explained that these were enormous bee swarms. A couple of tiny bee-proof shelters had been erected on the small plateau at the foot of the Lion's Paws for when the bees decided to go on the rampage. They wouldn't come near to accommodating the large numbers of visitors on an average day, let alone the poor sods stranded halfway up the climb to the summit. Luckily the bees remained torpid. The rock-cut steps of Sally's childhood had long since been replaced by a series of metal ladders bolted into the sheer rock face, with steps less than six inches wide in places. The summit consists of a series of small plateaux and contains the foundations of a complex of palace buildings together with a large rectangular water tank cut into the rock. The magnificent views out across the plains are of a dry, scrubby landscape dotted with solitary hills of all shapes and sizes.

On the way back down the touts re-emerged, this time not offering to guide us around but trying to sell souvenirs with alleged cultural and folkloric relevance.
"You want magic box? Sacred healing power!" "Traditional mask?" "Elephant on stick?" Jumbo or mumbo-jumbo, you take your pick. We found ways of getting the upper hand, though. Gabriel had the most effective technique, initially feigning interest and then explaining patiently that while he had no need of a sacred box, perhaps they had a magic spoon? Or custard? Or perhaps a self-flushing potty? There was no end to his inventiveness when he got going and the end result was some very nonplussed hawkers beginning to think that here was perhaps a dangerous lunatic rather than a potential customer, so they left us alone. Result!

Nearby Dambulla is a complex of ancient Buddhist rock temples. We managed to throw off yet another self-appointed 'guide' claiming to be a temple boy and made the long and very hot climb up the rock to the temples at our own pace. On the bare rock slope up to the temple we were simply very hot, but on entering the courtyard where one is obliged to cast off one's footwear we experienced the excruciating pain of walking barefoot on the dry-roasted pavement. We atheists must suffer for our lack of faith. Noticing a standpipe ahead we relished the prospect of splashing our faces but the water came out at about fifty degrees celsius. The water source is a reservoir at the top of the rocks and the fierce sun simply heats it up to that extent. The complex of caves that forms the ancient temple was at least a chance to cool off.

The unending giant representations of the Lord Buddha in every size and position managed to bore and impress me simultaneously. The new guide who had attached himself to us painstakingly explained the exact meaning of all the Buddha's bodily and hand positions and facial expressions. Forgive me, but I'm not a Buddhist and all of this is utterly irrelevant to me. What the Buddha taught – now that's different and interesting. But religious iconography is best left to the followers of that religion for whom it presumably has meaning, not the rest of us who don't share their faith. There is no denying the power of the exquisite wall paintings in the caves at Dambulla, but I yearned to be left to look at and contemplate them in peace and solitude rather than have some guy droning on about how many fingers the Buddha had raised and what this was supposed to signify. Philistine that I am.

Dambulla is as expensive for foreigners to visit as the rest of the 'Cultural Triangle' but for a while it was free. The typically Sri Lankan reason being that two different monkish factions controlled the lower (entrance) and upper (cave temples) levels of the site and could not agree on how to share the large amounts of entrance money shelled out by tourists. So until the day they managed to agree, Dambulla was declared free to enter.

Polonnaruwa is the other great ancient city of Sri Lanka, created when Anaradhapura fell in the 5th century so still pretty old. We approached from Dambulla via a back road that our driver knew. The road seemed like some kind of linear circus. Families living in roadside huts keep porcupines for food, much as English peasants of old used to keep a pig, and proudly came out to ruffle up the spines of their prize beasts to display them as we passed. Tiny children walked about on high stilts. Bonfires burned everywhere in the gathering gloom. There was also plenty of evidence of the herds of wild elephant which live hereabouts; broken trees and large turds. Vehicles are not allowed on the road after dark for fear of collisions with elephants. Collisions in which the vehicles and their occupants are likely to come off second best. So we had to make haste slowly through the chaos. Eventually we reached the main road to Polonnaruwa which is open after dark. Even out in the country the dark roads were thronged with unlit bullock-carts, unlit bicycles, unlit pedestrians, tractors and carts drawn by what looked at first sight to be large rotovators. In the distance a lorry approached at full tilt, headlights blazing, dazzling us and our driver. "Dip, you stupid *****!" But the lorry's headlights had two positions – full beam and off – so the dazzle was instantly replaced by darkness. We were disconcertingly aware of tons of invisible metal approaching at speed about thirty yards ahead. Hearts in mouths until it passed.

Where the wild things are

The war meant it was still not possible to visit either Trincomalee or Wilpattu, a continuing frustration for Sally. The upside for us was that tourist numbers were so low that even seven of us could just turn up at a place and find somewhere with room for us all to stay. Until we got to Nuwara Eliya, where we'd unwittingly timed our arrival to coincide with an international golf tournament. Nuwara Eliya is home to a top class golf course as well as a fabulously derelict-looking racecourse. Everywhere was full; even the option of splitting our group between two places wasn't on. We had one last throw, a guest house several miles out of town near the botanical gardens in Hakgala. We made our way there through the holiday traffic jams. Humbugs is indeed a lovely place but once again did not have enough spare room for all of us. The kindly owners, concerned at our plight as dusk approached, rang round every hotelier they knew but drew as many blanks as we had. But when Sri Lankans are determined to be helpful, as so many are, they don't stop until the problem is solved. So it was that we were finally found accommodation at the home of the Humbugs owner's daughter and her husband who lived several miles away near to Nanu Oya and didn't run a guest house. Instead Aruna and Nilanthi managed a division of the vast Somerset tea plantation in the area around Shortcut Road. They lived in an old, rambling planter's bungalow which they made over to all of us for the night, sleeping in a small back room themselves. But while the bungalow had space aplenty there were not enough beds for us all. So they borrowed some beds from a neighbour's house. 'Neighbour', of course, meaning someone who lived about a mile away. The operation involved commandeering tractors and trailers from the estate and fetching the beds in a convoy.

Meanwhile we headed back up to Nuwara Eliya for dinner at the Hill Club. Ah!, the Hill Club! The Athanaeum meets Fawlty Towers. A slab of grey stone set in manicured lawns with a forest backdrop, it looks like a minor English public school. Nor did the interior disappoint. There was a Reading Room, a Billiard Room, glass cases displaying trophy trout, antlered heads of all kinds adorning the walls, a bar that still claimed to be men only (though it isn't), a Ladies' Retiring Room (into which presumably men are now allowed on the basis of gender equality, though I've not tested that one out) and a vast dining-room-cum-drawing-room with an enormous open fireplace at one end, kept stocked with planks and small dead trees by men wearing white gloves. Upstairs there are ancient bathtubs and hot water bottles. Seven degrees north, but nearly seven thousand feet up; damned cold at night it can be here. You can join as a temporary member for a few hundred rupees per day but you still have to conform to the dress code. Not many male tourists come to the tropics bearing jackets and ties but you need these, plus long trousers, a suitable shirt, socks and shoes (not sandals). For once, women find it a lot easier. Just a nice floaty dress will do fine. But gentlemen, fear not! If you come inappropriately dressed the club will soon sort you out, footwear excepted. Whether you'll feel physically comfortable; whether you can catch sight of yourself in the mirror without bursting into tears – that's another matter. You are ushered into the gents from which a side door leads off into a spacious dressing-room where rails full of unlikely jackets, shirts and ties many of which make the seventies look like a model decade of sober good taste, awaits your approval. You emerge looking like a member of one of the odder beat combos of the past, *Madness* maybe. Or the *Bonzo Dog Doodah Band*.

Dinner was an extraordinary experience, a five course set meal for $10 plus burgundy, Armagnac and coffee to follow (it was a Poya day but this is not recognised at the Hill Club, which seems to operate as a mini-state). Pre-dinner G&Ts in front of a huge log fire, surrounded by the mounted heads of various beasts and occasionally plunged into darkness by the intermittent electricity supply. At the end of our meal a dessert of dramatically flambeed bananas in an ocean of brandy was carried off to perfection by the chef and the white-gloved waiter, somewhat to our disappointment, having read an account in the *Lonely Planet* of a disastrous attempt at the same dish, when the resultant kitchen fire had succeeded in plunging the entire town into darkness.

Nuwara Eliya is nicknamed 'Little England' and 'Little London' and was created in the same way as Simla in the Himalayan foothills as a colonials' retreat from the stickiness and oppressive heat of Colombo and the coast, particularly in the pre-monsoon season in April. I get the 'Little England' – as well as the racecourse and golf course there is a splendid pink Post Office which could conceivably fit in a Devon village, and a fine municipal park which could have come straight out of a Yorkshire mill town in its heyday. But anything even slightly reminiscent of London is way beyond the limits of my powers of imagination, I'm afraid.

Elephants are everywhere in Sri Lanka but if you want to see them in really large numbers there are two go-to places. One is Minneriya sanctuary, home every September to 'the gathering' when unprecedented numbers of the great beasts converge on a single lake. The world's largest gathering of elephants, or so the tourist websites would have us believe. I've not yet been to Minneriya so can't comment further. Though one of our guests commented dryly that Minneriya is also home to the world's largest gathering of jeeps so I may give it a miss. But we did go to Uda Walawe where we saw so many elephants that I was pleading for them to go away so we might see something else. I cheered when we saw a spotted deer and screamed in delight to see an Indian Roller perched on a rotting post. Anything but elephants, please! I don't actually dislike elephants but I just can't get that worked up about them like I can about birds, or leopards, bears or even snakes. They're just too common. I suppose the English equivalent would be the grey squirrel. Imagine if the grey squirrel were a rare sight – how special and cute it would be to glimpse one. But the damn things are all over your bird feeders the whole time and are just a bloody nuisance. Paddy farmers feel the same about elephants. They have to stay up all night lighting fires, singing till their throats are sore and letting off rockets just to keep the oversized pests from destroying their crops and livelihoods. And I'm sorry, but I'm with the farmers on this one. And as for monkeys – well, all in good time.

Our tracker, Samantha, spoke very little English but he was fluent in Elephant, which came in very handy. A female elephant seemed very agitated at our presence and after a short while we saw why. Under her belly on wobbly legs stood a tiny calf. She spoke to us in Elephant thus: "You come any closer to my baby and the jeep gets it!"

By this time we were a few yards away. We raised our cameras; she raised her trunk. Then charged at us. "Don't say you weren't warned!" she roared in Elephant.

Jemima headed straight for the small space below the bench seat, Gabriel looked ready to throw up or worse. I was too fascinated to be scared but was soon thrown from my seat by the diminutive tracker who held up his hand to the beast in the universal peace greeting and spoke soothing words in Elephant: "Aliya – it's me, Samantha. It's OK". The female's face and trunk were now almost inside the jeep but she'd stopped. "It was only a mock charge", said Sally knowingly. "If they mean business they put the tips of their trunks inside their mouths as they're tender and they don't want to get them hurt in the collision". She explained this in sign language to the tracker who confirmed she was right.

Then Samantha (one is tempted to preface the name by "the lovely", having listened too often to *I'm sorry, I haven't a clue* on the radio in England) told the driver to stay put and turn the engine off. Just the opposite of the 'Let's get the hell outa here!' that we were all feeling. The group of pachyderms, led by the angry female, gathered at the rear of our jeep, trunks almost inside the vehicle, and watched us intently. After what seemed ages our tracker told the driver to turn on the engine and drive very slowly indeed. The elephants followed us for maybe a hundred metres then stopped and almost waved us goodbye as we picked up speed and headed away, and I could relax and muse on the delights of being in a country where guys are called Samantha.

Sinharaja, our next stop, is among the world's oldest virgin rainforests. We took a break at the rest house in Deniyaya, the town closest to the south eastern entry-point for Sinharaja. The rainforest could be seen from the veranda, clothing the mountains beyond an intermediate range of hills. Our driver Norman was only familiar with the front door to Sinharaja, from Ratnapura, but was confident he knew how to get in from this side. In any case, he always stopped and asked people. Indeed he did this so often it could be maddening, especially when there had been no turning or junction since the last person he asked, and where it was obvious from the map and the road signs that we were on the right road anyway. However like most Sri Lankan drivers Norman could not read maps. In any case, Sinharaja was not signed from Deniyaya, or at least we spotted no signs, and despite repeated accosting of passers-by, all of whom confirmed we were on the right road, doubts began to creep in after an hour or so. The road entered a hamlet and became a pot-holed track with signs indicating various tea estates and their associated bungalows, offices, factories and muster stations but nothing else. This may have been *a* road to Sinharaja, but it manifestly was not *the* road to Sinharaja.

Onwards and upwards. Part of the van's undercarriage which had scraped intermittently all holiday was now making a continuous grating noise, eventually forcing even the determined Norman to a halt halfway up a mountainside in the mist. Three estate workers walking down the road were pressed into service and crawled under the van where, mainly using their bare feet, they managed to remove the offending piece of metal to allow further progress up the track. We offered them two hundred rupees which they declined, in conversation with Norman. We were mystified. Had we offended them in some way? Should we have offered more? "No", answered Norman, "They say if you give this money they will spend it on arrack. Then when they come home their wives beat them." Norman didn't understand why we all fell about with mirth at this. Once we'd recovered some composure we agreed, via Norman, to give them half that. "This they will spend on beer so not drunk getting." We never did find out what function, if any, was served by the piece of metal they removed. The van continued to operate in much the same way, but less noisily.

Half an hour more of steep climbing on the rutted and potholed road, at little more than walking pace, brought us to a barrier manned by a grinning chap in a bush hat who opened it for a hundred rupees and informed us that Sinharaja was another four or five kilometres further on. More climbing, across dizzying waterfalls, brought us to a battered sign which read: *TAKE A DEEP BREATH. YOU ARE GOING A STEEP CLIMB WITH ELBOW BENDS.* This warning came approximately eight kilometres and ninety minutes late and might as well have read *ABANDON HOPE ALL YE WHO ENTER HERE* given the level of dread we were feeling by this stage. We suggested to Norman that it was not too late to turn back, that we wouldn't hold it against him, he'd tried his best etc. etc. but the intrepid man would have none of this defeatist talk. A dozen or so 'elbow bends' later we came to a garlanded temple where a further road sign read *NOW YOU CAN RELAX. PUT SOME MONEY IN THE TILL.* We duly made a small contribution to temple funds and picked up a Tamil tracker to take us on to the rainforest which did indeed begin shortly, tea plantations giving way to dense jungle, the track now going downhill as often as up, but just as twisting.

At about three thousand feet we came out of the jungle and into another tea estate. Two telecommunications towers disappeared into the clouds. This, we were told, was the police post from where we had to seek permission to enter the rainforest on foot. Permission was duly sought and granted and Norman turned the van around to head back to the tea plantation's muster station from which our forest walk in the mist and drizzle would begin. Here two or three other men were gathered, one of them claiming to be the Chief of Police in the district and who promptly rescinded the permission we had just obtained. Despite his lack of uniform and general peasant demeanour Norman and the tracker obviously took this threat seriously. We could not enter, he told us, because there were suspected Tamil Tigers in the forest. We knew that this was arrant nonsense and we promptly changed his assessment of the security situation with a two hundred rupee bribe and a cigarette. He left us with an imprecation not to catch any butterflies.

Our tracker, who spoke no English, led us down through the tea fields and into the forest. Since Norman had elected to stay with the van, being afraid of leeches, this somewhat reduced the educational content of the experience. The visual experience wasn't great, either. We did see several butterflies including a couple the size of birds, and the jungle pools and streams we came across were delightful. But the weather was miserable and we had to keep our eyes downwards to watch for rocks, roots and above all, leeches. Our guide also set a cracking pace which was a mixed blessing. Too fast to appreciate the wonders of nature and exhausting for old limbs. On the other hand, we were outrunning the leeches, though every time we stopped they got us. They're remarkably fast for legless creatures and deeply unpleasant though harmless.

We'd anticipated them and dressed (as we thought) accordingly. Canvas shoes rather than sandals, long trousers rolled into socks. Gabrie in particular looked as though he was about to enter a nuclear reactor rather than a rainforest. Each of us had our own method of leech-disposal. I perfected a rapid scuffing of one foot across the other; Sally relied on a bag of salt she'd thoughtfully appropriated from a salt cellar at breakfast; Merigen, as ever the incendiary, preferred the cigarette-lighter approach; Dean developed a neat finger-and-thumb flick. In the event it was the heavily-defended Gabriel who was the only one of us from whom the evil creatures drew blood - his socks were too loosely woven. He was most stoical about it all. And canvas shoes are no protection against leeches, which insinuate themselves through the weaving, not to mention the lace-holes. We were told later that it is best to wear shorts and have bare legs and feet, on the grounds that although the little buggers can latch straight onto your skin, at least you can see them and remove them before they swell to the size of condoms with your blood. I used to think slugs were the vilest beings in creation, but now I'm not so sure. As they get to grips with you leeches inject a mild painkiller, so you're unaware of the bite, and an anti-coagulant to keep the blood flowing for longer. They're good at finding the bits you don't notice, especially in between the toes. In short, cunning little bleeders.

On the way back down the mountain we did spot one of the rainforest's famed giant centipedes sunning itself on a rock, looking rather like the caterpillar in Alice though without the hookah. We also saw an eight-foot rat-snake which slithered up a rock out of the roadside ditch as we passed. But Sinharaja was a disappointing experience on the whole, and we made a mental note to have a proper look at it another time. As yet we haven't made that return trip. We were told later that the US Government was offering to pay to 'safeguard' Sinharaja in a cynical deal to meet its carbon dioxide reduction targets and convince the world that it was committed to the Kyoto Protocol. Owning a carbon sink in Sri Lanka apparently counted towards meeting these targets due to the cynical arrangement known as carbon trading. I never did find out what happened to that proposal. I hope it was treated with the contempt it deserved.

Tourists trapped

On a brief stopover in Kandy en route to Nuwara Eliya we'd heard the news of the gun battle at Kataranaike Airport. The newspaper report the next morning informed us that the LTTE cadres 'came in an air-con bus to the Negombo area' and that they 'changed into battle clothes after dinner'. Not the done thing, you know, to take dinner in combats, dammit! Over the following days we became avid readers of the English language newspapers as details of the atrocity unfolded. It was indeed an audacious attack but it gradually became clear that the Tigers' action was made much more effective by the incompetence of the military and authorities. The full story ran thus:

A group of fourteen suicide bombers – known as Black Tigers (which I'd always thought were prawns) - arrived near to the air force base by the airport during a power cut. The power cut was planned to save electricity so its timing would have been known, providing the cover of darkness for a while. They alighted at a 'playground' (i.e. sports field) where they proceeded to eat a 'picnic' in the dark, all the while 'singing patriotic Sinhalese songs' to disguise their identity and intent. Not exactly sophisticated or designed to avoid attracting attention. They then changed into combat gear and took off with their guns, grenades, bazookas etc. into the jungle leaving behind the remains of their picnic. Their odd behaviour was reported to the police by residents but no action was taken.

The group cut the perimeter fence of the air force base and entered. Most of the guards 'were at a drinks party' and, according to the papers, pretty well gone. One guard did notice the intruders and contacted his superior officer who again ignored the information. The Tigers then attacked the base, destroying seven helicopters and fighter planes and damaging many more. It was the SLAF base and not the civilian airport which was their target. Putting a military target next door to the main civilian airport is not a very smart idea in a war situation, though it probably saves money on fuelling facilities and tarmac. Eight Tigers were killed in a shoot-out on the runways and the rest escaped in the only direction available to them, towards the airport. Four of the remaining six were also killed while trying to gain entry to the airport but before this they destroyed two Sri Lankan airbuses and seriously damaged a third.

Only two Tigers therefore actually entered the airport building, from which civilians and passengers fled in panic. Airmen mistakenly directed them all to flee straight towards where the two terrorists were. The military then started shooting in all directions while the civilians were trying to get out, wounding several people including a journalist, but no tourists, and killing one of their own men in the process but failing to hit either of the terrorists. Finally the two remaining Tigers blew themselves up, presumably as a demonstration to the military of how things should be done. This bungle in the jungle was compounded on the following day. Further gunfire was heard in the vicinity of the SLAF base and rumours spread that a second LTTE attack was under way. A senior air force spokesman explained the shooting, saying that after the attack fourteen pairs of shoes had been found at the picnic site, while one of the dead terrorists was still wearing shoes. The military therefore decided that a fifteenth gunman had escaped and was still at large. The alternative explanation, that one guy had two pairs of shoes, seems not to have occurred. The shots, he said, were from the soldiers 'firing at random positions in the jungle' in the hope of hitting the mysterious missing man. One innocent local farmer was shot in the leg and had to be taken to hospital. We learned also that the Army's 'Rapid Response Unit' had been called in to help but had arrived late 'as their leader had no feet'. Hmmm. The Sri Lankan civil war was Asia's longest and bloodiest. It was also possibly the most incompetently pursued conflict in history, but the joke is lost on the victims.

We returned to Colombo for a final couple of days at the Swimming Club before our return flight. Or so we thought. Since the airport battle we'd been reading the English language newspapers more or less daily and all of them reported that the airport was now back to normal except for Sri Lankan Airlines flights as they were a bit short of planes having had three of their top ones mangled. We were booked on Emirates, so no problem. No-one had told us that Emirates were locked in a management embrace with Sri Lankan. No-one had reported anything about the deal whereby Emirates had made their aircraft available to cover Sri Lankan flights, cancelling many of their own flights to make up for it, including ours. No-one had mentioned that in their infinite 'close the door after the horse has bolted' wisdom the amazingly clever people who insure the civil aviation industry had massively increased premiums which the airport was busy recouping by in turn massively increasing landing charges at Katanaiyake. Which in the inevitable chain of events meant that the airlines which might have provided some extra flights to help out Sri Lankan and its partner Emirates were now not going to do so. Meanwhile all the package tour operators were frantically pulling their often reluctant customers out of Sri Lanka using all available seats. And governments around the world were telling their citizens to cancel all travel plans to Sri Lanka. The response of the British Foreign and Commonwealth Office, which unthinkingly joined in this world attempt to crush the Sri Lankan tourism industry, seemed especially bone-headed given that only a short time had elapsed since their own tourist industry had been trashed by a similar international knee-jerk reaction to the foot and mouth outbreak. But governments are poor learning systems.

The consequence for us was a ten day delay in being able to fly home. We decided to split our group up and Sally, Jemima and I went off on an extra holiday on the coast, starting in Hikkaduwa. The afternoon train from Colombo ran along the coast for almost all the way, only venturing inland periodically to cross estuaries. On one such crossing an older abandoned railway bridge could be seen a little downstream. A fellow passenger helpfully explained that this bridge was abandoned as the girders were too close to the carriages, resulting in the decapitations of unwary passengers hanging out of the doors as I had been.

In Hikkaduwa we had rooms in a down-market place for a couple of nights. It had the air of a ghost town. Only a handful of tourists remained in the island. As we drank late afternoon beers in the bar, separated from the sea by dirty glass panels, we were befriended by a group of soldiers, here for the wedding reception of the sister of one of the group. They were also a band, the singer being now a non-combatant having had one hand mangled in an encounter with a land-mine. It was hard to reconcile their cheerful, innocent and indeed almost childlike conversation and questions with the stories of army atrocities carried out against Tamil civilians which I'd been

reading on the train on the way down. To us westerners the Asian peoples are enigmatic, as no doubt we are to them. Nowhere is this more true than in the matter of conflict and violence. We, who run our societies using what one might call 'managed violence', can't understand how, say, the Japanese could both be capable of such wartime atrocities and, immediately afterwards, renounce militarism and opt for a pacifist form of government. Or how some Myanmar monks who profess to follow the peaceful ways of Buddhism can behave so horribly towards the Muslim minority in their country. Such wild swings of approach which to us are inexplicable and contradictory seem normal across Asia and Sri Lanka is no exception. You'd be hard put to find friendlier, more helpful people anywhere in the world than Sri Lankans, whether Sinhalese or Tamil, but the civil war – whose roots of course go a long way back – was one of the bloodiest conflicts of its time. People whose religion forbids them to kill even the most insignificant creepy-crawly seem to have no qualms about hacking other humans to death. As A P Herbert put it in his 1950s satire of Sinhala nationalism:
'The Banyanese are charming folk.
Polite, they love to laugh and joke
Although, it cannot be denied
A trifle prone to homicide.'

Although they've since been exceeded by the likes of ISIS and Al Qaeda the Tamil Tigers more or less invented suicide bombing and used child conscripts, while Sinhala forces with covert or overt government backing were guilty of torture and murder on an industrial scale, both of Tamil activists and journalists who dared to tell the story as they saw it rather than how the government wanted it told. And all of it largely down to the matter of language – a mystifying battle for linguistic dominance between a language spoken only by the majority population of a small Indian Ocean island and one spoken by the minority in that same island and a small portion of its larger northern neighbour. No-one else in the world speaks either Sinhala or Tamil and no-one else in the world much cares. An agreement to settle for English would have been of enormous mutual benefit and might have saved countless lives. But English is, of course, the language of the colonial oppressor. Language is deeply symbolic.

After our chat with the friendly soldiers Jemima returned to her room to find it occupied by a giant Russian transvestite with big permed hair and clad only in a towel. It turned out he was staying in the next room and had locked himself out after taking a shower and, believing Jemima's room to be empty, was attempting to get back in via the adjoining balcony. He was covered with confusion as well as the towel, and very apologetic in what little English he had. "If he was just wearing a towel, how do you know he was a transvestite?" I hear you ask. Well, we'd come across him earlier, in Kandy – not a guy to be easily missed. We decided to look for a beachside restaurant for dinner, arriving at a very fine example of the species a little before a dramatic sunset. Evening beach scenes then, as dusk fell, watching baby turtles cavorting in the surf. Hermit crabs scuttled across the floor as we ate, putting on a kind of hermit crab catwalk show, inviting us to nominate which one was wearing the most outrageous or fashionable shell.

Breakfast the next morning was an unusual and very nasty experience involving scrambled eggs made with condensed milk, resulting in a sweet, grey splodge dumped on cold toast. Then out in a glass-bottomed boat to view life on the reef just offshore. Initially it was a disappointing affair: compared to our visit in1998 the rougher seas at this monsoonal time of year had churned up a lot of fine sand which now covered much of the live coral – only the occasional flashes of blue and brick-red shone through. Shoals of zebra fish and clown fish and a large, bright blue parrot fish. Then the boatman and guide took us over to an area where they said we might see turtles. Within a couple of minutes the head of a giant Olive Ridley reared out of the water less than twenty feet away, a seven-foot sea monster. Skilfully the boatman manoeuvred the craft right over the huge barnacled beast, swimming two feet below us, while the guide seemed to know exactly when and where it would next surface. The whole episode must have lasted less than ten minutes but seemed to go on for ever, and the crew's genuine surprise and excitement told us that this was not a common experience.

After Kandy and Colombo, Galle and its surrounding area has become the part of Sri Lanka we know best. Scarcely one of our visits to the island from 1998 to 2014 has not included staying in Galle or nearby Unawatuna or Talpe and we headed there after our sojourn in Hikkaduwa. When she was young Sally's family used to stay at the New Oriental in Galle Fort or the Closenberg on a promontory just south of the town. The New Oriental, now restyled the Amangalla, has become five star luxury; the Closenberg, by contrast, lies half-forgotten off the main tourist drag, next door to a police training camp, but it is a romantic old place with shady gardens and dark, heavy Victorian-eccentric furnishings and fittings in the dining room, including a spectacularly ugly aquarium, back-lit so the fish flitted about like ghosts.

Of all Sri Lanka's main towns and cities, Galle Fort is the most changed since we first knew it, though some districts of Colombo run it close. Anyone visiting the place now, with its trendy shops, posh hotels and eateries, would scarcely recognise the Galle we first came to in 1998 with eight year old Jemima. Smelly, down-at-heel, and infested by touts. Galle that is, not Jemima. The old town, within the walls, was still in 2001 devoid of shops other than soft drinks stalls and tourist merchandise outlets, especially antiques and lace, giving it a dead feel but the historic Dutch-era architecture did not disappoint. The restored Old Dutch House museum offered its exhibits for sale in a most un-museum-like way. Its main purpose was to entice the tourist beyond the antiquities to the much larger area of floor space given over to selling gems which have nothing to do with the history of the place. Galle stones, you might say.

At the time, to take a walk round the ramparts was to run the gauntlet of women selling lace and men selling fake antique coins and stamps. We'd walked over from the bus stand in the new town where we'd consumed quantities of delicious short eats in the South Ceylon Stores by the bus stand, an operation which listed its activities as *BAKERY, DELI, RESTAURANT, CATERERS AND TYRE DEALERS*. As USPs go, that's pretty U. We were trailed all the way to the fort by a pestilential character insisting we buy stamps and coins. It was a hot day and finally I lost my temper and gave him a torrent of loud and colourful language. Bad mistake. Although it put a stop to the endless sales pitch he continued to dog us from a safe distance across the road and waited until, some while later, we were seated on the veranda of the New Oriental Hotel. As soon as I got up to visit the gents he approached Merigen and explained: "Sir, I have offended your father. I must speak with him and tell him sorry and kiss his feet." "Thanks", said Merigen who although a fellow redhead has a much better ability than I to control his fiery temper, "but I don't think he will like that. Better you just go away." "But first I must apologise. I have offended your father". This exchange continued for a while before Merigen finally convinced the guy that he would convey his most sincere apologies as soon as I returned but that these would be more easily accepted if the fellow was by then out of sight.

Just down the coast road is Unawatuna about which I have mixed feelings. In 2001 Unawatuna was Scam Central. 'I was a stranger and ye took me in'. … and we've certainly been well taken-in on many occasions. Just when you think you've been the victim of every conceivable scam and con-trick someone manages to catch you with a new one. In 1998 we had fallen easy prey to the basic ones, such as: "I am schoolteacher. Teaching blind children. You give me five hundred rupees I can help them buy blind book". Though once, by Kandy Lake, I did meet a real schoolteacher and, having at first blanked him as a con-man, finally got into a fascinating conversation about his work and he never asked for a rupee.

In Galle we hadn't got out of the station when we were met by a guy offering a tuk-tuk to our guest house in Unawatuna. The tuk-tuk bore the slogan *MY LIFE IS NOT YOUR LIFE* (did I say it was?). After some haggling we agreed a great bargain price and got in, only to be immediately asked to squeeze up, Jemima on my knee, so a second guy could hitch a ride. A third man climbed on up front and the tiny vehicle set off. Not such a bargain after all. They all launched into the usual routine of explaining how the Sea View (no doubt run by a relative) was better than the Neptune which we'd booked: "Neptune full of smoking people" (i.e. narcotics users) "not good for baby. We can show you better place. Also do not buy anything Unawatuna, we can get everything local price. In Unawatuna water cost one hundred rupees one bottle. Small bottle." Of course the Neptune proved to be perfectly OK, and bottled water cost no more in Unawatuna than anywhere else.

Parting tourists from their cash in a non-violent way is something of a national sport for which I hold a grudging respect, even as a victim. But Unawatuna was infested with touts, either falsely claiming to be able to arrange or obtain things you wanted or insistently trying to sell you things you had no use for, like pieces of aloe vera. Unawatuna certainly has a beautiful setting and now has a huge variety of places to stay, eat and drink to suit any pocket. But in 2001 that was the sum total of Unawatuna's good points. Although the sea was clean, the beach had as much plastic as sand on it. It was very crowded and the most white-oriented place by far we'd been to. Packed full of Americans, Germans, Dutch, Aussies, Brits, Canadians, Italians and French and entirely geared to catering for western tastes. You couldn't get a Sri Lankan breakfast in Unawatuna. A lot of places didn't even do rice and curry in the evenings. It was, in short, a low-budget tropical tourist beach resort indistinguishable from hundreds of others from Barbados to Bali. Nothing Sri Lankan about the place at all.

But everything changes. Unawatuna has had a roller coaster ride of a time since we were first there. First the tsunami, though its sheltered setting meant it suffered less than most places. Nevertheless when our daughter Angela went snorkelling there four years later she had the unnerving experience of seeing barnacle-encrusted tuk-tuks, furniture and other household goods way below on the sea bed. Then the powers that be decided to build a breakwater off shore but hadn't taken the advice of any oceanographers with the result that Unawatuna's famous beach vanished almost overnight, and with it the bulk of the local economy. Smart move, that. Then the beach was reinstated. More than that, it was filled up to promenade level presumably to stop it washing away again and by way of apology. When we last visited, in 2016, Unawatuna was still just a mass-market tropical resort but it was now clean, had a great beach once more and remained free of high-rise developments so one can't be too hard on the place.

Beyond Unawatuna is the village of Talpe, a coastal strip of hotels and guest houses fronting fabulous sands and, in one section, a calm inshore lagoon protected by a reef. This is the to-die-for location of the Club Point de Galle where we have stayed on several occasions starting in 1998. The Club Point de Galle is not a club and, beyond the name, not in the least Gallic. Just a quiet hotel fronting an equally quiet beach and a lagoon inside an inshore reef, uncovered at low tide. A glance at the visitors' book showed that most guests at the Club Point de Galle were either well-heeled Sri Lankans or expats living in Sri Lanka including various embassy and consulate staff. We hired some ill-fitting snorkel masks from the café just up the beach and had a good look around the lagoon and the reef. Patches of bright pink and blue coral, a dozen different species of colourful reef fish, conger eels poking their snouts out of rock-holes, sea urchins. Careful where you tread. A walk along, or rather through, the edges of the ocean brought us to a rocky promontory covered with black crabs and sand-skippers, the latter a species endemic to Sri Lanka with a disarming ability to skim and hop across the water when dislodged from their rocky perches by an incoming wave. Just round the point a group of Sri Lanka's totemic stilt fishermen concentrated on their prey (tourists, not fish, you innocent fool!).

Back at the hotel we were making our way through the corridor towards the stairs when we noticed a large framed map of the island hanging on the wall. Keen to point out to Jemima where we were, where we'd been and where we were going I began jabbing an index finger into various points on the map. A large hairy leg appeared from behind the map, followed by another ... and an eighth. They belonged to easily the biggest spider I've ever seen – and, yes, I've been to Australia. Sally and Mima duly shrieked and I duly attempted to appear as though this was an everyday experience. The shrieking fetched the manager over from the desk to see what was the matter and, having ascertained the cause, he gently stroked the giant arachnid and with a few soothing words encouraged it to return to the safety of its home behind the map. "Madam, this one not poison", he gently berated us. But for the rest of our stay Sally and Jemima doubled speed when walking past that map.

And so, finally, the train back to Colombo and eventually our much-delayed departure for home. At Galle station we heard there had been an incident on the line and the disruption was going to be considerable. It wasn't clear whether there would be any more trains that day. We made the mistake of looking crestfallen, a sure-fire way of attracting unwanted attention. So a bloke comes up. Says he's the stationmaster. The train will be only one hour late, he asserts cheerfully. He will sort out our tickets, get us seats. Sits down with us and finds we're from Yorkshire which delights him. "Ah, Yorkshire! Freddie Truman! Feary Fred!" I mention Geoffrey Boycott and he screws up his face and replies simply "We like best your fast bowlers". He gives us news of an England batting collapse against the West Indies. "Curtly Ambrose four for twenty six and nine of these are no-balls! Atherton head again on block, I'm thinking". Jemima looks puzzled – Sinhala is easier to follow than cricket-speak. The 'stationmaster' (it seemed unlikely that the person in charge of a crowded station at a time when the rail system was in chaos would have nothing better to do than to hang around with a family of tourists) protected us from orange-salesmen and other would-be pesterers, apologised for the way some of his countrymen behave towards visitors. "I have one word for them: con-artists." Arguably that's two words, but I don't press the point. He reeks of arrack. We chat on. He may not be the stationmaster but he's good company. And Sri Lankan railwaymen have a hard-drinking reputation so maybe he is. Eventually the train pulls in, he hands us tickets, we say goodbye and prepare to board. Then, despite everything he has been saying about people who pester tourists for money, asks us for the price of a beer, alcoholic eyes pleading. We give it to him, of course, but with a little sadness that after all he wasn't that much different from the others, just more entertaining and crafty.

At last we reached the Swimming Club to reunite with the rest of our party and to compete as a team in the club's weekly quiz night. We called our team *The Castaways* and came second, winning six bottles of beer, one for each of us since Jemima was under age. Only four teams competed. We enjoyed more beer on an enforced overnight stop in Dubai where we found a bar which served a decent pint of Boddington's. We sleepily toasted Manchester and couldn't wait to get home.

Four

The big decision

They say that a year in Yorkshire is six months of winter followed by six months of bloody bad weather. Our idyllic cottage high in the Pennines was cheap to rent but cost a fortune to heat and was permanently damp and mouldy. By the early years of the new millennium we found we had a choice to make. Merigen had left home, Angela and Daniel our long-term foster children were about to, and Jemima was well into her teens. I had a secure public sector job (or so it seemed at the time, in those pre-crash years) and Sally was earning a half-decent salary though less secure, being in the arts. We no longer needed four bedrooms and we could afford to buy a house. But we'd be entering retirement not that far down the line with still a hefty chunk of mortgage to repay and then what?

"Well", said Sally, "We could live in Yorkshire and choose between having a bottle of wine and turning the heating on. Or we could live in Sri Lanka, keep the wine and remove the second half of the equation." It was a no-brainer financially. More complex emotionally, of course. But the more we thought about it, the more attractive an idea it seemed. "I'm up for it", Sally concluded, "on one condition. That we buy a house big enough for all our kids to come and visit us, including grandchildren. There must be lots of former planters' bungalows on sale – something like that would be spot on." "But we'd still be spending almost all the time just the two of us out on some tea estate, miles from anywhere, we'd drive each other mad". "Not if we started a guest house", countered Sally. My parents had run a guest house in Somerset when I was a boy and on the whole I'd rather enjoyed it – at least the bits about meeting lots of people who moved briefly and interestingly through one's life and occasionally did exciting things like taking me and my brother on all-night fishing trips. I was sold, and we decided that we would again visit Sri Lanka, but this time with the purpose of buying a place to live once I'd retired. Meanwhile we'd continue putting up with the cold and damp of Yorkshire.

As plans go, that wasn't much of one. Due diligence didn't come into it. What did we know about Sri Lanka, really? Could foreigners just walk in and buy a place? What were property prices like? How did the housing market work? Would a guest house make us money, or just wash its face, or be a pit to sink our earnings into and render us just as poor as the Yorkshire winters would come pension time? What would happen with the war? Would we be safe? Maybe it's because both of us had to spend so much time at work business planning that we entered into our own future with such reckless abandon. Do it first, plan it later.

Two friends had visited Sri Lanka the previous Christmas. We had given them various suggestions for places to visit or stay, one of which was our beloved Point de Galle hotel in Talpe, near Galle, where we'd stayed both in 1998 and on our second holiday in 2001. They had headed straight there from the airport and during their stay had met the owner, Bindu, a lawyer. They told him about our plans to buy property and live in Sri Lanka and he offered to help and advise, suggesting we get in touch with him, so we did. He told us we would need to set up a Sri Lanka registered company through which to purchase the property and eventually run the business and put us in touch with a Colombo legal firm, Simon and Associates, who specialised in working with foreigners and expats. We arranged to meet Simon as soon as we got to Sri Lanka in July 2004. We juggled our holiday entitlements, and we cobbled together a four week period in which to form a company and buy a house on an island six thousand miles away. No pressure, then.

Having nothing more practical to do beforehand we spent evenings thinking up a suitable name for our as yet unborn company, eventually settling on 'Jungle Tide'. *Jungle Tide* is the title of a book published in 1930 by a renegade colonial civil servant, John Still, who tired of the life of endless formality and parties, went native and joined up with a group of Veddha people, the aboriginal inhabitants of Sri Lanka who have been all but wiped out first by the invading Sinhalese and Tamils a couple of thousand years ago and more recently by the colonial powers, notably the British. Still's book meant a lot to Sally's family and to Sally as a child, and I came to love it too with its lyrical descriptive passages interspersed with wry sideswipes at his own people. The title stemmed from his accidental discovery of the Lotus Pool at the ancient ruined city of Polonnaruwa. The heart of the city had already been excavated but the Lotus Pool was a little way out in the jungle. He fell into it, thinking at first it was a natural vegetation-covered crater but, climbing out, realised the sides were of dressed stone. What had at first appeared as tree trunks covered in lianas were pillars of an ancient building. Much along the lines of Shelley's poem *Ozymandias* – my favourite poem – he mused on how ephemeral the works of man are, and how the 'jungle tide' relentlessly encroaches on and reclaims what belongs to nature.

There are still a few Veddhas left. The few remaining Veddha in a reservation in the centre of the island are no longer in physical danger but could perhaps be patronised to death. To visit their carefully preserved village close to Maduru Oya National Park is to be subjected to a toe-curling display of weapon-waving, pretend hunting and two guys dancing in the dust, followed by the usual outstretched palms and trinket sales. This is regarded by the tourist powers-that-be as respecting an ancient culture. Here's how one of the websites puts it:

A perfect place to observe Veddha is their last remaining village of Dambana and organise a camp close to or within the reservation and Veddha's will be more than glad to show you their ways of life, with an axe hanging from their shoulders and a bow slung behind them, gives you the impression nothing much has changed since the dawn of time for these proud warriors of the forest.

Quite a bit has, in fact, changed. These 'proud warriors' are no longer allowed to hunt, for example. The Buddhist authorities, who do not approve of killing animals, reluctantly offered to let the Veddha continue hunting with arrows and spears. The Veddha, though, wanted guns. Not on. Respecting an ancient culture isn't easy when the representatives of that culture aspire to modernity. On the positive side, the museum is actually quite good. But it doesn't come close to making up for the embarrassing experience of seeing human beings treated like zoo exhibits.

Simon's office was in an old colonial era building opposite the Galle Face Hotel. Galle Face Court had seen better days and was a warren of dingy offices served by an antiquated lift served in turn by an antiquated lift attendant. It's still pretty much unchanged. Simon Senaratne was a twinkling-eyed middle-aged lawyer with impeccable English and an immediate understanding of our situation. After our initial interview he introduced us to his assistant, Lilamani de Silva, who would be our day to day contact with the firm and conclude with us the business of setting up the company.

"What do you want to call your company?" he asked. "What we'd really like is to call it 'Jungle Tide' after a book we know and love, but that is quite a famous book, no? There will probably be another company with that name."

"Ah yes, I know the book. John Still, isn't it? I will check if another company has that name." We were surprised and delighted to find that the name 'Jungle Tide' had not been registered for any other Sri Lankan company, so we grabbed it. Various documents were required in order to set up the company and although we had sent these by registered post from England weeks earlier they had still not arrived at Simon's offices. Until they did, there was nothing we could do to complete the company registration. But that wouldn't stop us from house-hunting.

Unreal estate

On this occasion we'd taken along Jemima and her ex-boyfriend Ol. Why an ex-boyfriend? You may well ask. Ol had been Jemima's first real boyfriend and she was persistent in demanding he come with us on the holiday. He was equally keen and his parents, despite not being at all well-off, readily agreed to pay his fare. It was going to create further accommodation problems since they were fifteen and couldn't have their own room – sometimes we managed a room for the four of us; mostly Ol and I shared one room while Sally and Jemima shared another. But we believe in encouraging young love, as well as wanting to give Ol an experience he wouldn't easily forget, so we didn't take too much convincing. We booked the flights in June by which time Jemima and Ol had been together for nearly a year and were still professing undying love. Two weeks later they had split up. Who'd have teenagers? But Ol still wanted to go with us and Jemima faced up to her responsibilities. She had pleaded for him to come, and accepted that even though they were no longer together and she had a new boyfriend it was Ol not her current beau who would be going to Sri Lanka. In the event, all went smoothly but it was a bit of a pain having to spend most nights sharing a room with a teenage boy rather than being in bed with Sally.

Our shared ideal was to find and renovate an old planters' bungalow in the hill country, but it dawned on us that on our two previous visits we'd never set eyes on any shop or office in Colombo, Kandy or elsewhere that even vaguely resembled an estate agent. Just how did property get bought and sold? Searches on the internet had indicated very few properties for sale directly, hardly any of which were planters' bungalows. Almost all were in Colombo or along the coast. There were also many plots of building land for sale. The property market was unlike anything we were used to. So we contacted a couple of agents who operated online and who both said they could find us the kind of place we were looking for if we spent some time with them.

We headed off on the coastal train to the Point de Galle where we'd made an appointment to meet with one of them, Ikram, at nine the next morning. The train was packed and we all had to stand. I loved it, Sally hated it and poor Jemima being of small stature spent the first part of the journey with her head buried in a mass of sweaty and dirty sarongs, groins and armpits. At Ambalangoda a lot of folk got out and Sally, Ol and Jemima finally got a seat. I preferred to stay standing, hanging out of the doorway, dust in my eyes, diesel fumes in my nose, singing into the wind with the train bucking and heaving like a wild animal trying to escape the prison of parallel lines. Wonderful! Each curve and river crossing involved exaggerated braking then a great roaring as the engine picked up speed again. The sun set obligingly over the ocean. Near the doorway a notice explained how to operate the fire extinguisher. *FIRST FASTEN THE EXTINGUISHER TO THE FLOOR* it began rather dauntingly before adding *THE EXTINGUISHER MUST BE PROTECTED FROM TEMPERATURES ABOVE 40 DEGREES* (so not much use in a fire, then). It seems superfluous to add that the cavity above the notice, which should have housed the said appliance, was empty.

By ten thirty there was no sign of Ikram so we phoned him. He'd clearly forgotten the appointment but claimed he was 'delayed' and could we make it 11 o'clock? He duly turned up much later, accompanied by his father Odi and a friend who just seemed to have come along for the ride. Both Odi and Ikram were former international rugby players and it showed in their atypically Sri Lankan physiques, bull-necked and broad-shouldered. Ikram presumably recently since he was still a young man. Odi had been one of only three non-white players in the XV of his day. A former planter, he had known many of the families Sally knew in the old days and there was plenty of reminiscing and exchanges of information as well as many interruptions on Ikram's mobile. We were having our first lessons in doing business in Sri Lanka. Social chatter is seen as being of at least equal importance to money talk; and the cellphone is king and must be answered no matter what. In Britain it is regarded as highly unprofessional to answer one's phone, or even to allow it to ring, during a meeting. In Sri Lanka the number of times a person is interrupted by his phone during a meeting is a reflection of his status.

Ikram took the view that land would be a better bet than houses. Buying land was becoming a more attractive option to both of us, the attraction being the opportunity to realise our own ideas about architecture and design rather than making the best of someone else's. The counter-attraction of buying a traditional planter's bungalow remained that of inheriting and in some way continuing a part of the country's and Sally's history. Ikram said he dealt in the south and on the coast so he gave us contact details for someone we'll call Alwin, his up-country colleague who would be showing us round once we got to Kandy. Apparently, if it were noticed that we were looking to buy property it would be quite possible that a neighbouring property-owner would approach us with an offer to sell. One way and another, it seemed likely we'd have plenty to choose from. He said Alwin would negotiate prices on our behalf. "White people pay skin tax", he explained. He would pretend to be acting for another buyer, a Sri Lankan, to barter the price back down. We were familiar with the concept of 'local price' for hiring tuk-tuks, getting into places of interest or buying fruit in Kandy market, but the notion that there was also a dual market in property prices came as a shock.

Tall and gaunt, long greying black hair tied back, dressed in a loose flowing black robe, and as camp as they come, Alwin made an unlikely estate agent. He spoke English without a trace of an accent and peppered his speech with slang, obscenities and colloquialisms, the result of living in England for nearly thirty years from the age of eleven. Alwin told us he had left Sri Lanka with his mother in the 1950s as part of the exodus of which Sally's family formed the tail-end; an exodus of educated and ambitious people, foreigners, English-speaking burghers and politically active Tamils which had begun as the tide turned towards a narrow, isolationist Sinhala nationalism and a crude politics based on culture, nation, language and ethnicity.

Alwin's father had remained behind, prospered, had numerous affairs to which his mother turned a blind eye, and built him a house – Knuckles View – as a twenty first birthday present. As a young man, Alwin was in the thick of 1960s swinging London and developed a heroin habit which he'd overcome through the more or less continuous use of marijuana. He remained stoned for the latter part of every day and insisted his business didn't suffer. A chain-smoking teetotaller, we assumed he'd also had an alcohol problem though he put us right about this on a later visit by explaining that he "came from a long line of alcoholics and didn't fancy going down that road".

Our initial phone contact with Alwin was not encouraging. Ikram had given us his number and said he'd tell him to expect a call from us. Sally duly phoned at around ten thirty on the day we were travelling up to Kandy: "Hi Alwin, it's Sally Martin here. Ikram said we should call you to arrange for you to show us around the properties he's lined up for us to look at." "Who? What properties?" came the curmudgeonly response. Consternation. Five minutes later Ikram was on the line apologising profusely that he'd forgotten to talk to Alwin, that he now had done and everything was fine so would we ring him back please? He added that we'd probably got him out of bed by phoning so early in the morning as he's rarely up before eleven, which would explain his abrupt and grumpy manner. The phone call was made and a different, entirely friendly and business-like Alwin answered and we made arrangements to meet that evening at his home.

Knuckles View is a gorgeous place near to Kandy with, as you would expect, views across to the Knuckles mountain range and fronted by a large lawn and pond. A wide veranda with another *trompe l'oeuil* pond alongside connected the main two-storey house to the driveway via the utility rooms and the whole building was airy and light with high ceilings, architecturally different from both the Sri Lankan homes we'd seen and the European planters' bungalows, but with more of the feel of the latter for semi-outdoor living. Most Sri Lankan houses, even modern ones owned by well-off people, are dark warrens of small rooms. Alwin ran Knuckles View as an up-market guest house and said proudly he had no time for customers without fat wallets. He was equally proud that Knuckles View wasn't to be found in the guide books read by the hoi polloi such as us. As someone to do business with, the huge plus was his understanding of European and specifically English desires and needs. He conveyed the impression of someone who understood what we wanted, would make sure we got it, and also wouldn't try to sell us anything else on the side, unlike so many Sri Lankan business people. The downside, we suspected, was going to be the amount of power this man would have over our lives in the short term given that we were so dependent on him. But what the hell! He was interesting and promised us an exciting if bumpy ride.

Alwin had lined up a few places for us to look at the following day. "Can you meet me at the Suisse Hotel ten am?" Sure enough, a little before ten a van drew up at the hotel and we were summoned from our rooms. However, no Alwin, only the driver, named Lalith, and another man who was to act as our interpreter over the next two days but didn't speak much English. Not a great start. A phone call elicited the response that Alwin had been delayed on other business and to come to the HSBC bank in town a little after ten thirty. Sally went in to find him and was gone almost half an hour, emerging with Alwin who'd come out for a pavement fag or three (smoking had been banned in Sri Lankan banks in the three years since our encounter with Robert McNeish). He told us that the vendors of the property he was buying for another client had insisted on a cash payment. Since the sale price was four million rupees and since the thousand rupee note was then the largest Sri Lankan currency denomination, counting this amount out and double-checking the total was an operation of electoral proportions. We finally left, very sweaty and frustrated, just before noon.

First on our list of places to visit was Goomera, a bungalow and land nearly two hours' drive from Kandy, among the Knuckles mountains. Lovely ride, but at this rate we'd get to see maybe two properties a day and we had limited time available. The road eventually twisted around the head of a final valley and back down the other side and we reached Goomera. The design of the old bungalow seemed to be a hybrid of European planter and Sri Lankan styles – large-ish rooms but not very large, big bay windows along one side and a small front veranda, but all the rooms behind the reception hall ran off a long dark central corridor. All in all the house was a bit disappointing though with potential. The property for sale included three acres of land around the house and a separate forty two acres of tea higher up, under the rock. No-one seemed to know the name of the rock, despite its dominating the landscape for miles around. The gardens grew soursop, papaya, bananas, mango, avocado, coffee and various citrus fruits as well as cardamom and peppers. By the side of the house was a shed for drying cardamom, one of the two main cash crops of the estate, the other being, of course, tea. An external fire heated wooden drying racks via a flue passing through the shed. There were several chickens, a cow and a calf. The estate employed a resident manager and around twenty day labourers and apparently brought in a significant income.

Genuine reason for sale? The property was owned by a man who lives in Colombo and who needed to realise some cash, we were told. His sister lived in the bungalow. A middle-aged woman who spoke little English, she was mightily unhappy with her brother selling the property and forcing her to move. Our cheery *ayubowans* were met with a stony stare. Fortunately her niece, the daughter of the owner, had travelled up from Colombo expressly for our visit and spoke excellent English, showing us proudly around the house and outbuildings and helpfully and cheerfully answering our many questions. "Now you can see the estate also?" I demurred as it was now well after two pm and we'd seen precisely one property which, although fascinating, I didn't feel was close to what we were looking for. Too far from Kandy, too much work required, probably out of our price range, and managing a tea estate while living in England wasn't something I felt confident about, to put it mildly. And the estate was accessible only by a four wheel drive vehicle, which would need to be summoned from somewhere or other, followed by a short walk. But Sally was keen to revisit a working tea estate and my objections were overruled. A pickup and driver were summoned. The driver promptly disappeared into the bungalow complaining despite it being the afternoon that he hadn't had his breakfast and required feeding before he would take us anywhere.

Eventually we were driven to the end of a deeply rutted track halfway up the mountain from where we walked through a screechy, leechy jungle to emerge high up on the estate overlooking Goomera bungalow and with the great unnamed rock looming beside us. We met the estate manager and Sally was duly appreciative of his tea planting skills, then back to the pickup. Tired, dirty and bloodstained from leech bites we drove back to the van and thence the long drive back to Kandy.

The asking price of eighty five lakhs (a lakh is one hundred thousand rupees, at the time equivalent to £500, and the unit in which Sri Lankans and indeed Asian peoples generally calculate large sums of money), was indeed just over our budget though Alwin said it could be bargained down. He also pointed out that the income from the estate would probably have been enough to service a loan to improve the house, certainly together with what we could save ourselves over the next year or two. But I wasn't happy and on the drive back to Kandy I wondered whether I could stand living somewhere so remote. As a tourist business the location didn't seem to make sense, though perhaps we wouldn't need it to as the estate income plus my pension should give us enough to live on. But house guests would be another source of company, quite aside from the income. Did Sally feel the same or had she fallen in love with this undeniably beautiful and slightly crazy place? Fortunately, when we had the chance to discuss it back at the Suisse that evening, she felt the same way as I did. So Goomera was out. The place was eventually bought up, renamed and turned into an up-market guest house, catering for the kind of people who value the remoteness and want a base for trekking in the Knuckles mountains. Maybe we missed an opportunity. One day's house hunting, one property visited. At this rate we weren't going to find our dream home without a second visit, which given our finances would be another couple of years away.

But the pace picked up after that and in the two days we had available to look for properties from our base in Kandy we saw eight or nine more. A couple of them came close. Pinthaliya, a three-and-a-half acre fruit farm and guest house near Gampola, was a contender, for certain. It was a six-bedroomed bungalow already used as a restaurant and guest house. Our driver Lalith had once worked for the owner and was keen that we buy the place as Gampola is his home town. The land grew a mind-boggling range of fruits and spices. We listed soursop, verulu, guava, jak, mango, avocado, banana, custard apple, durian, rambutan, lime, vanilla, pepper and coffee. The house was situated on top of a small hill from where the land dropped away to two parallel valleys. Despite the rain, it was evident that the views on both sides across to higher hills would be a feature of the place. Good access road, big water tank, electricity and phone already installed and an asking price of 75 lakhs put it just within our budget and we were very tempted. The problem was the house which was Sri Lankan style, with small dark rooms and located away from the best views. We toyed with the possibility of gutting and extending it over four years with a combination of our savings and income from the land as it was in decent condition, but eventually concluded it would have to come down, and rebuilding from scratch would have put the costs beyond our reach. So reluctantly, Pinthaliya was also out.

Close to Meenawatte on the Elkaduwa road we looked at five acres with another Sri Lankan style bungalow. Stunningly beautiful setting though via an excessively potholed approach track, spectacular panoramic views over Kandy, a permanent spring on the land, mangoes, guava, mahogany trees. And tea, of course. Priced at fifty lakhs. The owner, an elderly Anglophile like so many of his generation, was delighted to show English visitors around his home and proudly showed us his 'library' – a cheap glass-fronted bookcase stuffed with old hardback editions of English classic novels. Interesting, but the dilapidated house was of no value to us and would have to be demolished and rebuilt, once again taking the project out of our price range.

Oorogala

The road to Oorogala - the name means 'Pig Rock' – climbs out of Kandy past the hospital and into the vast Hanthana tea estate, past the Ceylon Tea Museum and emerges after a lot of hairpin bends to meander on a roughly level contour, and a rough road, along the top of the estate. Eventually, just over half an hour from the city, a left turn at the Assistant Superintendent's bungalow, a twisting and picturesque downhill road through tea, rocks and trees for half a mile and a right turn up a concrete track brought us to a new bungalow on the left. We pulled up behind the bungalow, not yet completed and still uninhabited. The property for sale comprised the bungalow and five acres of tea with a small but perfectly formed garden sloping down to a babbling stream. Idyllic setting but more land than we really wanted and the three-bedroomed bungalow, though well designed and approximating to the style we were looking for, was too small for a guest house.

We'd seen ten properties over three days, only one of them a planter's bungalow.

"You've missed the boat there" was Alwin's comment when we complained mildly to him that nothing we had yet seen really met the specifications we'd e-mailed to his colleague Ikram. "All the ones that the Government hasn't nationalised have been snapped up in the last few years, mostly by foreigners and foreign companies to turn into 'boutique hotels'". So we'd had the right idea, just a few years too late and probably not the right depth of pockets anyway.

"Why don't we see if they will sell you some of the land at Oorogala and you can build something yourselves?" suggested Alwin. A phone call to the man we assumed was the owner but turned out to be his friend quickly confirmed that for thirty nine lakhs we could have just under three acres of land on the opposite side of the stream from the bungalow. That ought to leave us enough spare to build a decent sized house. We went back for another look and discovered that upstream the water flowed through the land we were looking to buy, creating romantic possibilities of dams, pools and small waterfalls. The plot crucially had a large area of fairly flat land at the top, with good views, easily big enough for a large bungalow, parking and outbuildings for servants' rooms and utilities. This was more like it, though Sally still harboured residual hopes of finding one of the last traditional planters' bungalows that hadn't already been discovered and picked up by some foreigner or multi-national company with more money than us. For the time being we'd keep looking, further afield, up in the real hills, around Maskeliya, Hatton and Nuwara Eliya.

So we set off for more property-hunting with a man from Lanka Real Estate, the other on-line agency we'd contacted who'd lined up several places allegedly based on what we said we wanted. It was frustrating. Back and forth they drove us in an irrational itinerary around the hill country almost to Nuwara Eliya then halfway back to Kandy in the other direction to see a variety of grot-holes bearing absolutely no relation to the list of properties they had e-mailed to us in England or to the kind of place we said we were interested in. We were learning another lesson, that in Sri Lanka business is done on the basis that 'the customer is always wrong'.

There was one exception among the places they showed us. Ottery Bungalow was around thirty minutes from the hill town of Dikoya. On a rainy day up a series of bumpy estate roads it was not a lot of fun reaching it in the van but well worth the discomfort once we got there. An enormous and ancient two-storey bungalow (the term is not oxymoronic in Sri Lanka or India) set in a vast tea estate, the house reeked of history. God knows who lived there, both in the distant and more recent past. It appeared to have been occupied only by droves of estate workers since around 1970 with the result that faded, water-damaged portraits of bewigged early Victorian English gentlemen jostled for wall space with washed-out coloured pin-up posters of pretty girls in hot pants. A cavernous downstairs room housed a mixture of Victorian colonial furniture, antique Sri Lankan carved furniture of unbelievable quality, and plain old seventies tat. Its centrepiece was a full-sized billiard table covered with a dusty cloth and with a set of broken and warped cues standing against the wall. Grotesquely contorted wooden-framed tennis rackets jostled one another in a stand. The adjacent dining-room was also stuffed with antiques. The kitchens (a whole series of them) were another time-capsule, kitted out with wall to wall wooden plate-racks, rusted cooking ranges and utensils and an ancient Aga, and littered with broken colonial era crockery. Upstairs we lost count at nine bedrooms and several bathrooms.

Jemima was reading *Gone with the Wind* at the time and went straight into Scarlett and Rhett fantasy mode.

The asking price of a hundred and fifty lakhs was double our budget, though this also included the enormous estate, and the place had such potential that we'd seriously have considered developing a business plan and looking for finance on that basis. All this was academic, however, since soon after our arrival a man turned up on a motorcycle and explained that he'd recently bought the place. Our less than impressive agents were unaware of this. The new owner was initially suspicious but warmed to us as soon as he found that we were English, that Sally was Sri Lanka born and that we were looking to start a small tourism business. He cheerfully showed us around his newly-acquired pile and ended by making a vague offer of a business partnership with us which he said he would follow up with his wife, or sister, or son, all of whom were living in the UK. Never heard from him again and he didn't reply to several e-mails. Yet another lesson about trying to do business in Sri Lanka, that we should expect a lot of initial enthusiasm and no follow-up. All in all, though, the experience at least served to remove the modicum of doubt we retained about buying the land at Oorogala and we phoned Alwin that evening to confirm, finally and absolutely, that this was the place we'd decided to buy. But nothing in Sri Lanka goes that smoothly …

Caveat Emptor

Back down to Colombo to try to clinch the deal. We had a 1pm appointment with Lilamani but she'd gone for lunch. Lesson seventeen: Sri Lankans don't keep diaries. However we were assured that her assistant had all the paperwork. Could we see her, then? "Sorry, also at lunch". Lilamani eventually turned up with the papers we had sent from England by registered air mail and which had arrived that morning after several weeks' travel. Soon sorted, leaving us just enough time to get to the HSBC in Fort to open our SIERA (foreign exchange investment) account before it closed at 3pm. Lilamani assured us that Jungle Tide would be registered as a company early the following week, at which point they would open the company account, we would fund it from the SIERA account, they would resign as temporary Directors and we would take their place as the two sole directors of our company Jungle Tide (Pvt) Ltd. Two's company, you might or might not say. And then we could purchase the land.

Alwin was pushing us for completion on the grounds – which may or may not have been true – that another local purchaser was interested in the land but first had to raise a bank loan. According to Alwin this could take him a few weeks, and put us in the driving seat so long as we could move quickly. So off in a tuk-tuk to HSBC in Fort. The tuk-tuk bore the slogan: *ALL THAT GLITTER IS NOT GOOD"* – couldn't agree more mate, never did go much for bling. The driver engaged us in the usual cheery banter. "Why not your Tony Blair come to be our president?" This being post-Iraq we were tempted to say: "Take him and welcome" but zipped it up. It was perhaps the flip side of the universal sense of despair about the war in particular and the corrupt nature of Sri Lankan politics in general.

Civil war hostilities had been temporarily suspended through a Norwegian-negotiated ceasefire but parts of Fort were still off limits to vehicles and we had to abandon the three-wheeler and walk the last bit through endless checkpoints. Streets which Sally remembered bustling with humanity were now almost deserted, with tinned-up shops on either side. There were further thorough security searches on entering the bank. Initially all went well. The woman we were directed to checked our papers in a brisk and efficient manner - for example she appeared to know without having to scrutinise them for ages just what each of her multitude of rubber stamps was for. Rubber stamps are revered throughout the island and presumably have some religious significance. They are carefully mounted on multi-layered turntables and are fingered in a state of meditative semi-trance like rosary beads. Aside from cellphone interruptions in meetings, the other reliable guide to a Sri Lankan's business status is the number of rubber stamps they possess. We were told that we had to deposit a minimum of twenty five thousand rupees before we could transfer any foreign currency to the account. This meant changing some travellers' cheques which fortunately we had with us. While Sally went to change the TCs I wrestled with the mysteries of internet banking – not my forte in those days though I'm a dab hand at it now. Accessing my account at the confusingly named Halifax Bank of Scotland (what's wrong with Yorkshire or Nova Scotia then?) was straightforward, if slow, but I could find no option to transfer funds to a non-HBOS account, let alone an overseas one. There was also a small-print 'important notice' which I hadn't previously seen – presumably because it only showed up when accessing the website from overseas. I clicked on it and dire warnings appeared to the effect that the site was only intended for use in the UK, use of it from overseas might be in breach of international or local banking regulations which it was my responsibility to check, and that I could not use it 'to purchase foreign products' which I suspected meant, in banking parlance, foreign bank accounts. I half expected the terminal to self-destruct in my face if I persisted. Panic set in.

Meanwhile, Sally was having an equally frustrating time at the counter. Compared to the truly local Sri Lankan banks 'the world's local bank' seemed to have great difficulty in understanding that she wanted rupees in exchange for sterling TCs.
"You want rupees?" (in an incredulous voice). "Yes, please". "You want money?" (even more incredulously).

Sally choked back the desire to say "No, cowrie shells and a couple of goats would be just fine, thanks" and eventually the deal was done and the SIERA account opened. They then gave us a card with the account number on it – but no contact information. By this time the bank had long since closed and we were fed up and desperate to get out so didn't think to ask sensible questions like contact details for the bank, how to access the account and so on. We were shown out into a dirty side street by the back door.

Later, I rang the HBOS international helpline, without much hope, to see if there was any possibility of being able to transfer the funds before I got back to the UK. A helpful chap called Neil confirmed that this could be done by fax provided all details were included and the fax signed. 'All details' included the various codes for the receiving branch – which of course we had not been given and had not thought to ask for. We didn't even have their telephone number. Since the HSBC was now shut, nothing to do but wait until the morning. Neil gave me the fax number of the branch where my account is held, and the next morning I found out the HSBC codes and faxed instructions from the Business Centre of the most prestigious hotel in Colombo to a branch of the Halifax in a small Yorkshire town – it all seemed a bit surreal. But with any luck the money we needed to buy the land would now be winging its electronic way to Sri Lanka. We, by contrast, were winging our way to Trinco and the Sea Anglers Club.

Internet cafes were booming in Sri Lanka at the time and were a godsend for us, having no portable devices. We even managed to find an especially dingy one in Trinco. I'd asked the branch manager of the Halifax to e-mail confirmation that the transfer had been made. Instead, I found an e-mail from him, one Tom Miles, that it had not been possible to make the transfer as he "could not validate the signature nor the origination of the fax". Since the fax was sent on Galle Face Hotel headed paper and I assumed that the branch where my account was held could verify my signature, this seemed curious as well as disconcerting. The e-mail referred me to the helpline. Fifteen minutes in a sweaty phone box full of spiders produced nothing except a sizeable telephone bill. I explained the situation to the helpline who concluded that they couldn't help and transferred me back to the Todmorden branch. Tom Miles was not in and not expected for an hour or so. Couldn't wait that long.

The next opportunity arose in Polonnaruwa. Tom answered the phone himself and after another half hour in an even more sweaty phone booth (it had a fan, but it was inoperative) and which was also festooned with large cobwebs I made some progress. Tom had been unable to decipher my signature or where the fax had come from due to the poor quality of the printout at his end, but also explained he couldn't do anything anyway. I won't bore you with the reasons which were all to do with the ways banks kept and accessed records. In sum, he explained that the act of confirming my signature in my absence would take two weeks. I explained that my account was on-line and I'd also provided on the fax my username and password. Since no-one else would know these, could not this count as proof that I was who I claimed to be? No, because he did not know that these were accurate and even if he contacted those who would know they would be unable to confirm the name and password to him. As a mere branch manager he was not permitted to be party to such information.

Was there anything I could now do? He said he'd try to contact telephone banking and put me on hold. The line went silent for a good five minutes and I hung up and re-dialled. A woman answered and said that Tom was still trying to connect to telephone banking and would I continue to hold? I reminded her I was phoning from Sri Lanka and this was costing me a small fortune but agreed to be patient. Another five minutes of making small-talk with spiders elapsed, and by this time I was ankle-deep in perspiration, before Tom finally came back on the line, full of apologies, and suggested a possible way forward. I was to re-send the fax in the hope that it would transmit more clearly this time, and provide a contact telephone number. He or a colleague would then call me back armed with the security questions I had been given when I opened the account and, provided I answered these correctly, he would then be able to authorise the transfer. I did as asked, and passed the security test with 100% so they agreed the money would now be transferred.

Back to Kandy via a flurry of indecipherable roadside announcements. *WELCOME DISCIPLINARY DRIVERS* it said at the entrance to one town. A clothing shop advertised *SARARAS. FLOWER GIRL DRESS. GENTS SATTY BACK*. A construction company's hoarding threatened that *WE BUILD BEYOND LIMITS*. A van which overtook us near the 'Roy Bin Hood' hotel offered the services of a *ONE MAN THREE PIECE BEAT BAND FOR ANY OCCASION*. In the city centre a sign warned that *NOT TO CROSS THE ROAD ON THE PEDESTRIAN CROSSING IS A PUNISHABLE OFFENCE* which may have explained the throngs of people forever trying to comply, and the consequent gridlock.

Alwin had asked us to a meeting with the vendor's agent who had Power of Attorney to act on the vendor's behalf, which was when we discovered that the people selling us the land were a Sri Lankan woman and her Scottish husband, resident in the UK but currently working in

Saudi Arabia. And we thought our lives were complicated. Knowing we were British he had promised the owners a proportion of the selling price in sterling but hadn't communicated this to us or Alwin. A phone call to Lilamani confirmed what Alwin had suspected – that this would be illegal under Sri Lankan exchange control legislation – so we could not help him out on this point. He squirmed around a bit but finally accepted that this was his problem.

"There is one point I have to check with you", Alwin said when the agent had left. "You are buying three acres of land but about one third of an acre is outside your fence. This is because local people use it to access the small temple next to your land. You have the right to this land, but I would suggest leaving it out of the purchase to avoid bad feeling with the locals. But it's up to you." We readily agreed; what's a third of an acre when you have nearly three?

Alwin also advised us that while we would be able to obtain mains electricity the supply might not be reliable, which proved to be the understatement of the year though at the time we were too focused on buying the land to think ahead about living on it. He suggested that we might want to consider sustainable and self-sufficient alternatives. And we did, but ruled them out quickly on grounds of initial cost – a decision we've lived to regret. He offered to arrange for someone to keep an eye on the place in our absence for as long as we needed. And he arranged for us to meet up with an architect, Dilhan Ratnatunga, on the site before we had to travel back to Colombo and the flight home. Dilhan didn't exactly come with Alwin's recommendation (no-one did) but he did say that he was a Colombo architect who tended to work on bigger projects but liked to turn his hand to houses from time to time.

The next morning a much larger party made its way up to Oorogala in two vehicles for our last look before returning to Colombo and home. We travelled in Lalith's van. In a car behind was Dilhan with two young men whose job was to measure up that part of the site on which we wanted to build so Dihan could work up some initial drawings. He was impressed by the site and showed a possibly feigned interest in the rough sketches and plans we left with him. Then stunned us by quoting thirty five thousand rupees per square foot as the price for a high quality building. This was almost double what both Ikram and Alwin had told us to expect. He also told us we would need to pay for a full topographical survey. After we'd exchanged contact details, said our goodbyes and were on the road down to Colombo Sally phoned Alwin to report our concerns over the likely building costs, which would put the kind of house we had in mind quite out of our range.

Alwin: "The man's mad. Does he think you want gold taps and marble floors? He could get it done for half that price."
Sally: "Good. We want polished cement floors and ordinary taps. What about the topographical survey? Can you arrange that?"
Alwin: "Topographical survey? The stupid fucker. Maybe I'll just sack him. It's almost level land, for fuck's sake – I've seen it myself. I mean, you're hardly talking about building on the Khyber bloody pass. I'll phone him and talk some sense into the daft bugger."
Sure enough, not ten minutes later our phone rang. It was Dilhan, anxious to assure us we could get a perfectly good job done for eighteen thousand rupees a square foot and that he *had* been thinking in terms of marble, mahogany and even gold plated plumbing. However he still insisted we'd need a topographical survey. Quite correctly as it turned out.

On the road back down to Colombo we passed a restaurant which urged passers-by to *VISIT US ONLY ONE TIME* and a hoarding advertising a tailoring firm with the slogan *QUALITY IS NOT AN OPTION*. You kind of know what they mean, but that's not the way you'd have put it. Due to a felicitous cancellation we were able to book into the Swimming Club for our last three nights, where a notice exhorted us *PLEASE DO NOT BATHE OUTSIDE THE BATHTUB* and a card in the room advised: *IN CASE YOU ARE UNABLE TO USE THE TV REMOTE TO SATISFY YOUR NEED PLEASE CONTACT THE ROOM BOY*. Although she doesn't possess my sewer of a mind this reduced Sally to uncontrollable giggles for some while.

It was good to be back in familiar and much-loved territory and within easy reach of Lilamani's office, the HSBC, Crescat Boulevard, Unity and Liberty Plazas, Barefoot – all the places we needed to be for business and last-minute shopping on our final two days. The sun dipped into the Indian Ocean as we arrived: bliss. But less of a sunset than a false dawn as it turned out.

When we left Kandy it seemed as though the whole deal was now virtually sewn up. True, the delay in transferring the money from the UK would mean we couldn't complete before returning to England but that was not of itself a problem. Purely emotionally, of course, we would rather have ended our holiday having actually achieved our objective rather than being 90% of the way there. But we were living in a fool's paradise. We called in on Lilamani as arranged, a routine visit to pick up our copies of the company Certificate of Incorporation and the Memorandum and Articles which duly awaited us. But she mentioned that Simon had asked for a word with us when we came in as a possible problem had cropped up. We waited until he had finished with other clients and went into his office, in some trepidation.

Simon told us that the government were in the process of rushing through emergency legislation via a Finance Bill which included two worrying clauses. The first of these would impose a 100% tax on any foreign companies buying property in Sri Lanka. 'Foreign' was defined as any company having more than 25% of its shares owned by non-nationals. This had come as a complete surprise to Simon who prided himself on his insider contacts. He had consistently advised us that while the government were considering imposing punitive taxes on foreign *individuals* buying property it would not apply to Sri Lanka registered *companies*, which was precisely why we'd formed and incorporated Jungle Tide. The second clause required that any such purchases be valued by a government valuer before the sale could proceed, a process likely to take around six months. During that time, of course, a Sri Lankan could step in and buy the property. It was due to become law in three days' time. There was no discernible reason why this should be regarded as 'emergency legislation' other than all legislation in Sri Lanka seems to be run through under emergency powers, presumably to avoid proper democratic scrutiny. We were assured that the new law would not contain any retrospective provisions so if we were able to complete the next day we would not be liable for the punitive tax. But would the money be there on time? What had an hour earlier seemed a minor irritation now assumed the dimensions of a fundamental problem.

So, off at speed to the HSBC to throw ourselves on their tender mercies. Sudarshan Sivamoorthy turned out to be helpful and understanding, and he was also to our surprise aware of our little company as soon as we introduced ourselves. We showed him the e-mail from Tom Miles confirming that HBOS had actioned the transfer. Sudarshan checked every recent transfer of sterling: "Sorry, Madam, we do not have this transfer in the system. But if the money has been transferred today it will not yet show up. So the transfer may go through tomorrow, I cannot tell."

"Is there anything we can do to speed things up?" "Maybe to contact your bank to get a reference number for the transfer, then let me know and I can see what I can do to speed things up at this end."

As it was still around 7.30am UK time we couldn't do this for a couple of hours. I rang Tom who was able to give me a reference number but also said he was not surprised the telegraphic transfer hadn't reached Colombo as this usually took seven to ten days. So far it had been five days. Things didn't look good. We passed the reference on to Sudarshan and went off to Crescat Boulevard shopping mall, feeling very dejected indeed, the whole project now hanging by a thread. In the mall we visited the internet café to check our e-mails. There was nothing of significance. I was about to turn off the computer when an e-mail popped in from someone at the HSBC confirming that a sum of 4.7 million rupees had just been deposited in our SIERA account. We immediately phoned Alwin and Sudarshan. We were back on track for completion before we left Sri Lanka.

The final act went smoothly. We headed off to the bank after breakfast and Sudarshan completed the transfers from the SIERA account to the company account and thence the 4.7million to Alwin's account from which he would pay out his own and everyone else's expenses and the 4% stamp duty. All this had to be completed before the meeting Alwin had arranged to transfer the title to us – or, more exactly, Jungle Tide (Private) Limited of which we were now the sole directors. As we tucked into our final lunch in Sri Lanka before heading for the airport a phone call came through from Alwin: "It's OK! The deal has been done!" he announced. "So now you can go back to Pinkieland." The documents would be posted on to us in the UK when he got them in the next couple of weeks, he added. We told Lilamani the good news and headed for Katanaiyake airport. I felt like the manager of a football team who'd just won the cup in stoppage time. But it was only Round One, not the Final.

Five

The Ceylon Sea Anglers Club

Every year throughout her childhood Sally's family took two weeks holiday. One week in Wilpattu national park, the other at the Ceylon Sea Anglers Club in China Bay, Trincomalee. Her brothers were home from boarding school in England and for a few brief weeks they were a family, enjoying the remote beaches of Sweat Bay and Marble Bay in the heat of the day, and going out on fishing trips in the early mornings and evenings. Going back to see what had happened to the Sea Anglers Club was one of Sally's top priorities but on our first two visits Trincomalee had been out of bounds to tourists due to the war. We finally made it in 2004 during a lull in the fighting and in the short break between deciding to buy our land at Oorogala and being able to complete the deal.

We had hired a man with a van for a few days. Our intrepid 2001 driver, Norman, who we had wanted to drive us again had seemingly vanished off the face of the earth. The new man's name was Lalith, who Alwin had engaged to drive us around to view properties in the Kandy area and he invariably began his phone calls to us in a stentorian voice with: "Madam, I am Lalith" – to which I always half-expected him to add "Look on my works, ye Mighty, and despair". We'd taken to his cheerful demeanour and helpful attitude and he turned out to be about as perfect a driver as one could hope for, every bit the equal of Norman. We had no idea whether the Ceylon Sea Anglers Club still existed let alone whether we could stay there. Before we left England Sally had managed to find a phone number on their creaky website but this subsequently proved to be out of date or out of order when we tried it. She had also found some kind of Trinco internet chat-room in which a guy resident in the town assured her the CSAC was still open for business but could provide no contact details. So off we went more in hope than expectation.

The road to Trinco runs through Sri Lanka's badlands – dry, scrubby brush and jungle scorched by fire and populated by skeletally thin cattle. As we came nearer to the town the evidence of war became apparent – wrecked buildings scarred with shell holes and a proliferation of armed encampments and road blocks. We knew that the Sea Anglers' Club was out of town, in China Bay, but Sally had only a child's hazy recollection of where China Bay was. Lalith didn't know either. After a lot of fruitless driving around and asking questions we finally located the road to China Bay, and at the junction a big sign indicated that the Sea Anglers' Club was eight kilometres down the road. Past China Bay and on past a Sri Lanka Air Force base another sign indicated that the club was off to the left down a dirt road. Halfway down the track, which crossed a tank range cutely named 'Tankodrome', we came to an army checkpoint. "We are going Sea Anglers' Club" we explained. "You have member permit?" the sentry asked. From our blank expressions the answer was obvious. "You can call for the club and ask them?" enquired Sally. "No madam, only the Air Force can call for the club. You must go back and talk to them." Back up the track to the Air Force base where Jemima announced she was desperate for a wee. She was given an armed escort to the toilets, which she found rather cool. Sally was allowed to phone the Sea Anglers Club and spoke to the manager, who was so interested in her story that he offered to come up to the Air Force base personally and sort out our permission to land. Having done so we returned with him to the roadblock, showed our freshly minted permit letter and the barrier was opened and we finally found ourselves at the Ceylon Sea Anglers' Club, a place Sally hadn't set eyes on for thirty four years.

Inside the clubhouse broken cane benches, faded photos of historic catches, old beds stacked against walls pitted with bullet holes. A shell hole, only partially patched up, in the ceiling. The ship's wheel mounted on the end wall was exactly as Sally remembered it. The club had never been known for comfort – the old iron beds had been replaced by slabs of concrete with thin mattresses on top – so for Sally its battle-scarred present didn't feel that different from its rough and ready past. The manager Erroll was an ex-planter and a serious huntin', shootin', fishin' type. He'd volunteered for the army near to the start of the war in the 1980s and paid the price with a bullet through his right forearm when in Jaffna, a large wound scar and withered arm bearing testimony to this. He showed us several albums of photographs which consisted mainly of pictures of large dead animals and fish with a triumphant Erroll standing by with rod or gun, but there was also an intriguing series of a much younger Erroll with a leopard he'd raised from birth and which he proudly told us was fine with him but a mortal danger to anyone who came visiting.

He filled in for us what had happened to the club since Sally had known it in its heyday. The Ceylon Sea Anglers' Club had remained open more or less continuously throughout the war, he explained. Early on, it was requisitioned as the local HQ of the ill-starred Indian Peace-Keeping Force whose soldiers looted it of most of its antique furniture and generally trashed the place. The IPKF has the dubious distinction of being the only 'peace-keeping' operation that actually worsened the conflict it was sent to resolve. It was apparently nicknamed the 'Innocent People Killing Force'. Their trigger-happy and often brutal behaviours left them equally hated by both sides and ironically led to the Sri Lankan government re-arming the LTTE so they could get rid of the IPKF. Which they did, and followed up by assassinating Rajiv Gandhi for an encore.

After the IPKF was withdrawn from the island the club was handed back to its committee who had ever since resisted persistent attempts by the Sri Lankan armed forces to take it over, with the result that it had become a civilian enclave within a militarised zone; on one side an air force base, on another an army camp and the navy patrolling the offshore waters. The clubhouse roof had taken stray shells on the occasions when the Tamil Tigers were busy bombarding the Sri Lankan navy from the other side of the headland. The Tigers were, by the way, the only terrorist/ guerrilla organisation in the world to have their own navy. And indeed a tiny air force which managed from time to time to drop a few hand-held bombs, World War 1 style. That the club had survived was entirely due to the prominence of some of its members. Top Sri Lankans – like top people everywhere, I guess – tend to like game fishing and aren't going to let the small matter of a war get in the way.

We walked out onto the ruined jetty, at the end of which the remains of the Tuna II, the fishing boat Sally's family had so often used, sat half-in, half-out of the water. A large man, dressed in shorts and a string vest, was walking along the beach and we took him for just a local guy until he opened his mouth and a string of perfectly enunciated English words came out. "Excuse me, I overheard you talking with Erroll. Did you say your family used to be members here?" He explained that he was the club President. Gerald de Saram was also the CEO of an important Sri Lankan company. He told us that the CSAC committee were now planning for a better future as at the time the war appeared to be drawing to a negotiated close – how wrong we all were. The restrictions on fishing the inner harbour were expected to be lifted soon and some   improvements   to   the   clubhouse   and accommodation blocks had begun with a soft loan from the Government for economic projects in former war zones. Fixing the bombarded roof would be the first priority.

Jemima had been feeling unwell and had retired to her concrete bed, rejecting the prospect of dinner. But when I discovered that roast chicken was on the menu I thought I'd better inform her as it was her favourite meal and not to be had in Sri Lanka. She perked up tremendously despite the lack of Yorkshire puddings and so it was that we all sat down to a three course traditional English roast dinner in a semi-derelict clubhouse with shell holes in the roof. Gerald, his wife Kisani, their daughter Salome and Kisani's's sister Tanya were the only other diners. At the end of the meal they suggested we all went outside for drinks on the seashore. Beckoning the two staff they commandeered threadbare sofas and easy chairs to be brought onto the beach and we all sat down under the stars, waves lapping gently at our feet. We ordered brandy – "Local brandy" insisted Sally, knowing that the alternatives could be punitively expensive and were invariably brought unless one specified otherwise.
"I am sorry, madam, local brandy all finish. You like Courvoisier?" So we settled for Courvoisier on a beach, by a ruined jetty and a wrecked fishing boat, in the lee of a shell-scarred clubhouse at what turned out to be the price we'd expected to pay for the local hooch. Gerald insisted on paying, anyway. And invited us out for a fishing trip early the next morning.

Up before dawn then for an attempt on the fish. Erroll and Gerald had both warned us that the fishing was poor at the moment, reasons varying from offshore winds to cool water temperatures to the activities of the navy patrols. The van took us to Kinniyai where our boatman was waiting alongside a ferry heavily laden with early-shift workers and their bicycles. We crossed to the opposite shore of the strait to pick up fuel for the outboard, then zigzagged to another point to change boats. Erroll had decided that he had a bigger, better and more comfortable boat that we should use but this entailed us hauling one boat up the beach and the other back down into the sea. Hard work at six in the morning. The whole operation had to be repeated on the return trip. Predictably we caught nothing. This may have been due to the factors just described or maybe to our failure to use the preferred local angling techniques. We encountered several boats full of people using dynamite and depth-charges. Not CSAC members, I hasten to add. Still and all, dawn fishing in tropical seas off jungle-backed beaches and with Brahminy kites wheeling overhead was its own reward, or so we told ourselves.

Having survived the war the club was temporarily defeated by the military who requisitioned the building in 2009. They wanted to turn the Tankodrome into a golf course as some of the top brass didn't like having to travel for their game. The club buildings were part of the project. Although the club had a lease on the buildings and land this was lost when the Trincomalee kachcheri (local government office) was burned down. Gerald resigned as President and the club sought a new location on the west coast. But nothing much happened and moves are now afoot to get the old place back. In 2016 we attended a fundraiser for the club in the splendid surroundings of the Dutch Burgher Union in Cinnamon Gardens, Colombo. It was a typically Sri Lankan event. Beyond the modest ticket price no fundraising was attempted, no speeches were made, no new members signed up. Dinner was eventually served sometime after ten pm, though it was worth waiting for. Dutch burgher cuisine is an interesting variation on mainstream Sri Lankan cooking and very tasty indeed. Lamprais is its signature dish but if you get a chance to try black pork curry don't miss it.

That first meeting with Gerald and Kisani turned into an enduring friendship and the beginnings of a network of people without whom we could never have built and run Jungle Tide. But we didn't know that at the time and headed off the next day after our unsuccessful fishing trip. Jemima and Sally had had enough of concrete beds after one night. Trincomalee town was impoverished and war-torn, with nowhere to stay so we had a quick look around before moving on. The magnificent Fort Frederick was scarcely signed and had no visitor facilities. Inside was a sprawling complex of army camps and parade grounds with the odd temple thrown in. Up on the walls we mingled with the herd of spotted deer who have made the battlements their home. Then on and out the other side to the great Konesvaram Temple, one of the country's most important Hindu places of worship. It was the day of a festival – a riot of colour and sound.

We made our way up the coast to Uppuveli and Nilaveli passing an evangelist church proclaiming: *JESUS I COME QUICK* – just a little punctuation required, I thought. With its miles of sweeping empty pure white sand, in 2004 with the war still on it was the unexplored end of paradise. Not so much now. Nilaveli boasts five star hotels while Uppuveli has gone down-market for pizza parlours. But the beaches are just as good and go on for so long that if you want a few hundred metres all to yourself that's still possible.

Inland from Nilaveli, Kanniyai hot wells are worth a look. Well worth a look, you might say. Or not. The dirt car park is the start of a souk of stalls selling soft drinks, sunglasses and cheap toys. Once you've run the gauntlet of these there's a minimal entry fee into a courtyard with half a dozen wells in which hot water bubbles up from underground. The site has some religious significance to both Buddhists and Hindus. We were the only white people there. It was a public holiday and the place was thronged. We were feted as whiteys with plenty of attempts to throw jugs of warm water over our heads and great merriment. We had to remind ourselves that this place of joyous celebration had only recently been at the heart of Asia's longest and bitterest civil war. A war which proved to be still far from over.

Wave of destruction

We'd returned home in August 2004 triumphant and optimistic. We'd formed our company and bought the land. But we knew we didn't have money left over to build a house, and we wouldn't be able to make another visit to get the ball rolling any time soon, either. It was going to be a matter of seeing what designs Dilhan would come up with, and doing a lot of calculations about costs and how we could put enough money together. Then, on Boxing Day morning we woke to the appalling news of the tsunami which had struck Sri Lanka among other countries. As the news unfolded over the next few days the extent of the tragedy became clear. Our shock and despair was mollified by seeing the dignified and patient way in which the wonderful people of the island responded, and hearing on TV travellers' stories of how hotel staff had put their guests first and themselves second, despite often having families nearby, close kin of whose fate they knew nothing. Feelings of sympathy jostled with feelings of pride in being associated, in however small and distant a way, with Sri Lanka and its people. We felt proud, too, to be British as the tremendous scale of the public response to the emergency was broadcast.

We gave, of course, to the emergency appeal. But we also supported a longer-term smaller project ourselves. The project was managed by Gerald, via the company of which he was the Sri Lankan CEO. The project focused on two villages, one in the mainly Sinhalese south coast near Tangalle and another in the mainly Tamil east coast south of Trincomalee. Various friends and colleagues contributed regular monthly amounts to support economic development in the two villages, such as rebuilding and refitting fishing boats. We got the chance to see at first hand the results of our friends' generosity when we managed to scrape together enough money for our next visit in 2006. The village near Trincomalee was again off limits due to the renewed fighting but Gerald and Kisani arranged for us to visit Kalametiya on the south coast.

Gerald chose the two villages because he had contacts there and could be sure the money was going directly to where it was needed. The Kalametiya connection was that he and Kisani had a small holiday house there. He made arrangements for us to be shown around by Sumith, the chairman of the local fisheries co-operative. He also arranged for the caretaker of their holiday chalet – a man ironically called 'Baby' as he was built like a super-heavyweight – to make us lunch. Despite this being still very much the dry season, and despite Kalametiya being on the edge of the southern dry zone, it rained steadily for most of the day. Not the usual torrential, short-lived tropical downpours but real Yorkshire rain, relentless and depressing.

The effects of the tsunami became evident south of Colombo. Wrecked catamarans in the scrub jungle, far from the beach; shells of houses; for mile after mile nothing had survived. Tented villages with the names of donor countries prominently displayed so we could all see who the good guys were. The beginnings of more permanent housing schemes, many of which might have been uprooted social housing estates from Europe – no understanding of or acknowledgement to local tradition and vernacular – though there were honourable exceptions. The A2 was for miles on end a potholed mess, diverted at various points on pontoons upstream from where the tsunami-destroyed bridges were being rebuilt. The track to Kalametiya, four kilometres off the main road, was barely passable by van and by no means for the first time we found ourselves apologising to our driver for what we were putting him and his vehicle through. Just beyond the bird sanctuary – an area of marshland teeming with avian life – all pretence at tarmac was finally abandoned and we were on a slippery red dirt road.

Sumith's house stood opposite an upturned wrecked boat and was by local standards large and well-appointed. By our standards, cavernous and gloomy with long-defunct fans and rusting kitchen equipment jostling for space with ropes and fishing gear. We met his family and were plied with the usual diet of sweet tea, cake and bananas while our driver acted as interpreter, for Sumith spoke little English. We felt like an official inspectorate, being shown schedules of repairs undertaken and receipts for costs incurred. Altogether some four hundred villagers had been helped out. Fifteen large boats and thirty seven catamarans and other small boats had been repaired and were operating once more. Ironically Sumith had been too busy sorting everyone else out to find the time to fix his own boat which stood out to sea, still afloat but not seaworthy. A maze of dirt tracks led eventually to the beach where we viewed and photographed the repaired boats and saw the wreckage of some that the tsunami had put beyond repair. I accidentally trod on the tail of a seven foot cabragoya (water monitor) lying on the sand between two beached boats. Luckily it wasn't up for a fight and shot off. Given the continuing downpour we passed on the chance to see yet more boats and climbed back into the van to travel a further maze of village tracks. We stopped outside Baby's house from which he emerged with our lunch in a red plastic bucket, two carrier bags and assorted other containers which we took up to Gerald and Kisani's chalet to eat, accompanied by a chorus of birdsong. An unseen pair of peacocks carried on a noisy conversation somewhere nearby.

A little further west the town of Dikwella featured official signs reading *TSUNAMI DANGER ZONE* and *TSUNAMI ESCAPE ROUTE* pointing away from the sea. Deconstructed, what these signs say is that tsunamis occur on the coast and if you want to survive one it's best not to head into the sea. Surprise, surprise! Aside from insulting the intelligence of the average stray dog these signs will have rusted away long before Sri Lanka is likely to suffer another tsunami. The previous one was in the early nineteenth century. But natural disasters have a way of creating folklore and several people have observed to us in all seriousness that climate change occurred as a direct result of the tsunami.

Enter Nissanka

By the time of our 2006 visit we had agreed the plans for the house with Dilhan and he had obtained what he told us was planning permission from the Kandy Urban Development Authority, though we needed to finalise this in person with the deeds. We also needed to be there to kick-start the building process and in particular to organise the construction of the access road and groundworks, without which there wasn't going to be any house. As usual, we began our visit at the Swimming Club, but this time there was no swimming to be had. The pool had been drained and was full of building materials, surrounded by mountains of sand and sheets of blue plastic. "Essential repairs, Madam" we were told, not open for another six weeks. Drinks and dinner in a building site was the best that was on offer. Two blocks away a floodlit crane heaved huge cubes of concrete across the night sky on a more substantial building project. Oh well, pretty soon we'd have our own building site.

It had dawned on us that we'd need to make an awful lot of phone calls on this trip, a daunting prospect. As we'd found previously the various Sri Lankan phone systems were complex, unreliable, expensive and sweaty. People would need to contact us, too. We discussed whether it would be worthwhile to buy a pay-as-you-go mobile. Sally had brought her mobile simply for the purpose of phoning home in case of flight delays or emergencies. I didn't possess one – or rather the one I had belonged to my employers. In those days we knew little of mobile phones and had no idea what a SIM card was. Some of our younger acquaintances would comment that little has changed since. A shop in Crescat Boulevard sorted out a local SIM for a ridiculously small sum and we bought a charger for an equally trivial amount of money. The phone proved vital and has been our constant companion in Sri Lanka ever since. Though its mortal remains – an ancient Nokia – have long been laid to rest its SIM-soul lives on in a smartphone.

We met Dilhan at the Galle Face Hotel next morning. Outside, Galle Face Green was full of tanks and regiments of squaddies lined up in blocks. Helicopters buzzed overhead and we were stopped and questioned three times on the short walk from the Swimming Club by soldiers enquiring as to our intentions. Independence Day was due in three days' time and this was some kind of dress-rehearsal. Dilhan presented us with a sheaf of detailed drawings in an outsize folder. They looked amazing and for the first time we could really visualise our new home. He'd already received one tender for the road construction and expected the other two imminently and promised to e-mail all three to us so we could select one. The euphoria was short-lived. We'd heard from Gerald among others that inflation in the construction industry had rocketed since the tsunami. The huge volume of reconstruction work had created a genuine shortage of building materials, but the price hike had been compounded by the ineptitude of the larger NGOs who had moved in with the mighty Yankee dollar and had been paying well over the going rate to local profiteer builders. Putting aside for the moment our selfish concerns about what this would do to the costs of building our house, it was annoying that so many more homes, health facilities, schools etc. could have been built for the money had the NGOs had the sense to hang tough and insist on the proper rate.

Jemima was impressed by Dilhan's metropolitan dress sense and rated him "a cool dude". We were more impressed with his taste in floor tiles. We'd also forgotten how good his spoken English was, including vernacular expressions and jokes, as his e-mails had been on the hard side of impenetrable. Dilhan had brought along his team – Saro the Surveyor (who sounded like a character in a comic book) and Nimal his QS. We had expected bad news on the costs front but this was worse than we'd prepared for. The tenders for building the road, bridge and associated earthworks were all almost half our budget for the whole project. If it cost that much to build a short road and small bridge we could forget about the house. Then Dilhan smilingly announced that the estimated costs of the house would now be 50% higher than his original quote. It looked as though we would just have to sell the land on and abandon our dream of living in Sri Lanka. We headed off to Kandy feeling utterly depressed. Again.

The Queens Hotel was back to being something like its old self, full of character and characters, faded grandeur managed by incompetence. We asked for more coat-hangers and a bedside table: "Yes, Madam." When we returned to the room a couple of hours later it had acquired an extra and superfluous bedside lamp but no table or coat-hangers. When Sally rang reception to ask for an adaptor to plug our phone charger into they replied: "You need doctor? Certainly madam, we fetch doctor. Doctor now coming".

We spent the morning with notebooks and a calculator, poring over ways of reducing costs, finding money and scheduling payments. Things were far from being resolved but at least we were clear about the size of the mountain we had to climb. First we needed someone to bat for our side – a project manager. We talked to Gerald, our only hope. He suggested someone called Pieter Ter Haar for the role. Pieter was a South African with a colourful past who had found Jesus and now did charitable works – but was by no means a pushover and would be a great guy to have on our side. We met Pieter and liked him but he said he couldn't commit to our project as he was already stretched and was about to go on an extended visit to his homeland. He suggested his friend Nissanka Perera. Nissanka was a former planter himself with a ten acre smallholding and we gathered he could do with a bit of extra income. A day rate of around two thousand rupees or a bit more would be fine and twice weekly visits should be enough. This was much less than Dilhan had said we should expect a project manager to cost. But as we knew, Dilhan came gold-plated, bells and whistles.

So we met Nissanka and his wife Lakshmi in the splendid lobby of the Queens. A tall, balding, handsome man in his sixties, though he looked younger, he listened carefully as we explained our situation and immediately confirmed that the quotes we had for the access road were outrageously expensive. He gave us the name of a contractor who could, he said, do the work for a fifth of what we had been quoted, to a lower but still perfectly adequate spec. Halfway through the conversation it dawned on us that we weren't interviewing Nissanka for the job of project manager, he was interviewing us to work out whether we would be worth doing business with. In particular asking about Sally's planter credentials and ancestry, which he later checked by consulting *Ferguson's Directory* wherein all the British planters are listed from the mid nineteenth century onwards. Having satisfied himself that Sally was from good planter stock he agreed to take us on. Although he had not known her parents, as a young trainee planter (or 'creeper' as they are called) he had known a number of other British planters who Sally also remembered. We had the immediate and strong sense that we were dealing with someone honest, trustworthy, knowledgeable and above all understanding, who was on our side. We arranged to go with him up to Oorogala to take a look around.

Uduwela (or Oodewella, depending on which sign you read – the name simply means 'high field') is the area where our land is situated. It's a division of the Hanthana (Hantane, Hanthane etc. etc.) estate which, according to Nissanka, would certainly have been one of the estates Sally's father Tony would have inspected since at the time, before nationalisation, it was owned by Gordon Fraser, the company he worked for. Not, I understand, the same Gordon Fraser which turns out cheap birthday cards, unless they'd diversified rather dramatically. Nissanka himself still owned and had restored an ancient Riley which had belonged to the family of Sally's best friend Catriona Cameron, and which she remembered well. Catriona herself got in touch after we moved to Sri Lanka and visited us with her family; she and Sally had not met for forty five years, and it was Catriona's first return visit to the land of her birth .

Nissanka and Lakshmi turned up promptly ("I work on British time, not Sri Lanka time" he explained almost apologetically) to take us up to look at the land and discuss the access road. On the way up I sat in the front of his ancient jeep to show him the way from memory, surprising myself by doing so impeccably. There are no maps in between Kandy street maps, which don't extend to Uduwela, and national road maps, which are nowhere near detailed enough to show the small tea estate roads. Actually, there is a Sri Lanka version of the Ordnance Survey and Nissanka had procured for us a copy of the section covering both Kandy and the Hanthana hills but it was a smudgy fourth generation black and white photocopy and near-impossible to read. Possession of these maps was apparently an offence, as they might fall into the hands of the LTTE. Quite how this would help the Tigers in these days of Google Earth was, as ever, beyond me. Incidentally it was years before I realised that the long, straight north-south Baseline Road in Colombo had been so named because it was from there that the British surveyed and mapped the island.

The road up to Uduwela was being improved, though it was still narrow and rough in short stretches. Our land was by now overgrown. It was hard to get around, and hard to see the views from the top but we were able, by parting various small trees, to confirm what we had suspected – that we would have some stunning views from the house once the land had been cleared. Or rather, I could confirm this as I scrambled with Nissanka across the stream and up to the summit. Too much for Sally, Jemima and Lakshmi who stayed down by the streamside and got leeched as a result. The tea was still being plucked and pruned, as a gash on my leg testified. A recently pruned tea bush is not a plant to be messed with. This was fine by us as, left un-pruned, tea can grow to thirty feet in height. On a flat patch by the stream a crude wooden frame had been erected. I asked Nissanka what it was. "It's a frame used to saw up the timber the local people are taking from your land. Don't worry, I'll soon put a stop to that."

.

So the deal was struck. Nissanka would organise the construction of the road and the bridge across the stream. As a planter, he'd built dozens of such roads and several bridges before, mostly on steeper terrain than ours. He would then act as our project manager during the construction of the house. We ended by roughly surveying a route for the access road and hit on the best place to bridge the stream. Next step was to get building permission from the Regional Council, which Dilhan had arranged.

The Regional Council offices covering Uduwela are almost an hour's drive out of Kandy, quite close to our land as the crow flies but separated by mountains across which there is no road, and we had no crow. We needed to visit them to obtain building permission and show them the original deeds which we'd brought with us from England. The council office buildings were a collection of grimy sheds with threadbare curtains and hand-me-down metal desks at which sat dozens of young women huddled over banks of manual typewriters, sheaves of carbon paper at the ready, in a scene that Dickens might have recognised. We were ushered into the grandly-named Environmental Management Unit, much of which was taken up by a large pile of refuse. During the long wait for attention I read the newspaper I'd brought with me and learned that a man had been 'nabbed' (they still use such endearingly Dixon-of-Dock-Green terms in crime reports) in the temple at Sri Pada, produced in court and fined five thousand rupees. The report went on to clarify that it is not an offence to worship in the temple 'but that he had 370 grams of ganja on him'.

The planning process consisted of first obtaining permission from the Kandy Urban Development Authority which Dilhan had already done, then obtaining Regional Council permission to build the bungalow (this bit) and finally a site inspection by the Regional Council where our presence would not be required. Thankfully, as by then we'd be back in Yorkshire. At that stage, and quite openly, a bribe of two thousand rupees was payable – plus an official fee of five hundred rupees – and building could proceed. The bribe later entered our company accounts, clearly stated as such. We were directed to sign an immense document in Sinhala in about a dozen places, with no translation or opportunity to read it; one has to take these things on trust and Dilhan said it was OK. Then the deeds were checked, the official fee paid and job done, relatively quickly and painlessly. We had our permission – though the Council now claim to have no record of it.

In Colombo before flying home we had a final meeting with Dilhan and Saro in their 'boardroom', possibly the least impressive example of its genre I'd ever set foot in. Dirty, dingy and sparse. Not the kind of place you'd expect a top architect to hang out in. We continued to emphasise our fixed budget, they continued to insist on the need for quality and to be deaf to our concerns. Stalemate. Oh well, off for some last-minute retail therapy in Odel and Barefoot.

In Barefoot we ran into Germaine Greer. "That's Germaine Greer over there" whispered Jemima. "Are you sure?" "I think so – I'll just go and ask." "Excuse me, but are you Germaine Greer?" "I certainly am". "Hi, I'm Jemima Martin" – and the *grande dame de lettres* was promptly ushered out by her entourage. Years later we met her properly at the Square Chapel Centre for the Arts in Halifax, which Sally ran and where she was performing, but not surprisingly she had no recollection of this encounter with our forward daughter in a shop in Colombo.

Slow, slow, quick, quick, slow

In between getting the ball rolling in February 2006 and first being able to stay under our own roof in August 2008 we visited twice, in March 2007 and March 2008, but the story unfolded as much in England as it did in Sri Lanka. Although unless we were there, things proceeded at a snail's pace.

"Dear Dilhan" we e-mailed at the end of April 2006, *"Could you let us know what progress you have made with drawing up the contract documents please? When can we expect to see them?"*

It was two weeks before a reply came:

"Sorry for the keep you waiting. All the tender documents are ready for your approvals but it need to complete with some inputs of your datas. So I'll currier it to you in this week. You can go through the document and give your comments but I don't think you need the set of architectural drawing with the document it is more or less the same thing that I have give to you, only few changes with the finishes and specifications but ill send the structural drawings take care and bye. Dilhan".

What "datas" did he want? Why was there no Bill of Quantities? How come his written English was so bad when his spoken English was impeccable? The tender document ran up to page 26 then jumped to page 56 then ran backwards to page 48, then started again from page 26 to 47 then jumped to page 57 from where it continued its meandering journey uninterrupted to the end. There were terms which meant nothing to us and were not explained. What was a 'bid bond'? What were 'liquidated damages'? What did the phrase 'Pantry unit measured under provisional sum trade' mean? Our comments and questions ran to several pages. Two months later he had still not responded to them. We were now more than a month into what should have been the build period.

He did eventually provide the answers. But still no Bill of Quantities and no contract, both of which had been long promised. They were promised again a couple of months later and the Bill of Quantities duly arrived soon after. It was an eye-watering 75% over what we'd given him as our maximum budget. We gave him a week to come up with revisions which might get us nearer what we could afford; needless to say he could not. We paid Dilhan for his work to date and told him we would regrettably be ending our relationship. Architects do tend to get carried away with their own ideas – and Dilhan's ideas were excellent – while forgetting the budget their clients have given them. Sri Lankan businessmen with white clients find it impossible to conceive that their client does not have unlimited access to money. And very few of them possess listening skills; we'd been talking to a brick wall. An architect-designed brick wall, but a brick wall nonetheless.

Meanwhile, back at our putative ranch, there was better news. Nissanka had found a contractor who could not only build the access road and the bridge over the stream but also level the house site, clear the overgrown tea bushes, dig two tube-wells and throw in an ornamental concrete dam for good measure, all for half the price Dilhan's contractors had tendered for, just for the road and bridge. A virtuoso first innings by our opening batsman. The bridge was the most expensive bit. In our unending naivety we'd failed to allow for this needing to be strong enough to carry construction traffic, not just the odd car or van. "And I added an arch to make it look more English" he reported proudly. "It cost very little".

Nissanka planted fruit of all kinds, from the obvious ones like papayas, bananas, avocados, passion fruit vines and various citrus bushes to lesser known ones such as amberellas, cherimoyas, grenadilla vines and star fruit. And an orchard of sixteen mango trees. There were already guavas, a jak tree and a lime tree on the land, and a durian just outside our boundary which conveniently dropped half its crop on our side of the fence. The porcupines and wild pigs soon saw off the papayas and bananas, rooting them up for their midnight feasts. He lined the driveways with bougainvillea, yellow-flowered cassia spectabilis and orange-flowered 'flamboyant trees', a stylised version of which we used as our logo.

There was an area of flattish land at the top of the site which was the obvious place to build the house. It commanded a view of Hunasgiriya, the mountain on whose lower slopes Meenawatte stands, so Sally can sit on our veranda and look out towards the house she did some of her growing up in, though the house itself is too far away to see. The land needed levelling before building could start, and Nissanka thought the house would look better facing onto a level lawn area rather than away down a slope. So he created an almost vertical bank more than ten metres high and in-filled the top side to make a level lawn area in front of the house, then planted trees and tough grasses to hold the bank in place. To level the house site he'd employed a man for thirty days to do nothing but blast rocks apart with dynamite – Oh how I wish I could have been there! A gigantic fissured rock still stands opposite our front entrance, others form a border to the lawn, while others still careened down the slopes and ended up in the stream, creating superb white water conditions after heavy rain. Well, brownish-red water anyway.

We were excited and though we still had no idea how we would find the money to build our dream home we resolved that we would somehow end up living on our land even if it were in a wooden shed. We determined to return a year later and do whatever we could to make things happen. And just before we left for Sri Lanka in March 2007 Nissanka contacted us to say he had come across a company in Colombo called Vijaya Builders who thought they could build the house within our budget. He suggested he take us to meet them once we arrived in Colombo. Their website was a curious affair, showing computer-generated images of a range of standard house types all in the garish colours beloved of Sri Lankans and none of which we could ever envision ourselves living in. But we e-mailed them, briefly stating what we wanted, mentioning Nissanka, explaining that we would be visiting Sri Lanka shortly and asking whether they thought they might be able to build a house something along the lines of our design. No reply. Oh well, off to Manchester Airport and see what to do once we got to Colombo.

The Vijaya dialogues

At the Galle Face Hotel the woman on reception apologised: "Your usual room is not available, Mrs Martin. But for an extra six dollars per night we can give you the Royal Dutch Suite." "Usual room"? What "usual room"? We weren't aware of one, but felt very chuffed to be remembered so. And a luxury suite for just $6 a night more! Over our budget, of course, but not to be missed, though Sally hinted darkly of a dietary regime of baked potatoes once we got back to England.

We were treated to a tuk-tuk ride back from the delightful Cricket Club Café to the Galle Face Hotel one night in a three wheeler driven by an Anglophile which had its rear panel covered with a large St George cross underneath which was written: ENGLAND, THE GODFATHER COUNTRY. Well, we assumed he was Anglophile though admittedly the slogan was open to interpretation. The interior of the hood of his vehicle was plastered with English phrases his various passengers had supplied. 'Hanky-panky'; 'Bangers and mash'; 'Well good'; 'Wotcher cock' and suchlike. We told him this was far too Cockney biased and that he should add some Yorkshire ones. He asked for a suggestion so we donated 'Ee bah gum' and 'Ecky thump' to his collection, writing the words out for him on a scrap of paper. He dropped us at the hotel and drove off into the night muttering "Ee bah gum. Ecky thump" and chuckling to himself.

Outside the Galle Face Hotel's splendid veranda, crow management was the responsibility of a trimly-uniformed man with a catapult who prowled the lawn at mealtimes, though there was a machine-gun nest on a blackened tower next to the hotel which may have served as back-up. As ever, Galle Face Green looked a mess. A hoarding proudly announced the complete refurbishment of the area, including a pier and a giant fountain. Work to commence May 2006, completion date December 2006. Three months ago. Needless to say, little sign of anything having even started save for a lot of metal fencing everywhere. Sri Lankans are very good at metal fencing. The joys to come apparently included 'reinforced grass'. Since our last visit the GFH had opened an 'English Pub' – Inn on the Green, very Robin Hood – along Galle Road so we called in to try it out. Quite impressed us, though whether the ability to eat shepherd's pie and drink Tetley's on draught in Colombo is a point in favour I wasn't sure. On the 'when in Rome' principle we stuck to Lion lager.

One of the world's lesser known sporting events is the GFH's 'Cannonball Run' and we witnessed it late one afternoon. It commemorates an incident in the nineteenth century when a cannonball was accidentally fired into the Galle Face Boarding House, forerunner of the GFH, during artillery practice on Galle Face Green. Each year the British High Commissioner takes on one of his fellow diplomats in the event, and this year it was the turn of the US Ambassador. We spectators were given the choice of a small paper union flag or a star spangled banner to hold aloft. The two men, suitably attired in towelled robes like boxing contenders, were brought to the seafront lawn of the hotel and paraded around amid much drumming and martial music blaring from loudspeakers then, to the strain of *Mad Dogs and Englishmen*, they were led off to the start of the sprint, an old cannon on the green from which, at the lowering of a flag, they raced back to the hotel. First to touch the cannonball, laid out in a kind of tented cannonball shrine, is the winner. All extremely silly. For the record, the High Commissioner won in a photo finish and many paper union flags were waved. It occurred to me that fitness to compete in the event might be on the person spec of would-be diplomats. Certainly the two contestants looked young and fit. Their CVs probably included their personal bests over two hundred metres. There was also, for some reason, an open topped London double decker parked by the seafront, and all the hotel's chefs paraded in their tall cheffy hats. After dark the celebrations continued, ending with an extremely noisy and exuberant firework display.

Nissanka had arranged our meeting with Vijaya Builders for 3pm down in their offices in Bambalapittiya. They began with an enthusiastic presentation of their standard house designs all in Lego colours on a loop playing on a large screen in the office. To the accompaniment of suitably schmaltzy music the presentation began with the on-screen words "Our specious houses ..." – what they call a Freudian slip, I believe. One of the grander versions on show included a room marked as 'Savant's Quarters' – what a good idea, to have one's own live-in sage to offer words of wisdom and good advice when needed. They told us that they could build the house more or less to Dilhan's original design by amending and combining some of their standard off-the-peg designs, all within our budget. There was no requirement to have their migraine-inducing Lego colours and the whole house could be finished in white inside and out. Lesson thirty four: Sri Lankans will always say they can do whatever you want for whatever you can afford, whether or not this is possible. So we agreed to return the next morning with twenty thousand rupees to pay them to produce detailed drawings and to be shown some of the other houses they'd built in the Colombo area. We then spent most of the following morning waiting around outside their offices with a fresh-faced jack-the-lad called Kalishka for a guy with a van to become available to show us around one of their houses, down the coast in Mount Lavinia.

As we waited a man sidled up and started the old "I am a schoolteacher" routine. As soon as he realised this was our fifth time in Sri Lanka and we knew the place and its customs rather well he had the good sense to give up and chat about the time he lived in Exeter. He told us he found Devon and Cornwall "very strange". We said that we did, too. Kalishka meanwhile engaged us in cheery small talk and showed that, like Dilhan's, his listening skills were close to zero. He seemed to have forgotten that they had agreed to build to a revised version of our floor plan and kept returning to his own 'solution' of sticking three of their Lego houses together to make one larger house. This, quite apart from the truly awful appearance of it, would have meant settling for a warren of tiny rooms which was absolutely not what we wanted. The doubts which were creeping in at the start began turn into a flood. Then he told us that in any case no-one could do anything until our cheque had cleared which will be several days away. Of course, if he'd explained that the previous day we would have drawn out the cash, but thinking ahead is not the way Sri Lankans tend to do business. Finally there was a terrific to-ing and fro-ing about the cheque since it was a company cheque and his boss at first refused to accept it. It took several visits to the man upstairs before they would finally agree to take our money.

Instead of the anticipated selection of houses we were finally taken to see just one house, in Mount Lavinia. It had been completed four years earlier but never occupied, for reasons no-one made clear. It was nothing like what we wanted, of course, being a two storey town house, but at least we could assess the quality of their work. We got out of the van and approached the house. To one side of the gate the words *VIJAYA BULLSHIT HOUSE* and to the other *NO CROOKS* had been prominently graffitied. The Vijaya team appeared unconcerned by this negative publicity and didn't comment on it. The house seemed flimsy but maybe that's what we'd have to settle for given our limited means. In truth, we left sadder but little the wiser and it was beginning to look like another false start.

We knew Nissanka had been busy. We knew he'd done all we'd asked and more, for less than we'd expected to pay. His e-mails had given us the impression that this was a personal project for him, not just a bit of extra paid work. But nothing had prepared us for the transformation of our land which we saw that morning. The entrance was already classy, even before the gates had been fitted. The approach road of rotting concrete slabs gave way to a smart driveway lined with a brilliant white low wall, complete with bollards at intervals and planted with young bougainvillea, already in showy flower. The drive dipped down to the white-railed bridge (complete with the faux English arch) then climbed back up to where the house would stand, dramatically overlooking the gardens as well as the long view towards the distant mountains. It was breathtaking. From just beyond the bridge a side road led off to the left, alongside the stream, down to the lower gardens where it ended up performing a circuit of what we intended would be a large pond. The land had been cleared of tea and all but a handful of useful mature trees plus the young fruiting and ornamental trees Nissanka had planted. It looked barren and rocky – a blank canvas.

The dam proved more of a mixed blessing. It looked great, with four big concrete pipes at the top out of which the water fairly hurtled during the monsoon. But dams take a while to fill up and while it was doing so the stream was temporarily stopped. This didn't endear us to the paddy farmers down below whose water supply we had just inadvertently caused to be cut off. So the plug had to be removed until such time as the rains gathered enough force to keep everyone happy. For a while our dam provided a pool deep enough to swim in but it leaked continually and eventually we decided to break it. It had been an expensive folly. The stream, Nissanka assured us, "will never run dry. You will always have water on your land." He was right in so many things but well out on that one, it later proved. It's dry for maybe half the year on average. Although we have now discovered the reason; one of the local temples and the next door hotel have tapped into the stream higher up to provide themselves with water rather than doing what they are supposed to and dig tube-wells.

Rajath, the Vijaya architect, came along to survey the site, confirmed it would be OK for the house we wanted – which of course we knew but they had to satisfy themselves – and without further ado or conversation climbed into his Indian cheap-jeep and departed for Colombo leaving us to explore the land at leisure with Nissanka and the ancient Tamil gardener from next door who was being paid to water and mulch the young trees. The following day Kalishka phoned yet again – full marks to that boy for enthusiasm and dogged pursuit of clients.

He now wanted us to pay a 3% deposit before we'd even agreed the design, let alone got any kind of contract. We were not happy with Vijaya Builders but what other options did we have? We stalled, for the time being.

We knew that Nissanka lived the simple life and Lakshmi, who is metropolitan by nature, seemed to spend most of her time living apart from him in her suburban house in Mount Lavinia. Just how simple we found out when he took us afterwards to see his modest house, down miles of remote dirt road near Wattegama and quite close to Sally's childhood home Meenawatte. It had a wide veranda under which he parked his car. His only use for electricity is lighting and he'd wired it up to run off his car battery which he simply connected up to the house when he got home. "What about a fridge?" we asked him. "I am vegetarian. I don't drink beer. So no need for a fridge". A stream coursed through the gardens by the house. Inside all was twisted tree trunks and home-made rustic furniture. As we chatted idly Lakshmi phoned to say she had been told by three separate people that Vijaya Builders were untrustworthy and shoddy. But she knew another architect with his own building company who was constructing a house near to hers and was interested in our project. Could he come up to see the land and talk to us? Fine in principle, but time was as ever getting short and even if the guy was good and could build something we wanted within our budget, whether we could finalise a deal before we left Sri Lanka was doubtful. Nevertheless we agreed to meet and talk further. We were desperate. Tuesday morning was the earliest Gamini Karunaratne could get up to Kandy, leaving us with three days to kill. So, as we'd predicted, all was going nicely pear-shaped and we were left nursing feelings of frustration and powerlessness. But we'd been in this territory more than once before and convinced ourselves that all may yet turn out fine. Well, you have to try to stay positive, don't you?

And come to think of it, the whole island is pear-shaped so it shouldn't have come as a surprise.

Third time lucky

We'd failed to agree with two architects and developers so we had no great expectations of our meeting with Gamini. He duly came up to Kandy and visited the land with us. We were taken with him. He seemed aware of our budgetary limitations and requirements and took a practical attitude. Being an architect, he was predictably dismissive of our attempts to redesign the house but said he would try to come up with an alternative sketch by Monday, our last day before flying home. Also, his fee would be only 5% which was half Dilhan's. Up went the roller coaster again, if only a small rise this time. And we spotted a golden oriole hopping around in our lime tree. At the time we were just hanging on grimly to any positives, however small, and a golden oriole fitted the bill nicely.

We shuttled back down the A1, probably the only trunk road in the world which has speed bumps on it, to Colombo. On the way we passed the Kandy-Colombo inter-city bus face down in a ditch. As we arrived in the city a drunk lay insensible in the middle of a busy main road, the traffic cheerfully swerving around him. The reason for this uncaring attitude being that to get involved with a road casualty of any kind is to court police action and probably an accusation that you had caused the casualty, though this was something we only found out years later. At the time we were mystified by the apparent callousness.

Duplication Road does what it says on the tin. It runs parallel to and inland from Galle Road for a couple of miles through Colpetty/Kolupittiya and Bambalapittiya. Since we were last here someone had had the bright idea of making the two roads one way, Galle Road running northbound only on this section, Duplication Road southbound. This has certainly improved traffic flows. But it had all been done without any alteration to road markings so one was constantly travelling down traffic lanes with big arrows pointing the opposite way, which is quite unnerving until you get used to it. The practice has recently spread to Kandy where alterations to the one-way system are made with alarming frequency, all of them carefully designed to maximise the amount of time each vehicle has to spend in the city centre, belching out exhaust fumes.

The next morning we noticed a larger than usual army and police presence and knots of people milling around on Galle Road. Someone told us that the President would be passing through on his way to view a parade of fifty elephants – a piece of information that gave rise to two thoughts (a) the poor man must be as bored with elephant parades as I am and probably regrets ever having taken on the job (b) doesn't he have anything more productive to do? There's a war on, you know. Shortly afterwards, as we sipped our mocha *frappes* on the terrace in front of the Deli France at Crescat, an eerie silence descended on an emptied Galle Road. Minutes later the motorcade sped past at a cracking pace – about a dozen motorcycle outriders followed by a convoy of jeeps packed with soldiers, then half a dozen or so limousines, one of which must have contained the President, with more motorcycles bringing up the rear. Another short period of silence, then back to the normal chaos of Colombo traffic.

Almost time to fly home nursing our wounds and contemplating whether our house would ever be built when Gamini phoned to say he'd worked up some drawings and could we meet at six? He picked us up at the Swimming Club and drove us to his sports club inside the Colombo cricket ground. While I gazed obliquely at the hallowed turf he and Sally inspected a set of excellent sketch drawings and plans which he said he could build for thirteen million rupees, close to our (massively upwardly revised) budget. As we'd expected, it was a totally different design from the thoughts we'd come up with and passed on to him but it did the business and was indeed better than our ideas – well, he is an architect. He's supposed to be good at this. And he'd even trained under the master himself, Geoffrey Bawa. We were particularly impressed with his understanding of how we wanted the house to look. Sally's vision was to combine the best of the planter style of bungalow architecture – spacious pillared verandas, high roofs and airy rooms – with a modern interior layout including far more glass and natural light than was traditionally the case, and a kitchen we could cook in rather than a dark hole separate from the house. Gamini got this. So we provisionally agreed terms and left Sri Lanka with the project almost ready to go. A start on site late May or June with completion nine months later was the intention. Our spirits were so high they probably powered the flight home. We fully expected to be back in a year or so with the house completed and ready to be furnished and staffed, and to open as a guest house. We never learn.

Six

Building blocks

When you're six thousand miles from your building project good communication is important, to put it mildly. And it's not something Sri Lankans are generally very good at. Nissanka, though, was an exception. He had no keyboard skills or familiarity with computers; he was strictly old-school planter stock. But he resolved the tricky problem of how to communicate weekly progress reports to us without relying on snail mail by the novel method of writing them out by hand, taking them into one of the internet cafes in Kandy and asking them to scan and e-mail them to us in England. His neat handwriting helped a lot. His written English was as good as Dilhan's had been bad, if somewhat Victorian in style. Over the following months as building began we became acquainted with some of Sri Lanka's more arcane and bureaucratic procedures and customs which we would later get to know on intimate terms – and with Nissanka's often novel methods for dealing with them.

27th June 2007
Dear Sally and Jerry
With difficulty I was able to obtain an appointment with the Technical Officer of the Local Administrative Council to visit the building site for his inspection to pass approval for the building. I took him to the site yesterday for the inspection, which satisfied his requirements. He informed me that at the end of next week Building Permission will be granted.
Currently I am working on obtaining the electricity connection for which the following items have to be attended to:
> *1) Construct a temporary hut on site so that the Ceylon Electricity Board has a dwelling on site to*

give a connection. This little building will be completed tomorrow.

2) Thereafter there is a set of application forms to be filled in and submitted which I hope to do on Friday 29th inst.

3) Then the Ceylon Electricity Board will visit the building site for inspection and estimation and will let me know the cost of the connection.

4) On payment of the connection costs to the CEB, electricity will be connected within a week.

6th July 2007

Dear Sally and Jerry

On the 2nd inst. I submitted an application to the Ceylon Electricity Board for the electricity connection to your building site. The delay was that the application form required the approval of two government officials, one of whom was on leave from work.

Gamini is very keen on starting work as early as possible; so rather than delay until electricity is available and the installation of the water pump is complete I have arranged a temporary water and electricity connection from your neighbour Mr Anton Perera.

Due to the recent heavy rains the earth embankment along the road from the entrance to the property adjacent to the chicken farm road has been subjected to a minor collapse. This requires it to be rebuilt with reinforced concrete to a height of three feet for a length of 125 feet otherwise part of their road will be on our road. As it is, most of their concrete fence posts are now lying on our road.

And so on. But those two e-mails illustrated the lessons we were having to learn quickly; that the wheels of bureaucracy grind slow and unpredictably; that we'd have to get on with the neighbours and that there were going to be a whole series of unforeseen costs and delays. Indeed the saga of the incompetence of the CEB continued for several months before a power supply was installed, and to this day they continue to occupy top spot in our pantheon of staggeringly inefficient and uncaring Sri Lankan bureaucracies, though Lanka Bell Telephones run them a close second and Dialog, another communications company which doesn't know how to communicate with its customers, has come up fast on the rails in recent times. And as for local government...

Work started on building the house in August 2007. Gamini sent a rare e-mail to say he had identified the auspicious time for laying the foundation stone and had travelled up from Colombo to take personal responsibility for this act. Since the auspicious time was around 4am we were impressed and mystified in equal measure. We know now how important astrologers are to everything that happens, from when exactly it is New Year (which, by the way, is some date in mid-April but not at midnight) to the start time for the Kandy Perahera procession, to the time to lay a foundation stone. But at the time all this seemed utterly strange. It was February 2008 before we could raise the funds to check on progress for ourselves.

Arriving at Katanaiyake Airport at daybreak we opted to go straight to Kandy to get started on business with Gamini and Nissanka. On the flight from Abu Dhabi the only whiteys were us and a couple from the midlands who also had Sri Lankan roots and friends. No white tourists. The war was scaring people off, with suicide bombings being the only non-cricket-related coverage of Sri Lanka in the British media. Yet we'd been told by more than one person that the war was almost over. To our surprise, not only was Trinco safe but so, according to some, was the rest of the east coast down to Batticaloa, Arugam Bay and Yala. Not that we'd have the time to check any of this out on this whirlwind site-seeing trip. We broke our journey up to the hills as usual at Ambepussa Rest House where I embarrassed Sally and flummoxed the waiter by ordering a beer, it being 8am local time but 2am by my internal drinking clock.

Our half-built house was well up to expectations, although progress was a little behind what we'd hoped. We particularly liked the splendid timber ceilings, the height of the roof and ensuing airiness, and the tapered columns and overhang on the verandas. The entrance porch was especially impressive and the area to the front, which would eventually be lawned, was larger than we'd expected. But Gamini had hinted that he wanted to discuss costs. We returned with him to the Queens where he presented us with an estimate a full 30% above what we'd agreed as our maximum a year ago. *Plus ca change. Déjà vu.* Why do the French have all the most useful expressions?

Nissanka came to see us at the Queens. He brought along his wife Lakshmi and a woman called Nilki whom Lakshmi had decided would make our curtains. Nilki in turn brought her husband, whose sole function seemed to be to operate her laptop so she could display examples of her work; also her young son and a lanky youth whose job it was to measure windows when we got to the house. Overstaffing seemed to be an aspect of family as well as working life in Sri Lanka. "Now I will prepare estimate using wild silk for the guest rooms, and for your bedroom and living room and blinds for the rest of the house". "Wild silk? No, I think too expensive. We use cotton" Sally replied. "Cotton, silk – same price. Silk is best", Silky Nilki explained patiently. And so to our amazement it proved.

Most of the trip was again spent shuttling between Kandy and Colombo and we needed urgently to talk money with Gamini. But he preferred to take us on a shopping trip: when the going gets tough, the tough go shopping. We met him again at the Colombo cricket ground. Having been warned of heavy traffic we set off ridiculously early and arrived twenty minutes before the appointed time. During our wait entertainment was provided by the army whose base was across the road and who used the cricket stadium car park as a parade ground. Two guys were practising two separate pieces on bugles when we arrived, which was cacophonous enough, and were soon joined by a lone piper playing something else again, and eventually by a full marching band performing to yet a different tune. Meanwhile a platoon was being marched around the car park with their hands in the air. I felt inclined to surrender, too. Maybe this was how the army was defeating the LTTE.

By the end of the day we'd agreed on flooring tiles for the whole house and bought a complete set of kitchen and bathroom equipment and fittings, all under our budget though not by a great deal. We also identified pretty much all the lighting we wanted, to be bought later. It all felt supremely unreal. We'd planned to continue the shopping the next day as we knew the day after was both Good Friday and Poya Day so nothing much would be open. But we hadn't reckoned on the Prophet's Birthday and give that so many businesses are Muslim-owned we couldn't do much more than window-shopping. God still trumps mammon in Sri Lanka.

We shuttled back to Kandy. Our farewell visit to Oorogala for this trip took place late the next day with Gamini. Arriving late afternoon we were surprised by how cool the air was. It had just finished raining as it had been doing daily in the afternoons or evenings. We were treated to a cloudy sunset of sulphur yellow and rose pink over the rock as we talked about seeds, crops, garden projects and – our main reason for meeting up – hiring staff. Then a couple of days touring around the Kandy area in a series of tuk-tuks (sample bewildering slogans: WASH POT NEVER BOIL; ROAD OF THE KING; PAIN IS THE ONLY THING THAT IS TELLING ME; "HO FLY NOT HIG

FALSE NOT LOW) looking at an equally bewildering array of furniture. And finally down to Colombo once more to see if we could get our costs back to somewhere close to our budget. Gamini joined us in the veranda bar of the Galle Face Hotel that evening. Ideally it should have been high noon but we managed a good – though invariably polite – showdown anyway. I suppose that if both sides leave a negotiation equally miserable then it must be presumed a fair result. We were still heavily out of pocket but so, he claimed, was Gamini. We shook hands on it, at least.

Gerald and Kisani yet again treated us to a sumptuous lunch, this time at the Taj Samudhra. We talked houses and furniture a lot. Kisani, as we knew, is an interior designer but we'd assumed her clientele were exclusively the super-rich so she'd be well out of our price range. Not so, it seemed. She reckoned she could get our house fully furnished for about seven lakhs, less than it would have cost us to buy everything at the retail prices we'd seen and to a higher standard, too. We left for the airport feeling our ship was leaky but still afloat.

Moving in

The plan was to come back, mob-handed with various family members, at the end of July and move into the house in early August after a week in Colombo. Gamini and Nissanka repeatedly assured us that the house would be ready by the end of July despite some delays caused by rain and holidays. There were warnings from Gamini about expecting further cost increases and from Nissanka about the inadequacy of the drainage system Gamini had installed given the amount of rainfall and the large roof area of our bungalow. But the general tone of Nissanka's reports was upbeat; our house was nearing completion and would be ready in time.

We arrived in Colombo to find the SAARCus was in town. SAARC, roughly the South Asian equivalent of the EU, had chosen this city and this week to hold its annual summit meeting. I didn't know exactly what SAARC stood for (literally or politically) but my favoured guess was 'South Asian Association of Rampant Capitalists'. People were busy painting the zebra crossings, madly sweeping the streets, pouring bubbling tar into potholes, lighting boulevard trees and erecting huge signs of welcome and solidarity across the main roads. Security was intense. Half the top hotels and, more to the point for us, the Swimming Club were closed for the week as was our company secretary Lilamani's office. Fort and Slave Island were no-go areas.

Sun City Apartments is a condo block between Galle Road and Duplication Road and we'd rented a spacious, clean if utilitarian three-bedroomed apartment on the sixth floor with a balcony (when you could force the sliding door open) and views of the city and the ocean. On the rooftop, another five floors up, were two small swimming pools, two gyms and a lawned garden, all free to residents. Could have been a lot worse. At first, the two of us rattled around in this empty space, but Merigen and Lucy joined us the next day, followed in short order by Angela, her friend Jay, Jemima and her friend Morgan. Later in the mammoth six week trip we were joined by our friend Melissa, her daughter Eloise and my granddaughter Megan.

Self-catering for a week gave us the chance to practise for being in our own house. The randomness and sparseness of the kitchen equipment in the apartment was no problem since we had our own house to equip. On Monday morning Nilki took us to pick up the bed linen, pillows and towels we'd ordered then in the afternoon we took a three-wheeler to Arpico on Union Place whose modest frontage conceals an emporium stretching way back from the road. Arpico not only sells the household goods we'd come to buy but also clothing, bedding, furniture, car spares, garden and DIY tools and a very good supermarket. We piled two trolleys full – as much as the tuk-tuk could hold – and returned to unpack the loot. Cooking for eight people was challenging in a strange and ill-equipped kitchen. I managed a fair impression of Gordon Ramsay before emerging, sweat-drenched, triumphant and to loud applause, with the food.

We had been in e-mail contact with Kisani since April, following our agreement that she would handle all the furnishing and the fitting of the kitchens, but due to a misunderstanding about payment arrangements nothing had been done to make the furniture – a fact we discovered a couple of days before we were due to fly out. There was no way the house could be furnished by the time we were due to descend on it with our family. Kisani, bless her, arranged with her supplier that he would ferry up a vanload of temporary furniture then replace it with the proper stuff once it had all been made. All without charge. The kitchen would be installed while we were there. Meantime we'd have a freestanding sink to wash up in, a cheap table to prepare food on and a two-ring table-top gas cooker which we'd bought. A bit like camping for the first few days but that would all be part of the fun.

Nissanka told us on the phone that Gamini, too, had predictably asked at the last minute – probably while we were in the air – for another fortnight to complete the house despite all his assurances to us. Nissanka's response was to get straight onto the contractor and give him a good blast, insisting that the work had to be finished by the agreed date. Good man. The building work would now be complete by the time we were due to move in, he told us. At least, to a liveable extent if not absolutely finalised.

And it won't surprise you one bit to learn that the house *wasn't* finished in time for our arrival. Not even a water supply or, therefore, functioning toilets so even camping was out. Gamini phoned us with this bad news the day before we were due to travel up to Kandy, utterly unapologetic and moaning about the bad weather preventing the work being done. Since we'd received his cast-iron assurances via Nissanka only the previous day, to say I was unimpressed by Gamini's excuses would be a wild understatement. He could have phoned or e-mailed us to warn us before we left England but, as with the cost overrun last time, chose to wait until we were over here with our family before dropping his bombshell. Needless to say, we'd e-mailed him several times over the past few months each time reminding him of the date of our arrival, to none of which he'd replied. As I've observed before and no doubt will again, Sri Lankans seem inherently incapable of communicating bad news, even when it is absolutely vital to do so in order that the other person can make alternative arrangements. It's either beaming smiles and good news, or total silence. No news is bad news in this country.

We phoned Nissanka who went over straight away to the house and later rang back to confirm the grim position. It was still a building site with next to nothing working and completely unfit for habitation of even the roughest sort. Nissanka held a negotiation with the baas (foreman) and later phoned again to say that by working through the weekend the bedrooms would all have functioning showers and toilets by Monday. We were unconvinced but committed to travelling to Kandy, our rental on Sun City having run out. So we booked into the Queens for a few nights. And if the house wasn't ready by Monday we'd just have to stay on until it was. The furniture would all have arrived – lord knows where they would put it. Meanwhile the rest of our crew took off to Hikkaduwa to a festival cum beach party leaving Sally and me alone to lick our wounds for a night.

The Sun City concierge informed us our van had arrived, bang on time, the next morning. We took the lift to the basement car park and met Dishantha who was to be our driver for the next few weeks. His company hadn't briefed him on what to expect – he assumed we were just holidaymakers embarking on a family tour. Being confronted with only two people was confusing enough. When they emerged from successive lift trips with mops, buckets, brooms, cleaning materials, bedding, towels, pots and pans, crockery, cutlery and small items of furniture the poor guy was clearly wondering what he'd let himself in for. "We have house in Kandy, we are coming to live Sri Lanka, so we have to buy many things" was as near as we could come to an explanation.

As we got to know him better on the trip and shared the essentials of our story Dishantha's initial nervousness about what we were doing turned to fascination and offering practical advice. By the time we spotted cane furniture land just beyond Pasyala – a village where every shop sells cane furniture – and stopped to cram the already well loaded van with veranda tables and chairs – Dishantha had become part of the team. We were going to get on. Fearful of what awaited us at Oorogala, as the journey wore on I tried to lighten my gloom by remarking on some of the products we'd bought. The brand name of the pillows we'd bought in Arpico was 'Fresh Arouse' – no doubt as used by the 'Randy Hotel' which we passed on the way. A disconcerting instruction on the gas bottle connector advised us to *ATTACH THE RUBBER HORSE TO THE GAS BOTTLE*. Smack it on the behind and off we go.

The house, which we visited on the Monday morning, was about as bad as we'd dreaded. Toilets and washbasins stood around the living room floor. Wires hung from the walls, discarded workers' lunch packets and other food containers littered the filthy kitchen and clouds of black houseflies swarmed around our faces. Within a few days, Gamini assured us, he would have the staff kitchen ready for use with reduced water pressure, enough for washing dishes and filling a kettle but insufficient for a shower. Again, no apologies. Just more whingeing about how he needed more money from us to finish the house and until we paid up he could not complete the work. We had already paid him 25% more than we'd originally agreed as a 'final price' but he held most of the cards. We put the rest of our crew into a cheap backpacker place up Saganankara Road and returned to the Queens to sit out the next few days.

———————

Home at last! Arriving late afternoon for our first night under our own roof we were met by a flurry of last-minute activity to get the place ready for us to sleep in. Among the many things which still didn't work was the electric backup for the solar water heating system (we have a receipt for 'Purchase of solar system' – step one to becoming Master of the Universe) which heats the water when the sun shines. Gamini now informed us that this would require a three phase electricity supply but he had only asked Nissanka to arrange for a single phase supply. No hint of apology, of course. This was the first move in a discussion of whether three phase electricity was essential to our needs – a discussion which continues to this day with the relevant experts divided fifty-fifty. Until we get a clear answer we're sticking with single phase. Meanwhile it was going to be cold water washes and pray for sunshine. And Gamini had us over a barrel as to extra costs – we couldn't very well leave the house in this uninhabitable state. We were haemorrhaging money but I started to look at it philosophically. Every extra grand would mean another month at work before we could retire and come to live here permanently. Seen like that, it wasn't too horrible a prospect. Gamini also appeared to be that odd specimen, an architect who genuinely had very little money. Judging, anyhow, by the battered old van he drove whose lights didn't work. Maybe they needed three phase electricity.

Kisani had dispatched a lorry with more temporary furniture and a team to put together the beds which were already stored at the house. They were due to arrive in the afternoon but the lorry was involved in a collision near Kegalle and broke its rear axle. Somehow the team got it fixed and were able to continue intrepidly on their journey, eventually reaching us around 2am. We were as excitable as small children, it being our first night, and not at all ready for bed, which was fortunate given the absence of any beds. Four excessively merry guys, none of whom spoke one word of English, leapt from the cab and set about arranging furniture and putting beds together. Even by Sri Lankan standards this was a high-spirited bunch despite their very long and arduous day. Through Dishantha (the one person who did have a bed, the drivers' bunks having already been erected) we found out that they were moving on to another job at one of the larger hotels once they'd finished with us. By 4am all was up and running and we bade them goodnight and were able to turn in ourselves.

Neither the escalating costs, nor the lack of some basic amenities, nor the chaos of late-night bed construction could dent the exhilaration we all felt on spending our first evening and night at Jungle Tide. Everyone was massively impressed by the opulent bits – the timber, ceilings, veranda, glass frontage; everyone worked like dogs to unpack, tidy up, sweep and mop and get things to somewhere close to their rightful places. Morgan and Jay managed to cook up a great vegetarian spag bol on our temporary surface-top cooker. After dinner we all went out to gaze at the Milky Way in a black night and felt we were a very long way from anywhere.

While the rest went off the following day to Peradeniya Gardens and to indulge in yet more shopping I spent a delicious day home alone – save for an electrician who spoke no English and was fixing the countless wall lights. Each lightbulb has to have its own personal switch, for some reason I still don't understand. Some of them have two, which is just greedy. So we have impressive banks of wall switches everywhere making the house look like some kind of command and control centre. I was happy playing houses. Tidying up, mopping muddy bathrooms, boiling water for drinking and getting through a week's worth of washing for eight people. When the machine reached the spin part of its cycle it charged around the laundry room like an elephant in musth until it detached itself from the socket and died. I later learned that this was because I'd failed to remove the transit bolts, but it was a scary experience. I'd never before heard of transit bolts. Aside from the silent electrician I had Fly TV for company and entertainment, a.k.a. the insectocutor we'd bought in Colombo. A combination of spraying and swatting had brought the housefly infestation partly under control and food hygiene was a constant preoccupation. On the positive side there were no mosquitoes to be seen. My housework was interrupted by random snapping and fizzing sounds as flies encountered their fates in the blue light of the Fly TV.

There was the inevitable rash of teething problems. One involved a leaking tap in one of the bathrooms. We phoned Gamini who started going on about the fittings being of poor quality, conveniently forgetting that he'd been with us and recommended them when we bought them in March. His plumber was in Colombo and being a Colombo architect he knew no plumber or other tradesman in Kandy, nor would he trust one if he did know one. Colombo people are like Londoners only worse, firmly believing that the world outside the capital is a dangerous and uncivilised place. So the plumber had to be sent up on a four hour each way journey to fix the tap and one or two other problems. Only then did Dishantha reveal to us that in a former life he'd been a plumber. "Why you send for plumber, Madam? I can fix these things." So our in-house plumber he duly became for the duration of our stay, and indeed on several subsequent occasions.

We decided to take everyone off on a bit of a tour and return in ten days' time when we were assured we'd have a fitted kitchen. Just to have an oven seemed a remote fantasy just then. The evening before our tour we were greeted by a power cut. Unlike the previous one, which ended within an hour, this continued all night and the power was still off when we left for Nuwara Eliya late the next morning. A power cut doesn't just mean loss of light. We had plenty of candles and a gas cooker so that was inconvenient but not disastrous. It also, eventually, means loss of water since there was no electricity to pump it from the well up to the tank. Much more mission-critical. This made us realise that getting a generator was an urgent matter, not something that could wait until the end of our stay. We'd found one in a shop in Kandy and been told they took one to two weeks to get delivered, plus we'd need to get housing built for it. So we phoned Nissanka to ask him to sort one out for us while we were away.

When we got back to Jungle Tide a fridge full of blackened food awaited us – the power cut when we left had continued for three whole days. The experience of opening the fridge door was akin to what I imagine grave-robbers would have encountered. Nissanka had forgotten about buying a generator while Kisani had run into problems with getting the granite cut for the kitchen surfaces. But with any luck all would now be complete in another few days' time. At least Gamini's crew had installed the shower screens and towel rails. The house became a hive of activity as our return to England approached, and with it people's loss of instant access to our cash. At one stage there were two vans and a lorry, as well as Dishantha's van, parked outside and a dozen people milling around inside installing wardrobes, fitting kitchen surfaces, plumbing in sinks and connecting the electric oven, hob and extractor. Since no-one arrived before mid-afternoon they were all over the place like flies until late at night with the sounds of drills, hammers, saws and granite cutters drowning out the frogs and cicadas for once. We fed several of them and put up three for the night so they could complete work on the kitchen the following morning. Result – we now had a functioning kitchen at last, but since Kisani organised the design and fittings and Gamini the electrics, and no-one talked to one another, let alone to Nissanka or to us, all the lights and sockets were in the wrong places. Taps didn't fit the sinks and wash basins they were allocated to. Nothing worked properly, though everything worked after a fashion.

So – time to talk about my generator, as The Who didn't quite say. Nissanka did get round to buying one soon after the house was built and it was installed on our next visit, in 2009, in a little lean-to construction around the back of the house which was built by a guy with the very un-Sri Lankan name of Sean. Sean, who had been recommended by Kisani, was also utterly dishy and had our friend Melissa swooning in ecstasy for the whole time he was there. She and Sally somehow kept finding him extra jobs to do to postpone his inevitable leaving date. We couldn't live without our generator. Power outages are an almost daily occurrence, often several times in a day. The Ceylon Electricity Board blames consumers for daring to have such things as washing machines and electric ovens rather than doing anything about their antiquated equipment and supply lines. And when they do deign to provide power the voltage is around 170 rather than the 220 it should be. We're sorely tempted to tell them that since they provide 75% of our power we'll pay 75% of their bills, but I guess we'd be on thin ice given the absence of consumer protection laws in Sri Lanka.

A trip down south

Putting the tribulations of our new home temporarily behind us we'd headed south on our ten day tour. The road to Kataragama passes through the fringes of the Yala (Ruhunu) National Park and in 2008 it was heavily militarised with small army bases every kilometre or so, interspersed with bunkers and numerous checkpoints. It brought to mind the milecastles on Hadrian's Wall. A stretch of land about fifty metres wide on either side of the road had been cleared of scrub jungle to prevent surprise attacks by the LTTE who still operated to some extent hereabouts. A lone wild elephant was grazing at the jungle's edge.

We'd booked into the Tissamaharama Resort. It used to be called the Tissa Rest House and is now the Tissa Safari – changing the names of hotels is a preoccupation which the cynic might feel is displacement activity to avoid doing something about how they operate. Though to be fair we've since stayed at the Safari and it is much improved – if you can avoid being dragooned into their buffet dinners. By this time our friend Melissa had joined us together with her then eight year old daughter Eloise and my then nine year old granddaughter Megan. On arrival a glance at the fetid swimming pool – the principal reason we'd chosen the hotel – changed our minds. But we decided nonetheless to quench our thirsts after the long, hot and crowded van journey from our overnight stop in Ella, before sorting out an alternative place to stay. In a corner of the foyer an old woman was making lace as a tourist attraction and Megan's curiosity sent her over for a closer look, soon joined by Melissa who bought herself a blouse and bought us a giant tablecloth as a housewarming present. The woman told them that she had learned lace making from her mother who had died some years ago at the age of eighty eight. When Sally heard this she wondered if this could possibly be the daughter of Old Alice, the blind lacemaker of Galle, at whose feet she'd sat as a child, enthralled by the old woman's ability to turn out delicate lacework entirely from memory. Sally's Mum had been one of Alice's best customers. It turned out to be indeed so and the two of them had an emotional and tearful conversation while the van was re-loaded with luggage for the short trip to the Waterfront Hotel which was our next choice. Sri Lanka is such a small place.

Not surprisingly, given its name, the Waterfront Hotel is also on Tissa Wewa, and it had a decent pool and slightly better rooms for about the same price. It looked out across a lake thronged with birds. In the foreground a small army of cleaners and pool attendants were busy de-insecting the place with brooms. It was the end of the dry season down south and the shrinking lakes and waterholes were excellent for wildlife spotting but also meant swarms of insect pests. The woman who managed the hotel suggested that we take a sunset boat trip on the wewa. The girls wanted to stay in the pool and she kindly offered to keep an eye on them so off we went, Sally, Melissa and I, in an astonishingly clapped-out boat whose outboard worked only sporadically. Out on the lake the motor finally gave up the ghost and we had to be rescued by the local maritime version of the AA – another boatman with tools though even this failed to get us re-started. We abandoned our craft and clambered precariously across into the other boat which we had to share with the owner's bicycle, and were eventually restored to dry land. As the sky turned pink and the fringing trees black we were treated to an ornithological spectacular of the kind Sri Lanka excels in. The various water birds started making their way home to roost – a flock of ibis in perfect V formation, a noisy crowd of flamingos, several giant herons and a white bellied fish eagle circling overhead.

Wildlife was the main focus of our tour but first we treated ourselves to a trip to Kataragama since we were close and it was perahera time. Sri Lanka is not short of deities. Each tea estate community has its own favourite but for the island as a whole you can't top the Kataragama Deviyo. Revered by Hindus and Buddhists alike, and with some special significance for Muslims which doesn't seem to fit with any chronology – but hey! we're talking religion here, not rationality. Revered also by Sally's father who would qualify every promise he made with the phrase "Kataragama Deviyo willing". This somewhat less than godlike deity (adulterer, seducer, trickster) is worshipped for reasons which lie beyond me. I suppose one can expect reverence when one has six heads and twelve arms and the ability to turn oneself into a tree at will. Though I don't quite get the point of being a tree. A tiger, or pterodactyl might be more effective. It seems his fellow gods expelled the chap from India and he found refuge in Kataragama. As a result the Buddhists simply accept him as their local deity but the Hindus constantly have to make reparations for their earlier maltreatment by walking on coals, sticking hooks into their backs and engaging in other forms of self-abuse. At the annual Kataragama Perahera the whole town becomes thronged with pilgrims creating as much mayhem as possible.

We headed into town, through the vibrant market and on towards the temple area across a river where the water was hardly visible through the throng of ritually bathing humanity. Even in the town the atmosphere was different - faster-paced, more excitable. We were adorned with bindis and later with lotus flowers. Megan underwent some form of ceremony which involved passing three times under an elephant. "What this for?" we asked. "Now this baby, she never have bad dream" came the answer. So if you have nightmares, forget psycho-analysis – get an elephant. Then we walked in single file through a Hindu temple at the end of which we were given holy water to wash our hands and faces.

The slow, barefoot walk in the setting sun up the sandy processional way to the great dagoba was trance-inducing, Chanting from the loudspeakers lining the route; cripples, mothers with babies and swirls of children begging, lotus-sellers, monks, wild-eyed bearded men – all of us flotsam on the tide of humanity. Near the dagoba a family released around twenty small birds from a tiny cardboard box, each a hope or dream ascending to heaven. Then back to the complex of smaller temples where a contrasting Hindu ceremony was going on. This involved a fifty-yard dash across a courtyard and into the temple led by a trumpeter, several drummers, dancers, and a penitent with hooks in his back to which were attached threads held by other devotees. Other Hindus smashed coconut shells into a deep pit of fire – a kind of incendiary wishing-well.

Outside the temple complex was an area which looked like an English agricultural showground experienced while on an acid trip, with small temples and shrines along the side. Shortly after we reached it, at dusk, a switch was thrown and the entire area of several acres was illuminated with coloured lights. Around this rectangle the local perahera would parade at 8pm, over an hour away. On Dishantha's advice we waited in a good spot rather than nipping into town for water, though we were all parched - Dishantha with his usual generosity insisted on going for bottles of water for all of us. Sally and I sneaked off for a quick smoke outside the sacred area. In the crowd of thousands we saw only one other white person.

The wait proved worthwhile. The perahera (about ten elephants worth, not big) was one of a nightly succession leading up to the big perahera on the full moon. As well as the bedecked elephants there were the expected drummers, fire jugglers and Kandyan dancers but also some less predictable acts including a tea-plucking dance and a mobile maypole dance. We wondered whether maypole dancing was an English colonial introduction but Dishantha assured us that it was an ancient tradition. Strange to think that the practice of wrapping coloured strings in patterns around a post to increase fertility – which is also its purpose here, we were told - has such ancient and global roots.

By mistake we had positioned ourselves on the inner side of the rectangle around which the perahera processed so once it had passed our vantage point we were trapped. In theory we were supposed to wait for it to come back round and disappear into the temple complex before we could escape to our guest house for a very late dinner. Dishantha somehow persuaded a policeman to allow us to cross to the other side in the middle of the perahera, the head of which was by now approaching from the other direction. Aware we were offending against various religious principles, and aware, too, that as virtually the only white people we would be even more prominently displaying our ignorance and disrespect, we scuttled shamefacedly across and made good our escape. The evening ended with a merry motorised beer hunt. The entire town of Kataragama, being sacred, is an alcohol-free zone at Perahera time except for one hotel (don't ask me why) which proved hard to locate. But the English ability to sniff out beer prevailed and we eventually managed it.

Back when English kings were preoccupied with claiming large tracts of land for their exclusive right to kill animals their Sri Lankan counterparts were busy inventing what we would now call wildlife sanctuaries. Sri Lanka is one of the top biodiversity hotspots in the world (something I learned, incidentally, not in Sri Lanka but on a visit to the Eden Project in Cornwall some time ago). My science isn't up to scratch but I understand it is partly to do with being an island which, at the times of ice ages when water gets locked up at the poles and sea levels fall, gets connected back to India allowing temporary migrations, which are later cut off and result in isolated evolutionary changes thereafter, and hence a great many endemic species. The Palk Strait between the two countries is about as wide as the Dover Strait but much shallower, with a series of small islands forming giant stepping stones – Adam's Bridge – across it.

Yala National Park is the best-known and most visited of Sri Lanka's many national parks. It is immense but only some parts (or 'blocks') are open to tourists. The main one is Yala West, accessed from the Tissa side. It's also possible to visit the north side of the park from Arugam Bay on the east coast. August and September, being towards the end of the south's dry season, are the best time to visit as the wildlife is more concentrated around the remaining, shrinking villus (tanks and waterholes). So it was that we hired two grey jeeps from self-styled 'King of the Jungle' Mr Jayantha and set off at 2pm for a half day safari ending when the park closed to visitors at dusk. We were not disappointed. Just the bird life would have been worth it, and in particular the sighting of a very rare (only four in the park), very large (5'6" tall) and very lugubrious-looking black-necked stork as well as peafowl, eagles, herons, jungle fowl, ibis, egrets, bee-eaters, pelicans and kingfishers.

We thought we'd probably see buffalo and crocodiles and might see elephant at a distance if we were lucky. In the event we saw countless buffalo, crocs spread out everywhere in and out of the water, wild boar, talagoyas (land monitors), a jackal and then an elephant, quite close in the bushes. Our tracker explained that more would soon come and indeed they did – as did more jeeps having got wind of our sighting. Soon a group of eight elephants appeared out of the jungle and crossed the track right among the assembled jeeps, close enough to touch. Even though Yala has the world's highest concentration of leopards, sighting one was always going to be a longshot but to cap the experience we saw a pair of them, again quite close though they didn't emerge from the scrub. As one of them strolled lazily into a clearing in full view a nearby talagoya got wind of it and shot off like a rocket, vertically up a tree. We followed them slowly, parallel on the dirt road, and saw them clearly every time they crossed a jungle path, no more than forty or fifty metres away. It was unforgettable, even despite having to compete for viewing with the drivers and occupants of about ten other jeeps. We saw them first, dammit! Get out of the way! Yes, Yala West is a crowded place and if you can avoid it and get into Block Ten from Kataragama or Yala North from Arugam Bay you'd be well advised to. It occurred to me that while we watch the wildlife, the wildlife might be watching us:

Yala: The leopard's perspective
"I was strolling through the jungle with the wife when I spotted it. A lone jeep. Quite a big one. Grey, so that meant a female. When I finally managed to get the missus to stop yakking we crouched down behind a bush to see what would happen. Jeeps are social animals so it's rare to see one on its own for long. Sure enough a smaller female, juvenile, soon joined its mother. We watched them playing peacefully for a while until more

and more joined them, all larger green ones, so adult males. I counted nine or maybe ten of them. What was this? Safety in numbers to get to the waterhole? Unlikely as jeeps are top of the food chain and have no known predators. Soon it became clear. The males were vying for the attention of the original female we'd seen who, judging from the exhaust fumes, was obviously in season. There was much harrumphing and ritualised movement back and forth. Two males confronted one another and made honking, squealing sounds. The others mostly just hung around, clearly not alpha males, watching to see who would win the contest and perhaps pick up some tips en route. Just as it was getting interesting the female decided she didn't want any of their attentions and slowly made off with her calf. Shame. I've always wondered how jeeps mate but I guess I'll have to find out another day."

The reason Sri Lanka has, for its size, so many leopards is that the leopard is the top predator. It has never had to compete with tigers, as in India, or lions, as in Africa. There are still viable leopard populations on the tops of the Hanthana range above Jungle Tide – some guests found and photographed what is definitely a leopard footprint while walking less than a mile from Jungle Tide recently – and when Sally's family lived at Meenawatte they certainly had them as close neighbours. She recalls one evening walk along a jungle track quite near the house, seeing a pair of eyes in the undergrowth, keeping quiet pace with her, sawing gently to remind her of its presence. Closer still, a leopard took to sleeping in the flower bed under her parents' open bedroom window at Meenawatte.

Close to Yala, in an area of coastal salt excavation, is the remarkable Bundala bird sanctuary. We were up at five to clamber into a jeep in Tissa to take us there the next day. By five thirty it was half light and we were bowling down the road towards the coast, standing up in the back, the cool wind whistling through our hair (or Sally's hair – I don't possess any). A screech of tyres, a sickening thud and my head banged hard against one of the jeep's roller bars. We'd hit a buffalo strolling down the road. It was clearly the buffalo's fault. He was on the wrong side, and not wearing lights. Neither was he insured. The jeep and I suffered minor damage. The animal walked nonchalantly away. But a slight injury couldn't take the shine off the sight of the hosts of unlikely birds that awaited us once we got into Bundala, many of them looking as though they'd stepped straight out of the imagination of Edward Lear. Lugubrious, morose and bored they all seemed as they formed into lines and groups to inspect us as we passed, or they waded in trios short-sightedly peering into the swampy waters. An imbecilic grin creased my face the whole time we were there.

Home from home

I don't much like raw coconut though I adore it as an ingredient in curries but Megan was obsessed with coconuts so when we returned to Jungle Tide we bought one for her. Then what to open it with? I got a heavy cleaver from Arpico, having checked with Dishantha that this would do the job, and went off to the kitchen sink. A few breathing exercises, a bit of meditation then I raised the blade and brought it down sharply on the coconut – with minimal effect. In a scene straight out of a Sri Lankan version of Fawlty Towers Dishantha came running into the kitchen shouting "NO!" and proceeded to do the job the right way. The blade is only used to get rid of the hairy bits, after which the coconut is cracked using the *back* of the cleaver. The nut being cracked, Megan duly lapped up the milk and Dishantha used our coconut scraper (a vicious sharp-toothed beast) to remove the flesh.

Around six one morning Sally nudged me awake and said "What's that noise?" A threatening rumbling sound was emanating from the kitchen, sounding for all the world like a serious plumbing disaster about to happen. She then admitted she'd accidentally left the water heater on overnight and we thought maybe the thermostat had failed and boiling water was coursing through the pipes. I shot out of bed like a scalded cat and ran stark naked into the kitchen where, too late, I discovered the source of the noise – Dishantha scraping out a coconut. He was making us a pol sambol – coconut, chilli, tomato and lime relish – for a breakfast treat. Maybe he was even more embarrassed than I was – we don't speak of it.

The pol sambol was delicious.

As our final day at Jungle Tide dawned we began to wonder whether or not we were going home. Jungle Tide had already come to feel completely like home, even if we had to pinch ourselves to be convinced that we now owned (give or take a few grand) such a splendid place. We had no property in England, having thrown everything we possessed into Sri Lanka. But home is more than just bricks and mortar, and for the first but not the last time we found ourselves torn between our two lives. It had begun to feel like being in Second Life; soon it would be time to turn off the computer and return to reality.

The last few days were gloriously sunny and around 4pm the birds would come out to play in the bushes near the house. We sat on the veranda and watched them. Best of all were the vermilion minivets. An eagle soared overhead until it was harassed away by the local crows. To cap it all, on our final day the sky became suffused with pinks, greys, yellows and electric blue. I'd rarely seen a sunset to compare then, though I've seen even better ones from our veranda since. When the setting of the sun coincides with a lightning storm over the Knuckles mountains the *son et lumiere* is indescribable.

Back to Colombo, and eventually back to the Veranda Bar at the Galle Face Hotel for a last brandy before being collected at 10.30 for the drive to the airport and the horrors of the 2.45am flight. At the airport we said goodbye to Dishantha – driver, interpreter, cleaner, cook and plumber though he was only paid for the first of these services. We all expressed hope that he would be our driver again on our next visit, and indeed he remains one of our regular drivers. At the GFH there was some kind of staff leaving do going on, with music and much speechifying. I found myself fantasising that it was all put on to say goodbye to us. "And so, with great regret, we finally say farewell to Sally Martin and Jerry Smith who have been with us these last six weeks but who now have to return to their humdrum lives in England. We very much hope we will see them again soon."

The applause dies away. Fade and cut.

Seven

You can't get the staff these days

What we would have liked to do at that point was to go home, put our affairs in order, give notice on our jobs and come back to Sri Lanka to run our guest house. But we knew that wasn't going to be possible for a few years. Lack of money for one thing. The house was built but not fully paid for and we had plans for a pool and some finishing jobs. We'd need to find wages for staff and running costs. A brand-new small business wasn't likely to pay its way for a while and we could only subsidise it if we kept working in England. And Jemima was still at home although about to go to University and we wanted to see her out the other side of that at least before we could flee the nest. Parents don't usually flee the nest, but we're birds of a different feather. Abandon your children before they abandon you. Get your retaliation in first. So we were thinking maybe three or four years of running Jungle Tide remotely, before we could move to live there. In the end it was double that.

Running a business from six thousand miles away in the face of language barriers, technological problems and time zone differences was always going to be a challenge, even with a great project manager, but mothballing Jungle Tide was not an option. Pests ranging in size from termites through monkeys to humans would soon destroy anything that wasn't being looked after. Perhaps we should have just hung onto the land and built once we were more or less ready to move. Twenty-twenty hindsight of course. But at the time everyone advised us to build quickly as costs were inflating rapidly and the pound was strong, giving us more bricks for our bucks. So we did. Once built, the first job was to find a live-in caretaker who could look after the place and keep it secure once we returned to England. If that person had the capacity to look after guests – maybe with casual help from outside – so much the better.

For a decent Christian, our project manager Nissanka's view of human nature is not the most charitable. It is, though, born of long experience, as he pointed out. He gloomily listed the risks attendant on employing a resident housekeeper, though he reluctantly accepted we'd need to do so as to leave the house unoccupied would be to invite burglars and squatters, an even worse prospect. Risk one: don't employ anyone from the local village. "If you make an enemy of him you will make an enemy of the whole village." Good point, which we hadn't considered. Risk two: Don't pay more than the going rate. We'd assumed that, provided we weren't paying so much that we'd be thought soft, this would buy loyalty. It wouldn't, according to Nissanka. Better to pay the basic rate and offer bonus payments every six months depending on good work and honesty. Once we'd established a viable business we should consider setting up a profit-sharing scheme with our staff. Not for the first time we found our western liberal principles at odds with, and no match for, the common sense of someone whose own principles were at least as strong as ours but who had tempered them with local knowledge and experience.

We agreed that ideally we should look for a childless couple on a single salary who between them would supervise a gardener, keep the house clean, do minor repairs and fixes, greet and help guests, shop and cook. So the advert was placed along these lines with the Sri Lankan *Sunday Observer* and its Sinhala equivalent. At the newspaper offices in Kandy the ad caused a ripple of excitement. *Sudus* taking on staff! Opportunity knocks! The newspaper employees huddled together to make suggestions as to which of their friends and relatives should get the job. One bloke phoned his nephew who hot-footed it over to the newspaper office for a quick job interview ahead of the field. A charming guy with loads of hotel experience as well as being a cook – all rather more than we needed or could pay for. We explained this, and also that the job is live-in and really only suitable for a single person or child-free couple (he had a wife and two kids). Only very slightly deterred he began thinking aloud about whether he should leave his family and come to work for us. A conversation later with a waiter at the Queens resulted in our adding a further candidate to the four Nissanka and we had shortlisted from the written applications – the waiter's father in law who was a retired police sergeant. Lucky we did as two of our original four were from Colombo and, when invited for interview, declined on the grounds that Kandy was not in Colombo. Never mind the fact that the ad opened with the location of our house. Maybe their confidence was so high they thought we would move the house to Colombo to obtain their services. Maybe they were just stupid.

And so it was that Mister Kingsley Reginald Francis became our new housekeeper. Being plain old Mister Smith I reckoned I must be one of the few people whose manservant sounded a deal posher than he did. Kingsley was our unanimous choice from the candidates we interviewed and started work immediately, moving in to live at the house when we left for England. As ever, things went up to the wire. We had arranged the interviews for a few days earlier but Nissanka had to go to Colombo for a funeral. Funerals are great occasions in Sri Lanka and attendance by a wide range of people only faintly related to the deceased is compulsory. The other two candidates were unsuitable. One, an overweight woman in her fifties, was simply too unfit for the physical work involved. She was also nervous about the requirement to live in (which had been made clear in the ad) and seemed to want to bring her niece to live with her. The retired police officer had got the wrong end of the stick, presumably from his son in law, and thought he would be managing a large hotel and supervising several staff. The routine and rather menial nature of the job didn't appeal to him. Even so, Nissanka had to tread carefully in conveying the rejection. It can go against you if you cross even a retired police officer. Equal opportunities recruitment this was not. The 'interviews' consisted of Sally or me briefly outlining the big picture then Nissanka took over, going through the list of tasks we'd drawn up and asking the candidate to confirm whether they were happy to do each one. Of course, answers were invariably affirmative but the decision was based entirely on feel – how convincing we all thought they were – rather than some more objective system.

Kingsley was middle aged but pretty fit and used to doing similar work. Although a quiet and shy man his written and spoken English were excellent if rather old-school, like Nissanka's. We all felt happy about him. When he turned up for his first day's work, our last day before returning to Yorkshire, he impressed us with his initiative, hard work and understanding of the job – a good start. Sally was discussing the housefly infestation problem with him and he suggested various alternatives to spraying which he intended to pursue. "But will that stop them?" asked Sally. "Madam, it will not eradicate them completely" came the astounding reply. We left feeling that Jungle Tide was in safe hands, with Kingsley and Nissanka both looking after our interests. We'd got a lovely house, classily if sparsely furnished, a trusted project manager and a caretaker who both seemed more English than we are, and the beginnings of a network of friends. Noses to the grindstone in England, then. A few years of remote control. There might be a few problems on the way…

Kingsley was the first. Nissanka called round unannounced twice and he wasn't in. We bought him a

phone and tried to call him from England; it was invariably switched off. Nissanka had no better luck. On the third occasion Nissanka visited he *was* in. Wandering drunkenly around, his room full of empty arrack bottles. Nissanka sought
our agreement for immediate dismissal and sacked him the next day. We lost our first employee after two months; we also lost most of our bed linen, towels, cutlery and so forth which he decided to take with him to sell, in lieu of notice payment. And we had no-one to maintain security – not that an absentee drunk is much good at that, though.

"Uduwela village is notorious", Nissanka sombrely informed us. "A lot of drug addicts who steal; a lot of illegal arrack stills. We need to secure your property. I can get a watcher to live there for the moment but we will need to put up a high and strong fence all around the property Also, we should not employ a watcher from the village as he may be in league with the local criminal gangs. But someone from outside will be vulnerable as he is not part of the community. What to do?"

What to do, indeed. Nissanka's favoured gulag option involved some very expensive heavy duty fencing around three acres of undulating land, not to speak of batteries of security lights and complex alarm systems. We half expected him to propose gun towers, booby traps and landmines as well. Not only could we not afford it, the whole idea of shutting ourselves off from the local community, however full of brigands and thieves it may be, went against the grain. It was to be a continuing argument with Nissanka over the next few years, only half resolved with a series of compromises and a series of thefts.

Wijeratne was a guy from the village who had been taken on from time to time to do some garden clearing and was now engaged temporarily as a 'watcher' – on-site security – and gardener, living in the staff accommodation but with no access to the main house which was steadily gathering dust and worse as we waited for Nissanka to find us a suitable housekeeper. He claimed to have building skills and offered to lay the lawn in front of the house and to build a flight of steps from it down to the lower gardens, which at the time could only be reached via a picturesque but tortuous path by the stream. Promises, promises. We came out to visit again in the spring of 2009. The start of the monsoon season and a time of year we'd not previously been in Sri Lanka. As the rain poured relentlessly down our dream was showing tendencies to turn into a nightmare. The lawn area in front of the veranda was a sea of mud into which Wijeratne had plonked strange circular patterns of bricks for reasons best known to himself. Every bedroom ceiling leaked and the unsealed gaps between lengths of guttering produced a series of waterfalls right around the house. The showers produced only a trickle of water. Half the light bulbs were missing or not working. When the weather relented sufficiently to take a walk around the gardens it became clear that Wijeratne's gardening skills started and finished with the ability to cut down foliage and burn it; the remains of small bonfires were everywhere but nothing else had been done. Far from being on the point of launch as a guest house, Jungle Tide was in danger of living up too closely to its name and returning to nature. What to do? The firm hand of management was required. Luckily, that's what Sally's good at – I'm rubbish.

We set Wijeratne a modest list of tasks. He didn't seem too happy but went off into the wilderness with mattock and billhook. And shortly after came back. "Madam, this work is too much. I cannot do this work. Now I go, I not working for you now." We feigned sadness at his leaving but said that if that's what he wanted, then goodbye and good luck. And off he went. And back he came the next morning, full of apologies. He hadn't meant it, he did want to continue working for us, please take him back. But we were resolute. We had three more weeks at the house and felt that with Nissanka's help we could find someone better. Employed two, sacked two. Not a great start to the season. Our architect-builder Gamini, meanwhile, was playing hardball with our requests that he deal with the roof leaks and endless other snagging problems before we made him his final payment. In the end, he had to forego this and Nissanka brought in local contractors to fix the leaks, the plumbing and the electrics, none of whom succeeded in their tasks. The one splash of brightness in the gloom was the bougainvilleas Nissanka had planted along the drive, now growing dramatically and bursting with flowers.

Our search for a replacement caretaker proved fruitless and we left the island with Nissanka having found another temporary watcher but with everything else unresolved and Jungle Tide miles away from starting life as a guest house. But the tide turns and a few weeks later an e-mail from Nissanka in his inimitable style gave us renewed hope: *I have found a suitable couple to maintain your home. Martin and Rani Fernando are Christian people, both of Tamil origin, who worship at Lakshmi's church and were recommended to me by her pastor. They have as yet no children and are willing and hard workers. Rani is experienced in domestic labours in Saudi Arabia. I propose that we give them a month's trial before confirming a contract of* employment. And so it was that Martin and Rani entered our lives. They moved into a house with no reliable water supply – the pump had been stolen and was awaiting replacement. But Martin and Rani are not the kind of people who let little things like a lack of tap water deter them when there's a stream in the garden and they set to with a will, cleaning and tidying and polishing until by

Nissanka's account the place shone. By the autumn of 2009 we were nervously ready to advertise for business. There was one big unknown – we knew Rani had all the domestic experience of cleaning and bed-making in spades, but could she cook?

Our first guests were friends of mine, former colleagues and Lancastrians. Well, they were our first *booked* guests but were beaten to it by a few days by passing trade. A couple of Swiss travel journalists were about to check out a nearby guest house and spotted the Jungle Tide sign so thought they'd take a look. They were so impressed they stayed the night. In our remote location the idea of passing trade was in itself almost a fantasy; that they should also be travel writers was pretty much beyond belief and got us all excited, though in the end all we got from it was a lovely note in the guest book and our first five star Trip Advisor review, rather than a feature article in a prestigious travel journal. But – nice start! My Burnley mates followed on and came back raving about Rani's amazing curries. Martin, meanwhile, was delighted that one of them, Razza – a man of Pakistani heritage – could chat with him in Urdu, a language which he knew from his former life in the merchant navy. It was all getting off to a very good start. We phoned to see how our friends were getting on and Martin put us on to Nissanka who happened to be visiting. He explained in his lovely antiquated English conjuring up images of wafting fans and loosened stays: "The ladies are yet resting from their journey to Sigiriya and unable to come to the telephone at present".

It was a few months before we were able to come out to Jungle Tide and meet Martin and Rani for the first time. We got on immediately and although it's been a bumpy ride at times we're delighted that they are still with us. They have been the soul of Jungle Tide for years and, more than us or Nissanka even, have made it what it is and laid the foundations for us to take it on now we live here.

Remote control

Nissanka, sadly, isn't still with us. He hasn't died or anything – simply he is no longer with *us*. We don't really understand why and theorising would be pointless and boring. At least part of it was to do with his forte being in the development of the land and overseeing the building works rather than project managing a guest house business for foreign owners. But we're sure there was a lot more to it than that, much of it nothing to do with us. He left abruptly in 2013 saying he was moving to Colombo "therefore I can no longer continue as your project manager". We tried to replace him with someone we'd met through him – Chanaka, an excellent guy – but found that Martin was not prepared to be accountable to anyone other than Nissanka or us. And with us being miles away in England, Martin held the cards. Had he resigned at that crucial time the business would have come crashing down just as it was taking off. So we reluctantly agreed to terminate Chanaka's contract though as far as we were concerned he'd done no wrong. Aaiyo! What to do? As they say here. Trying to find yet another project manager would be difficult and probably have the same end result. Equally, we couldn't continue without someone acting as go-between for us and Martin. Martin's English was good enough to look after our guests (Rani's wasn't, at first, though she is a quick learner) but long-distance phone communication with him was always difficult and he has no keyboard let alone computer skills and can only read Tamil.

In this land of serendipity one never has to wait long for the next bit of good fortune to turn up. Enter Anura Seneviratne, a Sri Lankan living in England who'd stayed at Jungle Tide with his English wife and taken an interest in our project and remained in touch with us. When we told him of our troubles Anura offered to phone and talk to Martin in Sinhala whenever we or he needed to discuss something complex or sensitive. Although we tried to keep our use of his generosity to a minimum it was invaluable and he wouldn't accept a penny or a rupee for it. Meanwhile we and Martin managed to scrape along with the practical stuff – details of guest arrivals, departures and requirements, and requests for cash cheques to pay for maintenance jobs or buy new or replacement items. Winging it, and looking back I'm still amazed there were no serious mishaps.

Later still we had the help of Anton, a building contractor who was introduced to us by a fellow Englishman running an already successful guest house in the Kandy area. The previous contractor, who our project manager Nissanka had engaged, had become a bit of a disappointment and also had no more English language or communication skills than Martin. Anton could use e-mail, understood how to work with westerners and has pretty good English. So that whole minefield of managing the maintenance of the property as well as developing some new projects while living thousands of miles away was neatly skirted. Even so, running Jungle Tide from England for that last couple of years stretched our nerves to snapping-point at times. And as for controlling the finances – forget it. They just spiralled away into the blue yonder.

When we bought the land we noticed that there was another small guest house further down the track from us, which proved a handy place for our architect/builder Gamini to stay in when he needed to be around for a couple of days during the build. It was also a sign, however small, that at least one other person thought the location good for tourism. Within a year of Jungle Tide being completed news came through that a larger hotel was to be built next door, on the two acres of land we hadn't bought – the land with the small bungalow. Several friends in England commiserated with us when we told them. We took the opposite view, and still do. Having the Mount Royal Hotel next door – actually a couple of minutes' walk beyond our gates, but completely invisible from our land – would be very good as it would put our end of Hanthana on the tourist map. It might also help put pressure on the authorities to do something about the rapidly deteriorating road. We arranged to meet the multi-millionaire Eriyagama brothers who were developing the hotel and who also owned other local hotels and shopping malls and they confirmed that they would be using their political influence to get the road fixed. The sign in the village proudly announcing the impending road works is dated 2004 (it's still there). At that time the last eight kilometres of the road to Jungle Tide was rough. It had once been surfaced, presumably by the British, but only patches of tarmac remained, surrounded by rocks and stones. By the end of 2006 four kilometres had been remade and re-surfaced. Then everything stopped. Depending on which account you believe the Chinese contractors simply walked off the job to do more profitable work elsewhere, or the Government failed to pay them so they could not continue.

The Eriyagama brothers certainly tried. They managed to get the then President Rajapaksa's brother – who in the dynastical ways of Sri Lankan politics just happened to be the cabinet minister for tourism development – to do the opening ceremony. There was no suitable site nearby for his chopper to land so he had to endure the bumpy track for the last stretch of his journey, and used his speech to berate the authorities for the state of the road, promising he would personally see to it that it got fixed. And that, we assumed, was that. But years passed, as did his ministerial position and his brother's presidency, before anything happened. The Mount Royal caters more for a local and wider Asian clientele but also, having a reception hall and restaurant, does a big side line in weddings. It is a common sight to see a convoy of be-ribboned saloon cars slowly bumping and grinding its way down or up the track. Nevertheless, even most tuk-tuk drivers baulk at taking guests to Jungle Tide. "Now road too bad Sir. I cannot go this road" they would tell guests on reaching the point in no-man's land where the tarmac ran out, and then 'relent' when the previously agreed fare was suitably doubled. The poor guests had no real alternative, they were too far from Kandy to return and too far from Jungle Tide to walk the rest of the way. Guests who had hired their own vehicles and drivers spent the last hour of their journey being driven at an exaggeratedly slow pace and listening to the whingeing of their driver bemoaning what the road was doing to his precious vehicle. We have had to put together a select band of intrepid drivers – from three wheelers to large vans – who are willing to make the trip, and where possible advise our guests in advance. Either no-one tells the wedding organisers about the road or there's so much money in weddings they don't care about wrecking a few cars. But the road is now being improved and by the time this book is published all these tribulations will be history. Hopefully.

The neighbourhood

I'm sure geographers and ethnographers have a technical term for villages like Uduwela. Something along the lines of 'dispersed multi-polar settlement' perhaps. What we had long assumed was the village centre – a small square where the bus terminates with a tatty *kade* (local shop), a muster shed for the tea estate where the pluckers take their haul to be weighed, and a kindergarten, with the Hindu temple close by – is only one of several 'centres' of Uduwela, a sprawling community of maybe ten thousand souls spread half-hidden in the jungles and tea fields clothing the Hanthana hills. Other 'centres' locate around other shops, the primary school, the tea factory, other temples both Hindu and Buddhist, and the post office respectively. In fact to date we have never visited our local post office – it's miles away along a dirt road that we never use. And as we'll see later it was Christmas 2015 before we were even aware of its existence. The facilities in Kandy are easier to get to.

Shops are informal affairs, cropping up in random places and selling limited goods. One of our earlier doomed attempts at controlling our spending was to ask Nissanka to ensure Martin only went shopping in Kandy for anything he could not buy in the village. But since almost nothing of use in a guest house is available in the village shops it made no difference unless we were prepared to insist our guests live on a diet of eggs, bananas and coconuts, and drink fizzy crap out of plastic bottles. I once asked Martin why the local shops did not sell fruit and vegetables. "Sir, transport too much costing." "But many people have some land here. Why do they not grow fruit and vegetables and sell in the village?" "Nobody doing that, sir". "Martin, when I come to live here we will grow vegetables and you and I will have small shop in village, no?" "Yes! This very good idea Sir!"
Maybe one day.

Martin often takes guests for walks around the village, or that part of the 'village' which is closest to Jungle Tide, including visits to various shops and the school and kindergarten, and most popular of all, our local bakery. The baker, who speaks no English, is a tiny, rotund and exceptionally cheery chap who turns out fantastic products in what amounts to a lean-to shed on the side of his house with an ancient wood-fired oven using techniques and materials that date back centuries. There are the narrow Sri Lankan plain loaves and a range of 'bunnis' from 'kimbola bunnis' ('crocodile buns', on account of their elongated shape) to buns filled with *seeni sambol* (sweet and powerfully hot) and complex shapes like French *chinoiserie* breads. If she's not at school his daughter sometimes translates a bit but most of our guests have to communicate by sign language, fingers in the air, pointing at the clock on the wall, or drawing pictures in the flour on the table.

Kandy, World Heritage City and cultural capital of Sri Lanka. Kandy, filthy and crowded with dangerous and potholed pavements, no place for pedestrians. Kandy, modernising with great shopping opportunities, new leisure facilities and restaurants. Kandy, run by the Buddhist establishment which frowns on all fun. Kandy, a place to explore traditional back-street shops and the vibrant market. Kandy, which shuts down at 7pm. Kandy, a city where water and greenery coexist with buildings. Kandy, a city throttled with traffic and noxious exhaust fumes. Kandy – all of the above. Kandy – our home town.

During the seven year period between the house being finished and coming to live here we began to get to know Kandy as almost-residents rather than tourists. "You are leaving here, no?" asked one stranger on the street a few years back. Not having any immediate plans to leave we were confused until we realised he had recognised us as being proto-residents rather than tourists. "You are living here". Increasingly we'd come across people we knew on the street, in shops and cafes. We were living a double life, spending most of our time in Yorkshire but with more and more of our hearts and minds in Sri Lanka. Even so, not everyone could see beyond the skin colour no matter how we were behaving. Tourists, after all, don't usually wander the streets with quantities of plastic housewares and tools as we were wont to. On one occasion Sally was strolling down Kotugodella Vidiya with a heavy crowbar over her shoulder when she was accosted by a tout: "Madam, you want see jewellery? Many good quality gems, local price. Just come look". Since, aside from a balaclava, she was well equipped for a smash-and-grab raid this might have accounted for a possible interest in gems but more likely it was down to the touts' equation of white skin = tourist = money irrespective of any countervailing evidence.

Compared with Galle and Colombo, public investment in Kandy has been meagre despite its being a major tourism centre and the nation's cultural capital and second city – in status if not in size. The pavements and the general environmental state of the city centre are a complete disgrace. Most of the smart private money goes to Colombo and the south west coast. Most of the public money goes either to rebuilding the wrecked infrastructure in the former war zones (rightly) or to ministerial and presidential vanity projects in their political heartlands (wrongly). But not all, and I have a sense that Kandy must by now be at the head of the queue (perhaps alongside Trincomalee and Jaffna) for far-seeing private investors even if public funds are these days hard to come by. The Kandy City Centre complex (KCC to us locals) opened in 2009. At the time it was an eerie and cavernous place containing only a bank and a supermarket as operating businesses. Now it's almost fully occupied and buzzing, with the usual retail suspects (phone shops, white goods stores, fashion and jewellery) plus many more banks, a juice bar and a Burger King. It's recently acquired a café and a food hall. There are a couple of bookshops. And of course the aforesaid supermarket. And an invariably unstaffed tourist information point. On the top floor alongside Burger King and the food hall is a children's entertainment area which our grandchildren loved when we took them there recently. It even includes a small, somewhat incongruous rooftop roller-coaster. Plans for the future include a cinema and theatre, a new bus station and – an unlikely one this – a cable car up to the Hanthana range. So we're expecting future guests to arrive by cable car – or not.

The key to Kandy is the state of tension which exists between the guardians of its role as the cultural and religious centre of Sri Lanka – for whom all change is at best suspect and at worst anathema – and a more inchoate group of business people and local visionaries who want to offer the area's crowds of tourists something more than the boring and over-priced *Dalada Maligawa* (Temple of the Tooth). And of course to cash in on it. Similar to the situation in Trincomalee except that there it is the military doing battle with the forces of economic progress, rather than the Buddhist establishment. There are other things for tourists to do in Kandy city but they're low-key and rarely included in organised tour itineraries meaning that most folk visit for a day and move on, and the local economy doesn't get a lot of benefit. Outside the city it's another matter with the wonderful Peradeniya Botanical Gardens, opportunities for trekking, cycling, immersion in the story of tea cultivation, bird-watching and so forth, but Kandy itself has a very limited appeal to visitors. Quite how this struggle will pan out – or if it ever will – I have no idea as yet.

One thing both sides might agree on, though, is the need to do something about the traffic. Kandy has easily the most congested street system in Sri Lanka and one wonders what training those responsible for traffic planning and management have had. The one-way system is Byzantine and forever being tinkered with, to no great effect. It seems to have been designed to maximise the amount of time vehicles spend in the city centre, slow-moving or stationary, belching out fumes. Obvious routes from A to B are blocked by traffic cones and police whistling incessantly – the police do so love to blow their whistles and have a suite of hand-gestures that seem more suited to 1970s nightclub life than traffic control. The two bus stations are places of utter chaos. So let's hop on the 655 bus and get back to Uduwella and Jungle Tide – if there's any room on board.

Slip slidin' away

Having a phone by your bed (or taking your mobile to bed) has its advantages and disadvantages. At weekends you can call or be called without having to get up first. You can have late-night conversations while comfortably propped-up on pillows. But you can also be raised from your slumbers at any hour when you might prefer not to. I once lived in a house which had previously been owned by the local undertaker which led to a few difficult middle-of-the-night calls (my number was also only one digit away from that of the Potato Marketing Board which gave rise to some amusing daytime exchanges of ignorance). One night in 2012, a few days before Christmas, the phone rang at an ungodly hour. A drowsy Sally answered to find Martin jabbering and sobbing unintelligibly, temporarily forgetting the five and a half hour time difference between Sri Lanka and the UK. She gathered, eventually, that there had been some kind of natural disaster, that no-one had been hurt and the house was still standing but we seemed no longer to have a swimming pool. The pool had only been completed two months previously and was easily our biggest investment since the house had been built. It was in the lower gardens, near to the stream and some distance from the house.

A few hours later we got Nissanka on the phone. He'd made his way over to Jungle Tide to assess the situation. Over the following days we pieced together what must have happened. Following three days of incessant heavy rain the stream had dammed itself when small trees and other debris had become lodged against a footbridge erected by the original owners of the land. Finally the dam burst and a torrent came over the banks where the stream turned sharp left. The flood washed straight over our swimming pool and beyond into our mango orchard. The land there was unstable and gave way. Result – a ten metre deep ravine where our mango trees had once been, leaving our pool teetering over a precipice and dumping the pumping house and pipework into the bottom of the ravine along with most of our mango trees. The land – hundreds of tons of earth and rocks – had been transferred to our neighbours' paddy fields below. The paddy farmers were understandably upset. The good news was that the pool had not been destroyed, although to this day it has a slight tilt as a reminder of the disaster. And of course it was not going to be usable for a very long time.

Christmas is our busiest time and our first job was to warn our guests. Typically people book Jungle Tide over Christmas for big family occasions and reunions and so it was this time. The *Grama Sevaka* – the nearest English equivalent would be the Clerk to the Parish Council – had got wind of the mishap and hot-footed it over to Jungle Tide where he informed Martin and Nissanka that the business would have to be closed forthwith until further notice. Minor officials the world over love to throw their weight around. Of course there was no need to close the business, the house was undamaged. Sure we'd lost half an acre of land, but that still left over two acres. The danger area could easily be roped off – and was.

And what about our guests? Anura Seneviratne and his English wife Annie had arranged a big family reunion at Jungle Tide with guests travelling from England as well as Sri Lanka. They were devastated when we phoned them with the news. How were they going to rearrange such a big event over Christmas with a few days' notice? But once they realised the house was fine they just suggested we ignore the *Grama Sevaka's* edict and carry on as normal. So we did. And that's how we became friends with Anura, who proved to be such a great help to us later on. Nissanka was mortified. Like most Sri Lankans he walks in fear and dread of even the most minor official, unlike we Brits who have an attitude to officialdom that perhaps goes too far in the other direction, bordering on contempt (I speak as a former local government officer...). So we carried on regardless. We'd already booked our plane tickets for late January so it would not be long before we could assess the damage for ourselves and see what could be done.

Though the worst of the debris had been removed (Martin had scrambled down to rescue the expensive swimming pool pump but it proved to be beyond repair) it was still a desolate scene that greeted us. Twelve of our sixteen mango trees lay roots upwards in the bottom of the ravine along with the remains of the pump house and the paving that had once run along the pool's edge. We had acquired an infinity pool by accident; one full of mud whose concrete underskirts showed, hanging dizzily over a ten metre drop. A few days later we travelled two hours into the Knuckles mountains to visit some of Rani's relatives. They pointed back towards the unmistakable shape of Pig Rock (which looks more like a recumbent Buddha than a pig) and, below it, a red scar clearly visible. "That is Jungle Tide landslip".

Sally always maintained that you could dig a hole anywhere in Sri Lanka and probably find some semi-precious stones. And there's lots of quartz on our land and one of our guests had told us that where there is quartz there will be gold. I knew that you could only find gold where there was quartz but didn't think the equation worked the other way round, and indeed it doesn't. But I had to find something to cheer myself up so I spent half a day scrabbling around in the dirt at the bottom of our canyon to see if I could make my fortune. I found nothing, but it kept the spirits up for a short while. Martin, meanwhile, had reconnected with his faith and assured us that "Nothing bad happen to Jungle Tide. All walls are covered with Jesus's blood." "Martin, that's good to know but best not tell the guests, OK?"

Aaiyo! What to do? Nissanka had been to see the National Building Research Organisation before our visit; the *Grama Sevaka* had told him to. They said the business must remain closed indefinitely (they didn't know we were still open) and that extensive drilling and subsoil and rock strata tests needed to be carried out before we could reopen. All of which Nissanka solemnly reported to us as the word of God. So off we went to the NBRO ourselves to sort them out. "How much will it cost for this drilling work?" we asked. "Maybe sixty lakhs" came the reply.

"Sixty lakhs? Are you sure?" (this is about £30,000. And that's just for the testing – who knows how much the remedial work would then have cost). "Yes, madam and sir. This is expensive work. But necessary, no?" "But we do not have this money". "Sorry, but this is essential work". "And if we were just local farmers or local people with small guest house would you expect people like this to pay this money?" "No, they do not have this money". "Nor do we!" "But this essential work, no?" And so on, round and round, until it suddenly dawned on me that the clue was in their name – Building Research Organisation. Were they assuming we wanted to build on the land? Yes indeed they were. Because neither the *Grama Sevaka* nor Nissanka had thought to check this out. Once we explained that the land in question was part of our garden and we had no intention of building on it, the matter was resolved.

But we still had to fix the land. It was dangerous and if there was another flood we could well lose our expensive swimming pool. Not to mention neighbourly relations. Some of the locals were already blaming us for swamping their paddy and thought the pool was the cause of the landslip when the opposite was the case – had it not been for the pool the stream would have permanently changed course and flowed through their paddy fields. Anura put us in touch with an architect friend who in turn put us onto an engineer from Peradeniya University. We visited his office and discussed options. He came to Jungle Tide and assessed the problem. And came up with a monster concrete structure which would have cost about £50,000 to install and made our garden look like a small hydro-electric scheme.

Fortunately we have a civil engineer friend, Ian, who fancied a trip to Sri Lanka and was more than happy to come out and advise. Having a British civil engineer at our disposal really impressed the Sri Lankan powers that be. Ian put together a solution with us and the Peradeniya University engineer which involved building a gabion embankment along the stream and three gabion walls at intervals down the canyon, putting in land drains at the bottom then infilling with compressed earth. The work took a year to complete, cost us in excess of £35,000 including reinstating the pool, and delayed for two years the date on which we could move to Jungle Tide as we had to raise the money. I'd just taken what at the time seemed a great early retirement deal so I had to put together some freelance work. Sally had just given her notice with a view to moving to Jungle Tide in 2013. Fortunately her Board were more than happy for her to withdraw it and stay on for two more years.

There was a final irony. Having invested huge amounts in flood defences we finally arrived to live at Jungle Tide in late 2015 to discover that our stream, far from running in a powerful torrent for most of the year as it originally had, was now reduced to a trickle which dried up completely for much of the year, only regaining a semblance of its former glory after a couple of weeks of monsoon weather. Mystified, we set off upstream to find out why, and discovered that one of the local temples and the Mount Royal Hotel had siphoned off the stream further up the hillside to provide themselves with water supplies, being too tight-fisted to dig themselves decent tube-wells as we had. Since the Eriyagama brothers, owners of the Mount Royal, are among the richest people on the island that grated considerably, though of course one doesn't get rich by being nice and generous. On the basis that the two things you really don't want to mess with in Sri Lanka (other than the police and the military) are organised Buddhism and money we bit our lips and decided we'd just have to live with having an occasional rather than a permanent stream. Anyone want to purchase a hundred metres of gabion wall? Buyer collects.

Onwards and upwards

Having made that enforced decision we thought we might as well use the rest of what we could save to make a couple of further improvements. Once we'd moved we'd be reliant on my pension and anything the business could bring in – which at the time was a negative sum – and investment would be out of the question for a long while at least. So first we built a pavilion next to the pool, with a shady veranda, a small kitchen, changing room and store room for pool equipment and furniture. Then there was the cowshed problem. Nissanka had earlier enthused Sally – who is easily enthused wherever animals are concerned – about the benefits of keeping a couple of cows. My objections were easily overruled. "Who'll do the milking?" "Rani will. I've asked her and she knows how". "What will we do with the excess milk?" "I'll learn to make cheese". And even I could see the benefits of a ready supply of garden manure and a means of keeping the grass down. So Nissanka had built us a cowshed. But the cows, which mercifully had not yet been bought, were to have grazed on the very land that now lay dumped on our neighbours' paddy fields. Aaiyo! What to do? We decided to convert the cowshed into another guest room – a budget room for families and perhaps backpackers. It was not on the unstable area of land and our new builder Anton obliged. The room has since proved popular with families who can't afford two rooms in the house. We also use it to house teams of volunteers in low season.

Sri Lankans don't do planning. They prefer to wait until something collapses – be it a roof, a car tyre or the economy – and then fix it. Usually at great expense and with a lot of disruption. The other side of the coin is that *everything* is urgent. Almost all legislation is 'emergency legislation'; the cynic might explain this as a means of avoiding or limiting proper democratic scrutiny, but it is at least partly down to the local inability to spot a problem until it overwhelms them. As with politics, so with house maintenance. Even Nissanka, one of the most Anglicised Sri Lankans we've met, would send us e-mails stressing the need for urgent action on our part over something or other. House repairs, getting permission for something or other, staff pay increases, whatever. When the matter was either something we didn't understand or simply couldn't afford to do, nine times out of ten the 'emergency' simply faded away. But from six thousand miles away it was hard to make a call on whether something really did require our immediate attention and cash or whether we could safely ignore it and it would go away.

Whenever we made our annual visit to Jungle Tide Martin quickly confronted us with a list of urgent problems that needed to be fixed. We got used to it and stuffed the company bank account in advance of our visits knowing it would all get spent in short order. The first two weeks of our month at the house was spent paying for materials and tradespeople. The third week was spent organising jobs to prevent such emergencies happening again and the fourth week, if we were lucky, some of that work might start. As soon as we headed back to England everything would stop once more, until the next guttering collapse or roof leak or pest infestation or washing machine breakdown or generator failure. Then we'd be back in emergency mode. We were in a classic Catch-22 situation: until we could live there permanently we wouldn't be able to get a grip on maintaining the place or growing the business, but as long as we were sinking silly amounts of money into a loss-making enterprise we couldn't afford to give up work and make the move we knew was as much needed as desired.

Martin does at least recognise the value of planning at a theoretical level. In between advising us on how to remediate our collapsed land our friend Ian and his partner Joan decided they would find a way up to the top of Oorogala (Pig Rock), the great inland cliff which looms over Jungle Tide. Martin had never been up there and did not know anyone who had. Undaunted, they talked with us and him the previous evening about a possible route and, armed with stout boots, sticks and a phone they set off early the next morning. A couple of hours later they phoned us from the summit and out came the binoculars; there they were, waving gaily at us. Martin took a look, shouted for Rani and they both stood and stared, amazed at this feat of derring-do. "Madam", opined Martin, "This is why the white man is great." "What on earth do you mean, Martin?" replied a shocked Sally. "You could climb up there if you wanted to. You're very strong and fit." "Ah, Madam, because the white man he has a plan. Last night these people they make plan to climb to the top of the rock and now they do the plan". "But Martin, you could also make a plan." "No, Madam, I cannot make plan. I start out, then too late and aaiyo! Sun going down, I have to come back."

Guest appearances

Meanwhile there were guests to be fed and housed. Two thirds of our guests are from Europe and about half of these in turn are British or Irish. We're also very big in Denmark. Don't ask me why, but I'm not complaining; the Danes are super people. The other third come from all over the world including Sri Lankans. The best thing about running a guest house is the guests. We've met and continue to meet scores of fascinating people most of whom are perfectly normal, but it's the oddballs you remember best.

Until recently we only got to meet a few of our guests, those whose stay coincided with our own annual state visits. The only true oddball among them was a hurdy-gurdy player from Luxembourg (not many of them around) called Hans Stiegler (not his real name). Hans had mysterious digestive problems, and hence some unique dietary requirements. Only certain vegetables and fruit agreed with him; no meat or fish; no additives or colourings whatsoever; and definitely nothing spicy. He stayed for two weeks, most of our time in Jungle Tide that year. To begin with we were sympathetic: "What is your condition called, Hans?" asked Sally. "It does not have a name. It is not simple and it is not known to conventional medicine." "Would it help if you prepared your own meals?" "That will not be necessary. Rani can prepare my food according to my instructions."

So we had to make sure the 'right' vegetables and fruit were always in store, and poor Rani had to prepare two meals each night, one for us and our other guests and one for Hans. When we discovered from her that his instructions included a stipulation that vegetables should be boiled only in bottled water – in his bizarre world view boiling tap water was still dangerously full of harmful bacteria – we realised why we were getting through such a lot of bottled water (we have since sensibly invested in water purifiers). At least buffalo curd and fruit (or certain fruits) were acceptable for breakfast. But when Hans had finished his plateful he began to look longingly at our curries. "Mmm, that looks nice. Is it OK if I try a little?" "Sure, there's more than enough" (which, as all our guests testify, is the understatement of the year where Rani's cooking is concerned). "I shouldn't be eating fish but that tuna curry tastes wonderful".

Hans's stay coincided with that of a retired Tory MP and his wife, with whom we got on famously despite our political differences. One morning at the breakfast table Hans began describing in some detail his bowel problems. Our other guests pulled hilarious faces at us which made it difficult to address the issue in a serious and adult manner and we found ourselves giggling uncontrollably into our *rotis* and *pol sambol.* Eventually Hans got the message: "Perhaps not a good subject for breakfast time" he admitted, to which the rest of us nodded enthusiastically and the subject was dropped.

One day our accountants were visiting and we were sitting with them at the dining table poring over figures, calculators at the ready, when in burst Hans in a state of high excitement. "Sally! Come quickly! I need your help" he exclaimed. "Whatever's wrong, Hans?" "There is a mosquito in my room!" We handed him a spray can of insect killer and went back to the accounts. A long time ago a friend of mine coined the term 'mimophant' for characters such as Hans – as sensitive as a mimosa to their own needs and as thick-skinned as an elephant to the needs of others. Mimosas themselves are mimophants – as you will find out if you ever try pulling one up.

Some of our most rewarding guests are those who choose Jungle Tide for a special occasion. We have had octogenarian former planters who've long since left the island using the house as a base to revisit their pasts; Sri Lankan expats booking the house for similar reasons; Sri Lankans living abroad who've married westerners and want to show them the country of their birth, and simpler occasions such as birthday celebrations young and old. Sri Lanka is also perfectly located for reunions of families split between the UK/Europe and Australia/New Zealand and we've had and continue to have more than a few of those. We've even hosted a wedding. No, not a honeymoon, the actual wedding. We were approached by a Scottish couple to see if they would be able to get married in Sri Lanka and specifically at Jungle Tide. We had no idea, but Nissanka offered to find out and make all necessary arrangements ('do the needful' in local parlance). And so it was that two people from Glasgow were married on our front lawn by the local registrar with Martin and Rani as the sole guests and witnesses. We were in England at the time; we'd have loved to have been present.

A medical interlude

Sally discovered house-swapping several years ago. She needed to spend some time at the Edinburgh Festival talent-spotting for her arts centre's new programme but neither she nor the arts centre could afford the sky-high rents in the city at festival time. Then she recalled that many years earlier, when Merigen was a baby, she'd arranged a house swap through the National Childbirth Trust and decided to look at whether these arrangements still existed. They certainly did – and the arrival of the internet had opened up a plethora of opportunities and websites. So she *was* able to go to the ball in Edinburgh – in fact we went every year for four years until we moved to Sri Lanka. Not only that, we've had several British and European short breaks and have house-swapped our way around Australia and New Zealand for a three month period. We now use house-swaps to make our visits to the UK affordable; three months B&B is out of the question and much as we love our family and friends, we'd all drive each other mad if we spent our whole time under their roofs. And these days we give house swaps as presents to our children and their families. Saves on postage.

A couple of our house-swapper guests have had interesting experiences with the Sri Lankan health care system. Susan and Dick were keen walkers and wanted to trek for a day in the Knuckles range. Rather than find them a professional guide Martin and Dishantha, the driver we'd recommended them to use, decided they would save them money by guiding the trek themselves. Needless to say the whole party got lost in the wilderness. Susan stepped into a concealed hole in the rocks and fractured her ankle – badly as it turned out. The others carried her a very long way back to the van which they eventually found after dropping her twice, thence a long and bumpy drive to Kandy General, who pronounced themselves incapable of doing more than a temporary fix and sent her on by ambulance to Colombo where, according to the British NHS, they did a marvellous job. But her injury and the complications from being manhandled over the mountains and bounced around in a van left her in a wheelchair for more than a year afterwards. She's now fully recovered and in her cheery, indomitable way claims it was all worthwhile for the free upgrade to business class on the return flight.

George and Silvia came to Jungle Tide a year later. One afternoon George developed a sore throat which over the next few days became so constricted he could hardly draw breath. Martin called for an ambulance. While they were waiting Silvia had to give him mouth-to-mouth resuscitation. At Kandy General they diagnosed severe asthma despite George having no history of asthma or anything related to it, and prescribed drugs which did ease his breathing, so the couple returned to Jungle Tide and, the next day, headed off as planned for a week on the coast. George's condition again worsened and he was rushed first to the local hospital where a sign on a door read *BEAST FEEDING ROOM* and from there – mercifully perhaps – to the private Durdan's Hospital in Colombo. After many tests and scary experiences the doctors finally identified the problem as a rare condition which causes massive inflammation of the vocal chords (I have no idea what it's called) and he was successfully treated. When they got back to the UK he sensibly went for check-ups and his consultant expressed considerable admiration for the diagnostic skills of the Durdan's team, given the extreme rarity of the condition.

In the hospital Silvia was told that the deal was that she would be given her own bed in the same private room as George, with a kitchenette attached. She would be expected to go out and shop and cook for herself and – once he was able to take in solid food – for her husband as well. She pronounced the hospital "the best hotel I've stayed in for the price" and appears to have had a great time once she knew George had been properly diagnosed, was out of danger and on the road to recovery. They sent the rest of their holiday in the hospital. And the cost? I'm not sure but Silvia told us later that it wasn't worth the trouble of claiming on their travel insurance as it was hardly more than the excess.

We have since availed ourselves of our local private hospital, though not as in-patients. The Kandy Lakeside Adventist Hospital hasn't had a lick of paint or a change of furniture since the 1950s, or so it would appear, and according to an unnerving mural Jesus is personally involved in patient care. I thought he was a carpenter, not a sawbones. Another mural for some unfathomable reason is a blow-up photograph of Pen-y-Ghent in the Yorkshire Dales. But it creaks along and costs a lot less than private medicine in the UK.

The system for getting to see a doctor is called 'channelling' and, like booking trains, takes a bit of learning for our unaccustomed western minds to get to grips with and I won't attempt to describe it here. If only because I don't yet understand it myself. Prescribing methods are also unfamiliar to us westerners. Sleeping pills can be obtained over the counter in most pharmacies, yet certain brands of mouthwash on British supermarket shelves can only be obtained from a pharmacist. Sally once tried to get some sleeping pills for a guest and was told they had sold out. "Do you have anything else? He just wants something to help him calm down". "Yes, Madam, we have something very good for calming the mind" – and produced a packet of Valium. This in a Buddhist country devoted to meditation and mindfulness. Doctors and, in my case, a dentist commonly prescribe just three days' worth of antibiotics, flying in the face of all medical advice. When a doctor does issue a prescription the pharmacist just puts all the pills in separate unmarked packets. On many occasions Martin has returned from a visit to the doctor and pharmacy claiming that some tablets are pain-killers when an examination of the brand and a little research on the internet reveals them to be blood-pressure tablets.

Needless to add, it's worse for the locals. There is free healthcare in the Democratic Socialist Republic of Sri Lanka but the NHS it ain't, even in its present reduced state. The healthcare is free, for sure, but to obtain it you have to be prepared to queue all day in the baking sun in the hospital yard. And if your condition requires you to be hospitalised you or your family have to pay for the overnight accommodation and all meals. Though the quality of the medical care is excellent, it must be said.

A friend of a friend was leading an effort to raise funds to build a centre in Kandy for cancer patients where they could stay rather than facing repeated long trips back and forth to their homes (Kandy hospital serves an area stretching out to the east coast where oncology is concerned). We were introduced to him and he immediately invited us to attend his board meeting on one of our visits as our mutual friend had mentioned that Sally had raised large sums for the arts. The meeting was a revelation. It was a one-man show by the chairman who showed no interest in getting the views of any member of his board. The meeting was frequently interrupted by his and others' mobile phones going off and needing to be answered. Eventually, after about two hours of this staccato monologue, he announced that "We have a very special guest here tonight, Sally Martin, who is a fundraiser and has come to tell us how we can raise money for our project." Talk about being thrown in at the deep end. Sally mumbled something about raising money for the arts in the UK not having all that much to do with raising money for healthcare in Sri Lanka and sat down. The centre was eventually built, floor by floor. When they had enough money they put in the foundations. Then started again to raise money for the ground floor. And so on through four floors. One is torn between admiration for sheer doggedness and a strong sense that they could be a whole lot more effective if they adopted a more strategic approach. But as I've already observed, Sri Lankans don't do planning.

Over the seven years since Jungle Tide was built we'd learned a lot. Strokes of great good fortune – especially finding a top-class project manager and housekeepers –

and a few disasters, notably the landslip. Beginning to find our way around the bureaucracies from the Electricity Board to the often bizarre requirements of our auditors (which were never the same from one year to the next). Not to mention wrestling with the National Building Research Organisation and the *Grama Sevaka*. Getting to know our new home town a lot better. Unravelling the mysteries of Trip Adviser algorithms to make sure we had enough reviews to get near to the top of the very big tree whose three hundred and sixty plus branches represent the guest houses and B&Bs just in the Kandy area. Finding out what our guests wanted, and sometimes didn't want, even when their needs were as odd as Hans's. We were ready to make the big jump and come to live in Sri Lanka – or so we thought. And that also gave us the opportunity to get to know the parts of the island I'd never been to, and Sally had not seen since she was a child. To wit, the war-ravaged north.

Eight

Wilpattu

In May 2009 our preoccupation with our own situation meant we'd lost contact with the wider world and indeed the wider island nation. We had no TV or radio, and didn't bother to buy newspapers when we were in town. We just wanted to do the shopping and get the hell back to sorting out Jungle Tide. One afternoon we were in Kandy. The sun was making a cameo appearance during the monsoon, Sally was buying sandals and I was off down a neighbouring street looking for light bulbs when the sound of gunfire broke out all around us. People were out in the streets shouting and waving flags. Revolution? No, the end of the war. On hearing the news that the LTTE had surrendered and their leader, Prabakharan, had been killed groups of young men had descended upon the city centre, cleared every street and produced quantities of firecrackers which they had presumably been stockpiling for the occasion and which were now being let off in the middle of the roads, flashing, banging and leaping in all directions with national flags being waved vigorously. The reek of cordite; a combination of warfare and the fifth of November. A shop-front TV started showing looped newsreel of Prabakharan's lifeless body to wild approbation. Sally and I had initially been concerned for each other's safety and it took us a while to reunite and witness the tumult of joy that had been released across the city. It was hours before we were able to locate our driver and his van and leave, by which time the authorities had re-established control of the streets and set up free *kiributh* stands at the main junctions and roundabouts. *Kiributh* – the name means 'milk rice' – is a traditional celebratory dish and is doled out free to the public on special occasions. And boy, was this one special! Later, back in England, we learned more of the details about the brutal way in which the war ended and the hosts of Tamil civilian casualties caught up and trapped in the endgame. It was sobering. But at the time we just felt like joining the vast majority of Sri Lankans, including most Tamils, in the mood of celebration.

I've said earlier that the Sri Lankan civil war was Asia's longest and bloodiest recent conflict and also a contender for the world's most haphazardly conducted war. It featured a peace-keeping force equally reviled by both sides and only removed when one side (the Sri Lankan military) armed the other (the Tamil Tigers/LTTE) to drive the 'peace keepers' back to India; a guerrilla army that had its own navy and mini-air force and was at the end in the process of constructing a full-scale submarine; third party brokerage by a northern European country (Norway) with no apparent links to or interest in Sri Lanka other than being jolly decent and well-meaning folk; and a Tamil 'liberation movement' which was only for the Jaffna Tamils rather than their lower-caste country cousins who had been brought in by the British and whose main aim was simply to be treated with equality and respect as Sri Lankan citizens. If there is one political idea more bonkers than Sinhala nationalism it is Tamil Eelam – a tiny independent Tamil state in the less fertile reaches of an already small island.

No part of Sri Lanka was untouched by the war. True, most of the country remained safe to live in or visit throughout – in the same way that London was still safe at the height of the IRA's activity or New York was still a safe place in the immediate aftermath of 9/11. Colombo suffered its share of atrocities; both the large-scale suicide bombings carried out by the LTTE and the myriad small-scale government-backed abductions of activists and journalists into the notorious unmarked white vans. Even the Sinhalese 'deep south' could be a dangerous place if you were deemed to have the wrong opinions or associated with the wrong people. But there is no doubt that the north and, to a slightly lesser extent, east of the country were the worst affected. We were both keen to get ourselves up north and down the east coast when the opportunity arose, not as war tourists but simply to get the flavour of what we knew would be a very different part of the island, culturally, economically, climatically and geographically.

Wilpattu in the north west of the island is for me the most beautiful of all Sri Lanka's national parks. In the mists of early dawn it is a magical place to be, irrespective of what wildlife you may see. For years it was LTTE territory. The Tamil Tigers decided at an early stage in the war that Wilpattu provided both ideal guerrilla training camp facilities and a ready source of protein and proceeded to kill the park rangers in order to take over the park and slaughter most of its four-legged inhabitants. Then when forced to retreat they left behind a legacy of landmines which claimed several civilian fatalities including most ironically the writer Nihal de Silva, author of the influential anti-war novel *The road from Elephant Pass*, who was on a post-war visit to the park he'd loved so dearly. The park is now clear of landmines and the animal populations are again flourishing. Sally was as keen to revisit Wilpattu as anywhere else but it was only after we'd moved to live in Sri Lanka that we were able to make the first of what have to date been four visits.

Sally's family took an annual week-long holiday in the park throughout the 1950s and 1960s, staying in one of the circuit bungalows deep in the park, invariably situated close to a *villu* (small lake or waterhole). You can still hire these bungalows if you can master the Department of Conservation's primitive website or have the time to turn up at their Colombo offices in person, but these days it's a tame experience. The bungalows have electricity and fans for one thing. In Sally's time there was a paraffin fridge as the sole nod to mod cons. Lighting was provided by pumped paraffin lamps with an unfortunate tendency to explode. Toilets were long drops. Showers were a perforated bucket precariously fixed to the top of a water pipe – a petrol pump took the water up from a well. Monikapola Utu, like the other park bungalows, was built on a platform. Underneath was the kitchen and dining area surrounded by a low stockade. Steps led up to a central hallway with a large bedroom either side. Each bedroom was crammed with wood and canvas donkey-beds but sleep was impossible in the heat, with no fans, so the family took the beds out onto the front veranda. Children and nannies in a row on one side, adults on the other. On one occasion Rose awoke all the children in a state of panic. "Quickly! Come inside! There is a wild animal on the veranda!" Having secured the safety of her charges she went back to rescue the parents who had been wakened by the commotion and wondered what the fuss was all about. The animal noises had mysteriously ceased, the reason being that Sally's Dad, having been rudely awakened, was no longer snoring.

There were and are some truly dangerous animals in Wilpattu, though. It is the most likely place to see sloth bears which, as I've already noted, combine stupidity with aggressive instincts. Sally recalls a bear which – in those bad old days when feeding wild animals was not prohibited – recognised Maradan Maduwa bungalow as a convenient food source and became well-known and tame as far as the regular human visitors were concerned. He was known as Kalu and had the habit of coming from behind and clutching you in a friendly bear-hug, a habit which understandably terrified those not in the know. So the park rangers fitted him with a bell around his neck and tourists would then know that a ringing sound prior to being clutched around the waist by a bear meant it was just Kalu up to his usual tricks. Which worked fine until the day Kalu managed to wrestle off his annoying bell before grabbing an unwary visitor in a bear hug...

Freshwater crocodiles abound in the *villus* and in those days swimming in them was permitted. Sally and her brothers, with their Mum's encouragement, used to swim out to groups of these small crocodiles which formed a semi-circle of reptilian snouts in the water ahead of them, sometimes sufficiently overcome by curiosity to paddle gingerly towards their human pool-sharers, at which point Sally was urged by her older brothers to swim out and splash their faces to make them return to a safe distance. Which she cheerfully did until one day brother Simon said to her:
"They're not man-eaters. Mummy said so." And brother Jeremy commented drily: "Yes, but have they read the same books as Mummy?"

But buffalo are the most dangerous of all, once they get it into their heads to run around in a herd. These days no-one is allowed out of a jeep; back then it was common to get out and stroll around, or indeed walk miles back to the bungalow due to the jeep having broken down. On one such occasion the family was charged by a large herd of buffalo and forced to climb into the trees to take refuge. Sally's Dad was a portly chap not given to tree climbing or other physical pursuits but Sally recalls seeing in amazement how he appeared to run vertically up a tree trunk to grab a branch and haul himself onto it. Adrenalin is powerful stuff.

There were other mishaps to which the Martin family seemed particularly prone on their visits to Wilpattu. Being ejected from vehicles was one. When Pamela was eight months pregnant with Sally she was perched in the back of a jeep, sitting on a crate of supplies. They were arriving at the park and had to bring a week's worth of food for themselves and the staff, which filled the jeep; the brothers were up front with Dad and Pamela was riding shotgun when the jeep went too fast over a bump in the track and the tailgate lynchpin came out. She and the crate shot out the back. Dazed, and half expecting to go into labour, she waited by the crate for more than half an hour before her husband, having asked her a shouted question repeatedly over the roar of the engine, finally turned around to see why he was getting no answer. This was only the most dramatic of a series of such accidental ejections over the years.

As I said, a week's worth of supplies had to be brought into the park by jeep on every visit. Supplies consisting of food, drink and fuel. The combination of bumpy roads and dodgy containers meant that on two occasions the family's prized joint of meat was contaminated, first by petrol when a jerry-can leaked all over it, the second more appetisingly perhaps when a gin bottle broke and marinaded the joint. No matter, the meat still had to be eaten. Flambeed mutton, anyone?

When we first visited Wilpattu in April 2016 it was Sinhala and Tamil New Year and we returned from our early evening safari to find preparations at our hotel in full swing. The staff were keen that we should participate as honoured guests. This chiefly involved lighting a great number of small wicks adorning an elaborate multi-layered floor-to-ceiling brass structure, and eating quantities of *kiributh*, oil cake and other traditional celebratory foods, all the while with one eye on the TV on the wall which was conducting not one but a series of countdowns to various 'auspicious times'. Not just for the precise start of the new year itself (sometime mid-evening) but the precise time at which the *kiributh* should be served, or some special oil lamp lit, or some other food preparation should commence. A kind of national OCD grips the island at New Year. And a big payday for astrologers. But what happens when astrologers disagree, I wonder? Maybe there's an astrological parallel court system to resolve differences.

Wilpattu is my favourite national park, though there are a couple I've yet to visit. The name translates from old Sinhala as 'Lake District' and although the flat landscape could hardly be more contrasting I find it every bit as beautiful as its English namesake. The early pearly light, the way the jungle tracks suddenly open out onto *villus* teeming with birds and animals, the chance of seeing pretty much anything if you're lucky and not minding much if you're not. I've yet to see a leopard in Wilpattu but it's the only park where I've seen a bear. OK it was near dusk, it had its arse end firmly pointed at us and was moving away slowly into the scrubby jungle, but you can't have everything. Wilpattu is a bit short of elephants (a further point in its favour as far as I'm concerned) but on one safari a large male burst out of the jungle by the side of the track, trunk raised and trumpeting loudly, almost up to our jeep. Even Sally was scared, while I dissolved into what must have been nervous giggles. Once I'd regained the power of speech I managed to explain that my immediate thought had been that this must be a virtual reality elephant, so sudden and noisy was its intervention in our lives. Only after it had gone did it occur to me that it had been a real beast. That's what the twenty first century does to our brains, I guess.

Peninsular oriental

Peninsulas are strange places, semi-detached from the countries they are joined to. Kalpitiya and Mannar are part of Sri Lanka yet each has a completely different feel. Both, but especially Mannar, were off limits on most of our earlier visits. Culturally Kalpitiya is half-Muslim, half-Catholic, both very much minorities in the wider country.

The economy is based on fishing, salt and, nowadays, tourism. Feral donkeys, the descendants of animals left behind by the retreating Portuguese centuries ago, or by early Arab traders depending which account you believe, roam around. Giant wind-farms pop up everywhere, unlike elsewhere in Sri Lanka where they are a rarity. On one side is the ocean, on the other a lagoon with the town of Puttalam visible through the heat haze on the opposite bank. The peninsula is approached across an isthmus via industrial salt lagoons, or salterns.

We have not yet made it to the far end of the peninsula, the town of Kalpitiya itself, but we did on one occasion venture out to sea. Or tried to. Kalpitiya is Sri Lanka's go-to venue for watching spinner dolphins. The owner of the place we were staying also owned a boat and offered to take us out one morning on a dolphin-watching trip. The venture began from a quay on a shallow river. Very shallow. So shallow that every few yards the boatman and the owner had to get out and push, as it were, to cross a sandbank and reach a short navigable stretch on the other side. Off we went as far as the next sandbank. The shores on either side were also pure sand, with the occasional leaf-thatched hut – an other-worldly landscape. We might have been on Mars, but for the water. And the huts. OK, perhaps not Mars then, but it really felt strange. After an hour we saw the breakers; the ocean lay just the other side of a final, giant sandbar. Out we all got and over we went and out to sea where the spinner dolphins eagerly awaited our visit. And so did a maritime picket line. Unbeknown to us, a fisherman had been beaten up by the police in a demonstration a couple of days earlier and in protest the fishing community was not putting out to sea until they could see justice being done. And if *they* weren't going fishing, no-one else was. Or even dolphin-watching, despite our protests. Apparently they knew the owner's brother and threatened to do him some serious damage if he persisted in taking his tourists out to sea. Discretion being the better part of valour, so ended our attempt at dolphin-watching.

Mannar is not technically a peninsula but you need keen eyes to spot on the map that it's an island, approached by a long causeway with shallow sea on both sides followed by a short bridge. There is also a railway line running parallel a mile away. Both have been recently reconstructed following their destruction, like much else of Mannar, in the war. At the furthest end of Mannar stands Talaimannar, once the ferry port for India which lies about twenty miles distant across the Palk Strait. It was from Talaimannar pier that Sally's family left what was then Ceylon at the start of their epic overland voyage to England in 1971. The pier is still there, fingering India in its desolate abandoned state; rotten timbers and rusted railway lines. A notice at the entrance says *'DANGEROUS STRUCTURE. ENTER AT YOUR OWN RISK'.* In England it would be *'DANGEROUS STRUCTURE. DO NOT ENTER'* which is one of the reasons I like living in Sri Lanka. Next to the pier is the empty cavern which used to be the customs shed. Beyond a roll of razor wire and a military lookout wrecked boats are grounded offshore. Aside from the brand new and incongruous railway station that's pretty much all there is to Talaimannar. The manager of the Palmyrah where we were staying took us in his jeep out to the piece of flat scrub where Sri Lanka ends with the intention of crossing the short stretch of shallow water to the first of the Adam's Bridge sandbanks that in times past have formed a land bridge to India. But it being the rainy season there proved to be too much water and mud for the jeep to tackle and we had to turn back, though we got up close and personal to a large flock of grazing partridge on the way which was a compensation.

Not as large a flock, though, as the collection of many hundreds of flamingos which cross to Mannar and which can be seen in the salterns along the coast. Not quite as pink as their African cousins owing to different diets they are nonetheless an impressive sight. "Madam, these tourist birds" offered our driver, who proved to be something of an ornithologist. We assumed he meant they are birds which tourists like us come to gawp at but eventually realised that this was his term for migratory birds. One imagines them touching down and heading for Immigration with their visas clutched tightly in their beaks.

Being in Mannar is like being in the Sri Lanka I first encountered in 1998. Dirt roads, dirt poor. Motorised and non-motorised two-wheeled transport dominates the traffic. Animals vying for the limited road space – goats, cows, dogs and yet more feral donkeys. Shacks for shops, only one small supermarket and no tourist outlets. You smell the fish market before you see it. Fishermen wade from their catamarans through twenty metres of polluted water with their catch in buckets. War-damaged buildings everywhere, and none more so than the fort in Mannar town which despite or maybe because of its sad state is my favourite of all the many sandcastles the Dutch built around the island. Originally a Portuguese fort, the Dutch took it over and massively increased its size. Then under British rule it fell into neglect and the tropical weather combined with the depredations of locals took their toll on the crumbling structures. Finally it was taken over by the Tamil Tigers as a base for operations in the Mannar area and heavily shelled as a result by the Sri Lankan army and navy. Given its history what is amazing is how much of it still stands, including a lovely though roofless chapel full of ancient Dutch inscriptions and tombs. There are no signs in any language, let alone English, and no-one around except you and the donkeys. Interpretation is a matter of informed imagination. And no doubt it helps if you can understand Dutch, which I can't.

The Arabs may have brought the donkeys' ancestors and certainly brought from modern Somalia the baobab trees which are another feature of this strange part of Sri Lanka; one is the largest by girth in the whole of Asia but little is made of it. A Marian shrine stands next to it despite its Muslim origins. But then another of Mannar's oddities is that it is mainly Christian and, within that, overwhelmingly Catholic. Churches, Catholic schools and shrines dot the place liberally. In a field stands a man-made grotto with a statue of the virgin. The cemeteries, though, nod to non-Christian traditions by being gaily multi-coloured rather than flat white. Yellows, greens and pinks are the favoured shades to be interred beneath. But some people live in the pink, or did until recently. Just up the road from the Palmyrah, across a salty lagoon, stands a new housing development entirely in shocking pink, including a shocking pink water tower. We asked and found out that it was built illegally by a corrupt local politician and has since been condemned. It stands on land prone to flooding and the houses quickly became uninhabitable. But no-one seemed to know why it was pink.

Mannar's Catholic shrines, churches and schools are numerous but for a dose of real heavy-duty Catholicism you have to go back to the mainland, though still in Mannar district, to the church and surrounding complex of Our Lady of Madhu. How a cathedral-sized church came to be located in the middle of nowhere I haven't yet discovered. I imagine the Virgin Mary put in one of her random appearances in this spot at some point in the past. Certainly its function is as a place of pilgrimage rather than a centre of community. All around the church are barrack-like buildings which can be hired by visiting pilgrims for the duration of their visits. Strictly bookable well in advance. Others choose to erect home-made tents in the nearby fields, using bamboo and stitched-together advertising banners. A building the size of an average supermarket is devoted to the sale of rosaries. There are many festivals, dedicated either to saints or to the faithful of the various Catholic enclaves around the island. But where the southern Europeans treat religious festivals as an opportunity for dancing in the streets and possibly imbibing a little too much, in Sri Lanka even Catholicism falls prey to the Asian cultural tradition that festivals and fun don't mix. Alcohol, smoking and music are prohibited and, just to make sure all loopholes are closed a sign proclaims *NO MERRYMAKING*. Inside the nave of the colourful church there are few places to sit. Instead people kneel or prostrate themselves on the floor praying loudly in cacophony despite signs all around imploring *SILENCE*. Our driver told us that, as in Kataragama in the south, the pilgrims are by no means all Catholics. Buddhists and Hindus regard the place as sacred and join in enthusiastically. Later, in Jaffna, we had a ride in possibly the world's smallest taxi – a kind of mini-minicab – where the driver sported, above his dashboard, a crucifix, a couple of Hindu deities, a Buddha and, for us non-believers, a nodding daffodil. Religious inclusion, or just hedging his bets?

Also off the island but still in Mannar district stands a memorial to British eccentricity – we Brits refuse to be outdone in the eccentricity stakes, of course. The Doric Bungalow was built by the first British Governor of Ceylon, Frederick North, at the beginning of the nineteenth century partly to impress his compatriots and partly as a lookout point to check up on the local pearl fishermen – the same ones Bizet wrote his opera *The Pearl Fishers* about, though their real lives were both more humdrum and more dangerous than the composer's romanticised version. The bungalow, on the edge of a low cliff, has partly crumbled onto the beach below but enough still stands to walk around and imagine its past glories. In this case there is a large and informative signboard despite the isolation of the place and the lack of visitors.

Jaffna

There's not a lot to do in Jaffna. Actually that's probably not true, it's just that there's no information and hardly anyone speaks much English. Or indeed Sinhala, which creates problems when you turn up with a Sinhalese driver who doesn't speak Tamil. The vestigial tourism industry appears to be run by a mix of NGOs (or former NGO wallahs) and the military, notably the Navy. Sound fellows all, no doubt, but not showing much of a clue about what visitors want or how to drain their pockets for the benefit of the local economy. The famed library, destroyed with its priceless collections at the start of the war and since rebuilt, is open only to its local members most of the time and to 'visitors' for an hour or so at the end of the day. The Information Desk was unstaffed when we went. There are several impressive Hindu temples and many good if less impressive churches for visitors who want to engulf themselves in religion, and a large but uninterpreted Dutch fort – like Mannar's heavily damaged in the recent war even more than it was in the historic past – but I'd seen so many of those that another one held little interest. What did fascinate me was the collection of ruined buildings. All over the north and east shelled and wrecked homes can be seen with depressing regularity, but in the north's 'capital', Jaffna, there are also the ruins of many civic or religious buildings which were clearly once of huge local importance. One in particular stands opposite the new Jetwing Hotel and the even newer Cargill's Square shopping complex. It was obviously destroyed some time ago as banyan trees grow up through its walls and foundations. We asked our taxi driver "What is this building?" "Ah, Sir, breaking in problem time" "Yes, we know, but before breaking, what was it used for?" "Sir, Government building" was all we could get from him. I'm not a ghoulish war tourist, but I don't think I'm the only visitor who would love to know more about these places, and what Jaffna was like before the war. How much would it cost to put up a few signs? A lot less than the cost of the lavish 'war memorials', which I'll come to.

Jaffna may have a proud library but as far as I could discover it possesses not a single bookshop – other than the usual outlets selling school textbooks. There is no local guidebook and no city website. Needless to add, no publicly viewable map of the city. But as noted it does now possess a brand new shopping centre and a Jetwing hotel. The former houses a large and well stocked supermarket so full marks to Messrs Cargill for that, but the rest of the small complex is of limited range. The Jetwing charges Jetwing prices but doesn't deliver the level of quality one associates with their other hotels and doesn't even have a swimming pool. The guest house we stayed in was clean and run by a well-meaning and hard-working woman with little English; the rooms were small and dark and the food dull. Two oases we did discover were Morgan's, a delightful garden bar on Temple Street, and the nearby Mangoes restaurant – fabulous *dosas* at knockdown prices. But Jaffna is a gem waiting to be unearthed, or maybe unearthed and waiting to be cut and polished.

To the west of Jaffna Sri Lanka peters out in a series of flat islands joined by causeways or ferries. Some have Dutch names (Kayts, Delft), others Tamil names (Punkudutivu, Karaitivu). Up early and clambering into our van to catch the 8am ferry from Punkudutivu to Delft, the first causeway which links Jaffna to Kayts is a well-surfaced road, presumably rebuilt since the war, flanked in the dawn light by rectangles of prawn and crab nets and traps in the flat calm waters. Jaffna has a reputation for the best crabs – and the best mangoes. Silhouetted fishermen check their traps soundlessly; the tide flows left to right under the causeway making no fuss at all. An honour guard of pelicans, Brahminy kites and spoonbills mans the wooden and concrete posts alongside the causeway. Further out stilts and flamingos go about their business paying us no attention. Once on Kayts, the road becomes potholed and the second causeway, from there out to Punkudutivu and the ferry, is a bumpy old ride with a couple of inches either side separating the van from the briny. But buses somehow do the trip.

They, along with bicycles, motorcycles, tuk-tuks and the occasional car or van congregate at the end of the pier. The eight o'clock ferry is free and is a motorised sardine tin run by the Navy. We were warned we'd have to pay a few rupees on the return journey in a 'private boat'. Packed into the hold on hard benches we waited for the engines to start and therefore, more importantly, the fans. Even at this early hour it was stifling. The fan nearest to us had a union flag emblazoned on its middle and a notice informing us that it was 'sponsored by the Delft Society (UK)' – hard to think of a more niche organisation. A genuine fan club. It was non-operational, having a round-pin plug next to a square pin socket. Perhaps a metaphor for the relationship between the UK and Sri Lanka. A sailor eventually turned up with an adaptor and put us out of our sweaty misery.

On the quay at Delft Sally and I had the same immediate reaction: "Isn't this like Rottnest?" she said. A year earlier we'd spent a day on that island off Perth and the similarities were surprising and hit us both. It was also a lot like Sark. Perhaps there's something in the way small islands speak to us, something that connects their visual language and geography irrespective of latitude and climate. Of course there were differences. No giant marsupial rats, for a start. Delft is built not of pottery as one might wish but it is built of dead coral. Great lumps of it making everything from dry-stone field and garden walls to churches and forts. It doesn't look anything like anywhere else in Sri Lanka. One piece of coral stands about six feet high and is revered as it is apparently growing by itself. Carved deities, incense burners and coloured cloths sit on and around it. We were bounced around the island in a converted pickup truck, stopping to admire a baobab tree; a ruined and atmospheric British hospital with a Dutch pigeon cote in the back garden from a time when the birds were the only form of communication with the mainland; a Buddhist temple dating to the Anaradhapura kingdom when the whole island was for a relatively brief time Buddhist; an indent in the ground looking like a giant footprint said to have been made by Hanuman as he hopped across from India; the nearby remains of a hundred metre long building constructed by the Dutch simply to stable their vast collection of horses, then on to 'the wilderness' – a barren seaside plain populated by wild horses descended from the inhabitants of those stables and left behind when the Dutch abandoned Ceylon following its takeover by the British. Some of the horses appeared to have elaborately permed manes and looked quite fetching. Perhaps they shopped at the place on the road to Jungle Tide which advertises 'BRIDLE WEAR'.

The whistle-stop tour over, there were still two hours to kill before lunch and the return ferry so they took us to the beach. Small problem: no shade, nowhere to get anything to drink, no changing facilities or toilets. We and a few other hapless tourists moped disconsolately around for a while then asked our drivers to take us back into town, 'town' being a relative term on Delft as the only settlement is the size of a small village by the ferry dock. Here we managed to kill the remaining time in a café where no-one spoke any English, then in the other café where we had booked lunch, which was actually rather good. Then off to the jetty to claim first place in the queue and prime seats on the return boat, due to leave at two thirty. A jolly-looking waterfront bar turned out to be exclusively for the Navy. Next to it a building declared itself to be the 'Naval Sewing Centre'. I'm still trying to work out what might go on in there now that sail has given way to steam. Maybe it's where the horses come to have their manes touched up.

There were a couple of false starts as groups of Sri Lankans pushed past us and on to the jetty. Thinking they were the usual queue-jumpers we tried to race them only to be turned back by the Navy. These were not returning tourists but the WAGs of naval personnel off on a jolly on a gunboat. Among the many boats tied up at the quay in various stages of dereliction and seaworthiness one had attracted my camera's attention earlier. It was a large open boat whose wheelhouse was an elderly tuk-tuk roped across it towards the stern. A curiosity to photograph was all I'd thought. Until it emerged that this was our return transport. We all clambered aboard the hulk and arranged ourselves on the various planks serving as seats. The captain sat sidelong to the action in the tuk-tuk's driver seat, gazing out to sea and wearing a headset, though whether this was anything to do with running the ship or just his personal in-boat entertainment system I couldn't be sure. It was equally unclear whether the two guys in the passenger seat behind him were the bosun, first mate, purser or cabin boy, or just his friends, or even the first two passengers to clamber aboard who grabbed the only upholstered seating in the boat. Although thunderclouds menaced in the distance the sea remained obligingly calm and we made it back to Punkudutivu without mishap. I couldn't remove an imbecilic grin from my face for the whole bizarre trip.

War memorials

We'd arrived in Jaffna by the relatively little-used coast road from Mannar; stretches of recently applied tarmac frequently interrupted by lengths of dirt-track where a blown-up bridge waited to be replaced and a diversion took us over the river on a few concrete pipes. We returned south on the A9 through the famed Elephant Pass where a long causeway and bridge connects the almost-island of the Jaffna region to the main part of Sri Lanka. Elephant Pass was of great strategic importance during the war and two contrasting memorials stand at either end. To the north is the war memorial itself which tells how former President Mahinda Rajapaksa beat the Tamil Tigers almost single-handedly with just a little help from one of his brothers who happened to be Defence Minister. Oh, and a few words are added about how nice it would be if everyone lived in peace and harmony. I know history is written by the victors but this is a particularly crass example and leaves a nasty taste in the mouth.

At the southern end of the causeway, by the new train station, stands a more interesting and more touching memorial. The eye-catching bit is not the statue of the soldier whose self-sacrificial gallantry is commemorated (Corporal Gamini Kularatne) but what stands in front and to one side of it: the rusted and shell-pocked remains of the strange Tamil Tiger vehicle he disabled – a converted armoured bulldozer which, armed and packed with explosives, was trundling towards the strategic army base before Cpl. Kularatne managed to climb aboard and throw a couple of grenades into it, killing himself in the process. The event happened in 1991 but the memorial is of course post-war. It records that the soldier was posthumously awarded Sri Lanka's equivalent of the Victoria Cross by the President. The President's name is not recorded, since it was not Rajapaksa.

Chewy as it is for us pacifists to swallow, it is an unfortunate fact that war (or the preparation for imagined future wars) acts as midwife to a lot of technology which may be adapted for more peaceful uses. And that's true of both conventional warfare – radar and the internet both come to mind – and less conventional conflicts such as the civil war in Sri Lanka, although here it is more likely to be intermediate or alternative technology. There is no doubting the resourcefulness of the Tamil Tigers whatever view one may take of their aims or morality. They had field artillery, a miniature air force, converted bulldozers to tanks as we have seen, and a navy, known as the Sea Tigers. In 2006 the Sea Tigers captured a Jordanian freighter, the *Farah III*, which had anchored off Mullaitivu with engine trouble. Having conveyed the crew to safety (the LTTE were merciless with their Sinhalese foes and with Tamils who disagreed with them but had no quarrel with foreigners) they raised the anchor and let the ship run aground, where they began by nicking its cargo of rice and other goods. Then they systematically stripped it of everything of value to be turned into military hardware. The skeletal remains of the ship stood on the beach for years after the war ended – and feature as the cover photograph of John Gimlette's wonderful book *Elephant Complex.* I was very keen to see and explore it but turned up a year too late. What was left of the ship had been sold for salvage and removed. It had become something of a tourist attraction and we were told that the Government was worried that this may lead to it becoming a kind of shrine to the Sea Tigers.

Strange, then, that the Sea Tigers' dockyard 'museum' remains open close by, though it's hard to find. As museums go it has to be one of the oddest. Head south east down the A35 until you pass another contender for the world's most tasteless war memorial – a phenomenally ugly and garish erection featuring raised guns flanking the Sri Lankan flag – then look for a red dirt track on the left with a small sign indicating 'Sea Tiger Museum'. If you then take the correct fork in the road (unsigned but pssst, it's the one on the right) you emerge into a yard with a lone soldier standing sullenly and wordlessly in a kind of home-made sentry box. Ranged around the edges of a dirt yard the size of a football pitch are the war-damaged remains of what I gather was only a small part of the Tigers' sea power, ranging from a converted jet ski up to quite sizeable fast launches. This being Sri Lanka I was most disappointed not to find an armoured swan pedalo among them. But it's the submarines that grab the attention, from one-man jobs not fully submersible to a full-sized vessel under construction when time was called on the Tigers' war effort. At the far end is a test and launch tank whose gates once led into the ocean. Information is minimal and the soldier speaks no English but even in such an off the beaten track visitor attraction the local nose for a tourist proved to have its usual sensitivity. We'd been there maybe twenty minutes when a lad with a refrigerated box on the back of a small motorcycle rolled up. "Ice cream? You like ice cream?" We did. It was astonishingly hot and the container promised choc ices which we selected. "You have chocolate ice cream?" "Yes, Madam. Chocolate have". A rummage in the box led to a revision of this statement. "Sorry, only orange have". "OK, then, five orange ice cream". Who cares? Anyway, we'd probably have rewarded him for his entrepreneurship if he'd been selling sand. Sadly the 'orange' iced lollies were fluorescent pink and tasted abominable. I ate three of the five (I hate waste), we gave one to the soldier and our driver ate his own uncomplainingly.

Batticaloa

For much of the time the war zone extended beyond the northern quarter, down the length of the east coast. The strategic military importance of Trincomalee meant that it and its surrounds and approaches remained mainly in Government hands though that did not prevent it from being a highly dangerous place to live for much of the war's twenty six year span. Not so Batticaloa, further south. It was 2014 before we made it there.

The Kinniyai ferry we encountered on our 2004 visit to the Ceylon Sea Anglers Club has been replaced by a bridge as have all the other river crossing points so the journey south from Trincomalee on the A15 to Batticaloa takes a fraction of the time it once did. On the way, a short detour off the main road, the burgeoning new resort towns of Passikudah and Kalkudah offer one vision of the post-war future for the east coast. Identikit luxury and semi-luxury multi-storey hotels weren't exactly our cup of tea and certainly had little Sri Lankan about them. But Passikudah is also a day-trip destination for the locals so the beachfront hotels rub shoulders with a more typically Sri Lankan assortment of ice cream sellers, purveyors of cheap inflatable toys and a beach café run by the army, all fringing a bus park with buses arriving from all parts of the island at weekends and holidays. *PROTECT THE ENVIRONMENT. DO NOT USE POLYTHENE IN THIS AREA* implores a battered sign, futilely. The beach itself is segregated. Masses of brown bodies frolic in the waves with luxury yachts moored just beyond them. On the other side of a fence the private beaches belonging to the hotels contain a much smaller number of people, mostly though not exclusively white. 1980s Cape Town it isn't – but the feeling of a kind of apartheid persists.

Like Jaffna, Batticaloa is still bringing up the rear as far as tourism goes. It has huge potential but no-one much seems interested in realising it. The town makes next to nothing of its magnificent Dutch fort. The famed singing fish are featured on the town's logo as well as in something called 'The Singing Fish Association of

Batticaloa' which sounds like a surrealist choir but seems to be a property development company. On Kallady Bridge, where the piscean vocalists congregate (allegedly) there are no signs, no guides or touts, nowhere to park and explore and certainly no boat trips on offer. Boat trips *are* available from a jetty on the seaward end of the lagoon, by the road out to the lighthouse, another building with unrealised visitor potential. Nothing is signed in English and nor do the operators have any real command of the universal language of tourism. We took a punt – excuse the pun – and went for a ride in one of their two boats (the other being yet another swan pedalo) which was fun but of limited value when the boatman could only communicate with us in gestures.

On our first visit to Batticaloa in 2014 the fort wasn't signed in any way. Sure, it was easy to spot in its prominent waterfront position but, as with Sigiriya, there was no indication of where the entrance might be. We found ourselves scrambling through a building site – the nearby law courts were being renovated and extended – and after a clamber over a particularly large pile of stones there was the entrance. Or at least *an* entrance. No sign, no ticket office and no charge, so in we went. Where we'd expected a military-looking central courtyard-cum-parade ground we were confronted with a higgledy-piggledy collection of buildings dating from the late nineteenth to mid twentieth centuries by the looks of them, and housing a bewildering variety of uses. Registry offices, local TV and radio stations, surgeries, notaries public, council depots, you name it, Batticaloa fort seemed to contain it. Still no signage or information to be had. We strolled disconsolately around for a while and were about to leave when a uniformed guy beckoned us over. Oops! Maybe we weren't allowed in here? But he merely indicated a flight of stairs we hadn't noticed and, speaking no English, pointed us upwards. Up to the spacious battlements, littered with rusting cannon, crumbling watchtowers – and litter. And crows. Hundreds of them. A murder is the collective noun for crows and if you wonder why, come to Batticaloa fort towards sunset. Flying in over the water, flapping on and above the walls, standing sentry on the watchtowers and commandeering the cannon barrels. Cawing fit to bust. It was all quite Hitchcockian but we made our way gingerly around the entire circuit of long-abandoned military hardware with its panoramic views across the lagoon, over the town and out to sea. There was no-one else around, it was fascinating if a little on the eerie side.

When we came again two years later with Merigen, Lucy and our two grandsons Finlay and Louis we'd discovered the main entrance, close by the stairway, so we headed in there after a brief refreshment stop at the nearby rest house, itself a curious time-warp of a place. Next to the arched gates was a shiny new sign which announced that in 2014, just a couple of months after our previous visit, the fort had been 'renovated and beautified'. A feeling of dread came over me. Had they cleared out all the random courtyard buildings? Had they painted the place? Built a visitor interpretation centre? And a souvenir shop? Of course not, this is Sri Lanka not England; this is Batticaloa not Galle. There was now a ticket office but there was no-one in it. The signs presumably indicating entry charges were in Sinhala and Tamil but not English. The courtyard buildings were still there though looking a little bit better maintained than I recalled. Nothing else had changed; not the staircase, not the battlements, not the cannon or structures on the walls. Certainly not the litter. Oh, except for the bird population. The crows had been replaced by a flock of over thirty white bellied fish eagles, wheeling around our heads in between forays out over the lagoon. Maybe it was just the time of day – midday rather than sunset when perhaps the crows resume air superiority. It was a welcome change whatever the reason.

But more fundamental change is a-coming, maybe. On our second visit to the fort we were not the only visitors. There was a Sri Lankan family and a group of Dutch tourists with a guide, who was proudly showing them an ancient 'Dutch cannon'. Since the rusted hardware still bore the insignia of Britain and the letters 'GR' as a patriot I had to intervene . And seaplanes from Colombo – three of them a day – now splash down on the lagoon and taxi over to a rickety landing stage. One suspects their occupants are mainly well-heeled tourists transferring to cars to take them up to Passikudah, but one can at least hope they might take the time for a quick look around Batticaloa on the way.

The end of the war in 2009 took us news-starved foreigners by surprise, but didn't come as a surprise to Sri Lankans who had been expecting it for months. And stockpiling celebratory fireworks accordingly. Ironically, according to a friend of ours, the photographer Stephen Champion who recorded so much of the horror of the civil war from start to finish, and who therefore should know what he's on about, the defeat of the LTTE was partly due to their decision to diversify from guerrilla attacks and suicide bombings into full-scale frontal assaults using their home-made military hardware. Taking on the Sri Lankan army in battlefield conditions amounted to a kind of fatal hubris; they could never hope to win a conventional war with unconventional weaponry. International events over which the LTTE had neither control, influence nor even interest, namely 9/11, then led to their being caught up in the widely spread net of the west's 'war on terror', proscribed and demonised by governments some of which had previously been vaguely sympathetic. The result was a drastic reduction of a great part of their foreign arms supplies and their foreign media influence. Defeat was only a matter of time. Though it still took another seven years. And the sheer bloody-mindedness of Rajapaksa who understood (rightly) that only overwhelming military force would defeat the Tigers and (wrongly) didn't care who else got hurt or killed in the process. So long as they weren't Sinhalese.

I never know what to make about the tendency some people have to diminish war: those people in Northern Ireland who refer to 'the troubles' or in Sri Lanka to 'problem time'. Is it an understandable reluctance to face up to the horrors, or, more positively, an attempt to move on? 'Problem time' to me is redolent of something like the washing machine breaking down and flooding the kitchen, not the deaths of thousands. "Now problem all gone, Sir" our Jaffna taxi driver had continued. "Now all good". Which it clearly is not. But if we pretend things are OK does that increase or decrease the likelihood that they will become so? Answers on a postcard.

Nine

Living the Dream – illegally

There is no way we can live legally in Sri Lanka and run our guest house. Indeed there was no way we could even live in England and visit Sri Lanka legally to run our guest house. I won't bore you with the details but the way Sri Lankan citizenship laws and visa categories are written precludes us. Being an optimist I believe that this is due simply to poor drafting and the lack of joined-up legislation. I think that despite our illegal status we're actually welcome here. But there is that scintilla of doubt, and if someone wanted to make our lives difficult they wouldn't have far to look for ways of doing so.

The first dead-end street we explored was trying to get dual nationality for Sally who was born in Colombo as was her grandfather. This would have conferred full rights on both of us to live in the country without restrictions on time, or on what we could and could not do, and without the need to pay fees or invest foreign currency. But a Sri Lankan-born foreigner seeking dual citizenship has to demonstrate either that there is Sri Lankan blood in their ancestry or that three successive generations were born in Sri Lanka. None of Sally's ancestors married a Sri Lankan or – to the best of her knowledge – fathered any babies with a Sri Lankan on the wrong side of the blanket. Crucially, her grandmother decided that it would be safer to take a sea voyage to England in 1915, braving the attentions of U-boats as well as storm and tempest, than to give birth in Ceylon. An interesting decision which says much about colonial attitudes but which also, as an accidental by-product, deprived her future granddaughter of the right to dual nationality. Sally's grandfather was born and died in Sri Lanka. Her father came to Sri Lanka as a babe in arms and lived there until the age of fifty six, but this cuts no ice with the Sri Lankan authorities.

Other cul-de-sacs we explored were registering our business with the Board of Investment (Nope –although we've invested far more than the minimum requirement we had to have done this all in one go, not spread out over ten years); joining a scheme run by the Tourism Development Authority for the owners of small guest houses (Nope – even the owners of small guest houses are expected to have £50,000 in spare foreign currency to put into a Sri Lankan bank and not touch – we don't). The third route was the 'My Dream Home' scheme aimed at retired people and requiring a more modest £10,000 or so to be invested, which we could just about scrape together. This seemed to be the answer, but the information on the government website was unclear. It forbade people entering under the scheme to take on any employment, paid or unpaid, but did running our own business constitute 'employment'? We tried e-mailing the immigration department via their website with the anticipated lack of any response.

For some years we'd been members of the UK-based Friends of Sri Lanka Association and their secretary kindly agreed to circulate a letter from us setting out our dilemma about how we could legally move to live in Sri Lanka to run our Sri Lanka-registered business, and asking for advice. We had several replies including one from a prominent Sri Lankan barrister practising in London who was amazed that Sally could not have dual citizenship. One Sunday morning we took a phone call from Lord Naseby, who chaired the parliamentary all-party committee on Sri Lanka. He offered to sound out various members of the great and the good on our behalf. Once we had convinced ourselves that it was the good lord himself and not some practical joker we were genuinely grateful but declined as we didn't want to make waves. But three were from British expats living in Sri

Lanka on the 'My Dream Home' scheme and all told us that the scheme did allow for people like us to run their own small business. The intention of the legislation was simply to prevent foreigners taking local jobs. We were doing the opposite – providing employment to local people – and we would be welcomed, they assured us. So that's what we did. There were the usual bureaucratic hurdles to jump over, nets to climb and tunnels to crawl through but the assault course which we started in Britain was eventually completed several months later, a week after we'd arrived in Colombo in October 2015. And we duly received two-year Residence Visa stamps on our passports. Which read in part: '...so long as the holder does not engage himself/herself in any employment paid or unpaid *or in any business* ...'.

By then we had no home in Britain and our worldly goods were on the high seas aboard the *Maersk Enfield*. I mused about why a foreign shipping company would name its vessels after obscure London boroughs until it dawned on me that it was possibly named after a rifle. Or a motorcycle. The crew who had packed up our things in Stonesheygate seemed more Sri Lankan than Yorkshire despite their accents; they worked merrily and hard but without any attempt at communication with us. "You've missed this" I pointed out, carrying down the stairs a *barong* – a large machete in a carved wooden sheath, a present some years back from Sally's brother Kim in the Philippines, and a potentially prized garden tool for Jungle Tide which had already proved its worth on my Yorkshire allotment. "No, mate, can't take that. It's a weapon". "No it's not. It's a gardening tool." "Customs won't see it that way. Take it from me, it's not worth the risk". There was no point in arguing, and he was probably right. We'd brought it in from the Philippines on a plane in our hold luggage years before with no questions asked, but shipping is different, and maybe times have changed. So the *barong* had to be left behind.

Our home and twenty years of our lives in it steadily emptied. Tea and sympathy were provided by our lovely neighbour Caroline. Sally was distraught as we pulled out onto the road, car heavily laden with things to leave at her brother Jeremy's from whose home in Kent we'd be making our final trip to Heathrow a couple of days later. Being slow on the uptake it didn't hit me until we were halfway down the M1. What on earth had we just done? Was I right in the head?

Planes are somewhat quicker than ships so our belongings were not due to dock in Colombo for five weeks after we arrived. Which was fortunate given the procedures we had to follow to re-engage with our worldly goods. As ever, the Sri Lankan company handling things at this end kept changing the rules about what paperwork and bank guarantees were required so we were kept on our toes, and kept waiting for almost a week in Colombo. No-one seemed to know the whereabouts of the *Maersk Enfield* other than its due date of arrival. Even that couldn't be confirmed. We knew the day after was a *poya* day so unless it arrived early customs would not be dealing with our goods for two days. It was three days after the good ship docked and five days spent kicking our heels in a Colombo apartment before anything of ours could be unloaded and inspected. Then Maersk dropped a bombshell and said they had not been provided with the correct paperwork by the company who organised our shipping so our container could not be unpacked. We had visions of it roaming the high seas indefinitely. It all turned out to be a communications problem and was resolved after another two days' wait. Then a hefty payment to customs for things never specified (there's no point in arguing about this stuff, we decided) and finally our belongings were packed into two big vans for the journey up to Jungle Tide.

The week in Colombo had included Sally's first birthday in Sri Lanka – well, the first since her thirteenth, anyway. A bit of a non-event, just the two of us, but we did splash out on a meal at the *Ministry of Crab*, where one eats nothing but crustaceans of all conceivable sizes, and the customers are provided with large plastic bibs. I felt we should all have been seated in giant high chairs to pull off the full effect. I would certainly have enjoyed screaming at the top of my lungs and throwing cutlery and claws onto the floor. Very yummy, very costly. It's owned by two former Sri Lankan cricketers – Jayawardene and Sangakkara.

We'd closed the guest house for the week it took to unpack and sort out our former lives, bits of Yorkshire erupting into Sri Lanka, transforming a smart but minimalist house into a family home under the intrigued gazes of Mervyn and Rushi as a succession of weird pictures, housewares, utensils and even weirder foodstuffs emerged from the chaos of packing crates. Not to mention the many boxes of Christmas decorations we'd brought out.

Jungle Yuletide

And before we knew it Christmas was upon us. It doesn't start quite as early here as in the UK but the great festival of commerce is just as enthusiastically celebrated in this Buddhist land. By the end of November the shops are full of decorations and cake-making ingredients and soon afterwards the checkout girls don Santa hats. That's the signal for carols and schmaltzy songs to take over the shopping mall public address systems. Inflatable Santas for some reason tooting inflatable saxophones stand on street corners. Fake snow covers the floors of banking halls and shop windows are frosted in the corners or have plastic icicles hanging from their top edges. Something we'd discovered the previous year, on our final visit in November and early December, was that it is cheaper to post Christmas cards to the UK from Sri Lanka than it is to post them internally in the UK. Not many people know that.

At Christmas the house was taken over by an exceptionally cheery three-generation family distributed between Australia and Scotland. We'd been naturally worried that we'd have a miserable first Christmas away from our own family but this lot put paid to that concern. Their infectious enthusiasm was apparent even before they arrived. Unusually they'd decided to hire a big van and drive themselves; a rash move in Sri Lanka and not for the faint-hearted. More rashly still they'd trusted heir satnav to get them to Jungle Tide. We were in the echoing cavern of Kandy train station when we took a call on the mobile: "We think we're getting close, but we just wanted you to tell us the last bit of the way from the Post Office." "What, Kandy Post Office? We're standing opposite it right now." "No, Uduwela Post Office." "Uduwela doesn't have a Post Office." "Yes it does, we've just passed it. There's a sign on it saying 'Uduwela Post Office'." "What road are you on? Have you passed the Tea Museum? You need to be on the Hanthana Road." "No, we didn't see any museum. We took the Kandy by-pass." "Kandy doesn't have a by-pass. We can't work out where you are." "Our satnav says it's less than a kilometre to Jungle Tide." "Satnav! What are you using satnav for? It will take you up roads you can't manage unless you're driving a tank. What about the directions we sent you?" "We thought it would be quicker to avoid Kandy as the traffic there's so bad." "It certainly is, but at least the roads have tarmac on them." "Never mind, we're so close now we'll get there somehow."

And get there they did, completely unfazed by the experience. We'd decided to attempt an English Christmas in the tropics, or as close as we could get to one. Some compromises would be necessary. Sally had made the cake, the pudding and many jars of mincemeat before we left Yorkshire and we'd shipped them out. But our other traditions – salmon and a ham on Christmas Eve, and half an ox for Christmas dinner – were going to be more of a challenge. And of course we could forget the parsnips, chestnuts and Brussels sprouts. Most people would prefer to forget the sprouts anyway.

Salmon, too, was quickly abandoned. It's virtually unobtainable outside Colombo and the price is extortionate; there are no local alternatives. Whole hams – smoked or unsmoked – were advertised in Keells supermarket, though not displayed. They had to be ordered in from Nuwara Eliya, home of everything in Sri Lanka considered 'exotic' (meaning carrots, leeks, turnips, cabbages – well, in the tropics such plain European fare is indeed as exotic as, say, mangoes in Britain). "Is the smoked ham cooked or uncooked?" enquired Sally. "Madam, I do not know" came the uncharacteristically honest reply. We bought one anyway. After four visits it had still not turned up at the store. "Madam, I will deliver it personally on Sunday" said the person in charge of the meat counter, grovelingly. It would certainly need to arrive before Christmas Eve which was another *poya* day so no meat could be purchased. Though the turkey would probably be OK. Poultry are regarded by Buddhists as a kind of flying vegetable (and fish as swimming vegetables) and hence not subject to religious restrictions. We did get it, finally, on the twenty third. It looked cooked but when we cut into it we soon found it wasn't. There was just time to boil it for several hours before preparing it for its final roasting. And though the taste didn't compare to a proper English ham it was perfectly OK.

The beef had been abandoned in favour of an easily available turkey. Buying beef in Sri Lanka is a hit-and-miss affair. They hang the beasts, lights and all, on fly-infested market stalls and charge the same price per kilo irrespective of what bit of the animal you want. Which would be great – to buy rib, or fillet, at the same price as shin – if they had any notion of butchery. But they don't. Our method of buying beef is to get five kilos of randomly selected anatomy, take it home and butcher and sort it ourselves ranging from bits you might just about consider using as steaks through tasty pieces for stew and curry, to other bits that go through our mincer, down to the remainder to be boiled up for the dogs. Good fun, but not for Christmas. You can buy beef in the supermarkets but only either minced or cubed for curry. What they do with the more toothsome bits of the animal remains a mystery. Maybe the President gets to distribute them personally.

But the challenge of sourcing meat paled beside the difficulties of getting a tree. Ironically a large pine forest dominates the hillside to the east of Jungle Tide, but a tree is for timber, not just for Christmas, to paraphrase. Sally insisted on one suitably big to grace our high-ceilinged living room. "Christmas tree can get in Nuwara Eliya, Sir" Martin assured us. But he appeared not to know where and a potential six hour wild goose chase in an expensive hired vehicle big enough to take a tree which met Sally's exacting criteria for size and shape didn't seem sensible. The internet was of no help. We asked around various local expats we'd begun to know but they either didn't bother with a tree or had an artificial one they pulled out each year or were of the 'Bah! Humbug!' persuasion. We spread the dragnet to Colombo where friends told us you could buy a real tree, but they were not on sale until the twenty third. Too late – we'd be far too busy with guests by then to have time to erect and decorate a tree. With a heavy heart Sally conceded that we would have to buy an artificial tree. Off to Arpico, home of all things plastic.

There was only one tree of suitable size on display so we asked to buy it. "Madam, this tree already sold" came the reply. "But there is no sign saying it is sold! Why is it still on sale?" "Madam, I will enquire". Ten minutes later: "Madam, I have spoken to the man who has bought the tree, He does not want it. He says you can have it." So we took it back to Jungle Tide, unpacked it and tried to set it up. With hindsight it was probably due to our incompetence that the thing looked a dreadful sight (there were no instructions) but we decided it was a faulty product and took it back; Arpico willingly returned our money but it seemed that Christmas would have to take place without a tree.

But Martin would have none of such defeatist talk. "I will go to Colombo and find tree. Tomorrow morning early, come back evening time." We gave the go-ahead for him to hire a van and he'd left before dawn. Throughout the day he kept in touch, explaining the various false leads he'd been given on a motorised tour of greater Colombo, everyone saying they had no tree but of course everyone knew someone else who did. Eventually late in the evening he located a tree which he pronounced to be of suitable size so we told him to buy it and we'd pay for him to spend the night in Colombo and come back the next day. But no, he strapped the tree to the van roof and drove through the night back to Jungle Tide, getting a police fine on the way for having a dangerous load. I got up at first light to find a van carrying an outsize fir tree parked by the front door; Martin had gone to grab a couple of hours' sleep.

It was not by any stretch of the imagination a Christmas tree. But it was a pine tree and when it was put up in a corner of the living room it almost reached the high ceiling. Once decorated it had a faintly haunted quality, a kind of Addams Family Christmas tree. It passed muster with the Aussies who said that their Christmas trees looked pretty similar; the Scots contingent were less impressed. Meanwhile the house, the veranda and the *nelli* and guava trees around the lawn had been lit and decorated and we had lit the 'circus' with fairy lights. Some years before we had had a set of forty eight steps built as a quick way between the lawn by the house and the lower gardens and swimming pool. Martin had phoned to tell us the good news:

"Madam, now circus have. Big circus in garden." We gulped. What on earth did he mean? It was weeks before we came to realise that he meant 'staircase'.

We'd started using volunteers to do various mostly garden jobs and one young lad, Dan, stayed almost to Christmas. He could climb trees like a monkey and managed to rig up a spectacular lightshow in the *nelli* and Chinese guavas in front of the house. Though it was I who had to take the rig down on Twelfth Night, which I eventually managed with bamboos and the garden rake, my tree-climbing days having long since passed.

Christmas Eve was warm and clear. We and our Scotstralian guests sat out on the lawn after dinner with tumblers of scotch, looking up at the Milky Way. The guests spent much of Christmas Day wearing silly hats and playing croquet on our bumpy lawn. We were exhausted and cooked-out but well content with our first Christmas at Jungle Tide.

New Year's Eve was both less fraught and less exciting. Our only guests were a lovely British family who unfortunately had to leave at 5am on New Year's Day to head for the airport and their flight home. Nonetheless Dad and one of the children bravely stayed up to midnight and sang *Auld Lang Syne* with us. This was also our first encounter with the deadly, noisy and none-too-colourful Sri Lankan fireworks, and a few others could be heard banging away from the direction of the village. One of the big hotels in Kandy was holding a proper display but too far away for us to see.

Hard work

"What will you find to do when you get out there?" was a question asked by several friends in England. As they saw it, we were moving to live in a tropical paradise with servants waiting on us hand and foot. And up to a point that's true. I'm not allowed to do the laundry or the ironing – both jobs I enjoy – and can only occasionally manage a stint at the equally enjoyable activity of washing dishes when Rani is out gardening and I can duck under her radar. Yes, I know you probably think all that's bullshit but it's true. Rani and Martin also cover many of the things I like less, including cleaning, bed-making and DIY. But we're as busy as we ever were when working full time. Just running the business takes silly amounts of time, plus we like to offer guests a choice of Sri Lankan cooking at which Rani excels, or western food which we do – for kids, spice-phobics, or people who've already spent two weeks in the island eating nothing but rice and curry and really fancy a shepherd's pie.

When Sally was young her parents had between six and ten staff, which was seen as normal for a family in a three bedroomed bungalow. We had two to run a four bedroomed guest house as well as look after us. But taming three acres of garden is beyond us and them. Martin looks after the pool and tackles the worst of the encroaching jungle when at least one of his growing collection of substandard Chinese brushcutters works. Rani makes big efforts to grow flowers around the house and keep the lawn looking good. Anything English, preferably planted in military formation, is her preferred gardening style which Sally is slowly trying to erode. Though we did have another linguistic phone episode a couple of years ago when Martin proudly announced that "Rani now putting rice everywhere. All gardens now too much rice Madam!" We knew that in Martin-speak "too much" simply means "a lot". "Now too much rain coming" is good news after a drought, for instance. But we didn't fancy living in a paddy. What was all this rice business about? It finally dawned on us that for them 'rice' is a generic term for 'seeds'. We need not have worried. Rani had simply been sowing quantities of marigolds and nasturtiums.

Though we've since taken on another full-time worker, Noni, from the local village as the guest house has become busier we still lacked the time to create a much-needed kitchen garden as well as improving some other areas of our jungle-covered land which had great potential. Then Sally had an idea: "How about seeing if we can get some volunteers?" "Why would anyone volunteer to help us? We're not a good cause" I replied. "That's not the point" she patiently explained. "They volunteer so they can see the world on a limited budget, not to be good citizens of Toytown. We feed and house them, they help us out." "OK, so how do we go about finding a volunteer or two?" Sally as ever was a couple of steps ahead. She'd found two websites where we could advertise and – joy of joys – it was the poor volunteers who had to pay to have their profiles published. We hosts could just use it for free. I couldn't very well disagree so she went ahead. And two days later reported that six people had already signed up.

Our first volunteers were a Czech couple, Martina and David. "What are their profiles like?" I asked Sally. "They're vegetarians, into yoga and meditation, interested in Buddhism" she answered. "God, no!" I groaned. "We're going to have to eat veggie mush with them all the time and be treated to little homilies about how we should live and the evils of drink. I'd rather do the garden myself. And you can count me out of any yoga sessions." "OK, if you want to do everything yourself, good luck. I'm sure you can manage three acres." Point taken, as usual. And as usual I was wrong in my off-the-cuff assessment of people. Martina and David proved to be remarkably normal and had an English vocabulary which extended well beyond droning "ommmm" all the time as I'd half expected. Shared my love of word games, pretty much shared my views on the world – and worked like two demons. David is probably the physically strongest guy I've ever come across but Martina – tall and built like a supermodel – also proved to be an enthusiastic user of the pick and *mamoty* (mattock), which she used to wield clad in a bikini until we politely suggested that the owners of the chicken farm next door might resent their male workers spending all their time peering over our fence.

Since then more than fifty volunteers have passed through Jungle Tide. They have come from all the expected places – UK, USA, mainland Europe, Australia – and from a lot of unexpected ones – Vietnam, Colombia, Iran, South Africa, China, South Korea. One has even been a Sri Lankan. They have built walls, flights of steps, a pond, fences, compost bins and a chicken shed and yard. They have painted rooms, fixed wonky doors, put up shelves and filled cracks in walls. They have created raised beds, weeded, kept the jungle tide at bay, and climbed trees to pick mangoes, soursops, avocados and star fruit before the monkeys got to them. They often bring with them added extras such as helping us with IT problems, taking professional standard publicity photos and making a short video for our website. One was a trained French *patissier* who put on the most splendid breakfast for everyone one morning. Another an experienced cocktail chef who helped make Sally's second birthday back in Sri Lanka somewhat more enjoyable than her first. They're tremendous company and we get to spend evenings playing parlour games just like we used to with our family and friends in Stonesheygate. It's like having all your grown-up kids back, except all they want to do is to be useful.

Never a dull moment

"Aren't you going to be bored? Will you have any social life?" was another FAQ from some of our British friends before we moved here. We're never bored. Far from it – we relish the occasional evening when there is just the two of us in the house. Most of the time we have guests to spend evenings socialising with – and volunteers at the times of year when guests are few and far between. Most of our guests are Europeans and either speak English as their first language or are utterly fluent. With a constantly changing cast of characters we get into more fascinating conversations than we ever did when living in England and working and socialising with the same relatively small crowd of people – wonderful though they are. Of course the downside is not having anyone around permanently we can start to develop a deeper relationship with and rely on. And as I've already related we do get very occasional guests who are more trouble than they're worth.

Jungle Tide is not everyone's cup of green tea. Some guests really should have read the large print, let alone the small print. "We hadn't realised you were not in Kandy." "How far is the local supermarket?" "We can't pay you now as we've run out of cash – is there an ATM in the village?" "We didn't know about the bad road." So exactly whose website were you looking at when you booked your stay with us? One large extended family of Russians who booked the whole house for three days spent the entire time sitting in the lounge watching TV on Sinhala channels they couldn't understand, smoking and drinking vodka. They did venture once to the swimming pool but didn't think much of it. In their Trip Advisor review they complained that "the pool has a shallow end and a deep end. This is dangerous for my grandmother." We've had Muslims who expect other guests not to use the pool when their womenfolk are in it; Sri Lankans who treat Martin and Rani as their personal servants: "Bring me a glass of water"; and people of all faiths and nationalities who expect Rani to act as a free nanny and us to act as surrogate grandparents to their children while they relax and have a good time. But I'm not going to say any more about them. I'd rather concentrate on the truly lovely guests.

Such as John and Anna. John and Anna Boyd-Moss used to be planters in Ceylon/ Sri Lanka and still plant in Kenya despite John being well into his eighties and Anna not that much younger. Like all the other ex-planters who've stayed, John was horrified by the parlous state of the local tea and began fomenting plans to start a small specialist production scheme. His philosophy is pretty much that if you keep on trying new things you stay alive longer and I say Amen to that. At the time of their visit we had a bunch of volunteers working in the vegetable garden and John went with me to have a look. Within minutes he was showing the volunteers how to use a *mamoty*. Meanwhile Anna was up on the lawn with Sally and said she couldn't possibly sit and watch while other people worked and how about giving her a hand-fork and letting her weed the rockery. People like John and Anna are my role models as I get older – it used to be singer-songwriters and political activists, but there you are.

And the Popsicles – a wordplay on their real name – an extended family of New Yorkers hailing originally (most of them) from Romania who made our second Christmas at Jungle Tide if anything even more memorable than the first one. Particularly as Jemima and her partner Ed were also staying with us. More silly hats, more silly games. Singing English, American and Romanian carols. But above all having four children who gave Santa the opportunity he'd been waiting for to drop in on Jungle Tide. I have a bad habit of christening most of our guests with an alternative punning name before they arrive, in the firm hope and expectation that Sally will forget and address them as such. So far I haven't scored, but give me time.

Our local friends, volunteers and guests all bring us fun and enlightenment, and sometimes inspiration. But nothing compares to having your family visit. Before Jemima came for Christmas Merigen, Lucy and our two grandchildren Finlay and Louis spent a month with us in July and August 2016. Louis had his third birthday at Jungle Tide and Sally was not to be denied this possibly final chance of laying on a full-blown kids' party. A Dutch couple staying with us kindly donated their two children for the occasion; Martin and Rani rounded up the kids who live at the chicken farm; and we knew a couple in town who run a children's charity and they came with their own two small children.

Parties for three year olds can be daunting, and when only two of the eight children present have English as their first language, four can understand it a bit and two not at all things can get very interesting. But Sally, resourceful as ever, came up with a series of non-linguistic games tried and tested on Jemima many years ago: pennies (rupees) scattered on the lawn just to be found and collected and kept (to the amazement of the chicken farm kids who kept trying to give the money back to us); pin the tail on the donkey (monkey); pass the parcel; and the marvellous Jar Game. This highly adaptable game, which can be played by three year olds or graduate students depending on the complexity of the category chosen, consists of concealing a series of glass jars each representing a category. Each participant is given a slip of paper (in this case a coloured shape) with their initial on the back and has to find the corresponding jar and drop it in, before returning for their next random slip of paper. The winner is the one whose initials appear most in the correct jars when counted up at the end. It starts slowly and builds to a great crescendo when everyone has found where all the jars are hidden and is racing to maximise their score. For three year olds different coloured shapes work well, but you can play the game using the names of authors on the jars and titles of their works on the slips of paper, for example. Finally, more dangerous Sri Lankan fireworks and plenty of silly gifts and sweets in party bags to end the day.

Incidentally, the traditional game of 'pin the tail on the donkey' has, as I later discovered, a Sri Lankan equivalent called 'Elephant Eye'. I was out for a walk with a group of friends when we came across the sounds of a local village festival. In one corner a man was blindfolding children, turning them around several times and arming them with a marker pen. Their mission was to find the whiteboard hung from a nearby tree on which was drawn the crude outline of an elephant, and to make a mark where the eye should be. The intervention of a few inquisitive *sudus* was an opportunity to make gentle fun of us all and I rashly offered to go first. The MC, who had evidently been hitting the arrack, tied the blindfold and whirled me around several times. I thought I'd remembered which direction I would be facing but couldn't have been more wrong. With a lot of steering from the villagers I did eventually find the whiteboard, but I didn't exactly cover myself with glory in this children's game.

Conned

In the year since we moved to Jungle Tide the number of guests, and hence the income, has doubled. Unfortunately so have the costs, so we're still only breaking even. Some of that has been improvements and a backlog of maintenance that greeted us when we came out from England. But some is simply down to our own gullibility in the face of Sri Lankan builders and tradesmen, police and authorities, and in one case an extraordinarily charming con-man.

We should have seen him coming. After all, we'd both just read Jon Ronson's *The Psychopath Test* and he ticked all the boxes available to us to spot: low boredom threshold, high activity level, loquacious, impulsive. But although as a confidence trickster his life is lived through lies, nothing he said during the five days he spent with us was known to me to be false. On the contrary he had an encyclopaedic knowledge of topics from US politics to Sri Lankan geography and history to gem stones. All subjects which Sally and/or I know a fair bit about and everything he said about them was true. Like all conmen he exuded charm and was highly entertaining company. And began by paying us upfront in cash for the two nights he'd originally booked although we normally take payment on checkout. To instil confidence, of course, we see now.

Joe Samarasinghe turned up with a companion, Agna, a solo traveller he'd met in a Mirissa hostel. Joe's story was that he worked for Maersk line as a first mate and had come ashore in Colombo for a couple of days before going on to Singapore. He'd gone down the coast to Mirissa, got drunk at a beach party and had his passport stolen. He claimed to be a US citizen having been born in a small town in Alabama to Sri Lankan expat parents (the small Alabama town even checked out). His captain told him to stay in Sri Lanka to get his passport sorted out and then fly to rejoin the ship in Singapore. He embellished his story with lots of detail about the workings of container shipping in general and the Maersk line in particular. Although we know next to nothing about either subject the level of unnecessary detail he provided also served to make the story more plausible.

He'd visited Sri Lanka many times and seen all the usual sights and most of the less visited ones – all of which checked out with our knowledge. He and Agna were not in a relationship – he was just showing an impecunious traveller around Sri Lanka at his own expense because, he said, ship's officers had money to burn when they were in port due to their high salaries and the lack of anything much to spend it on while at sea. And he just loved what he'd read about Jungle Tide and was full of (real or pretended) admiration for what we'd achieved. We had two sets of other guests and everyone got on like a house on fire. Dinner times and pre-dinner drinks and chats on the veranda were hugely entertaining – exactly what our place is all about, we felt.

Having gained our confidence and interest Joe began stage two of his strategy – to make our dreams come true. We remarked that we'd once had plans to travel to live in Sri Lanka by ship but couldn't afford the costs so we ended up just flying here. No problem – Maersk captains have carte blanche to give free lifts to anyone they choose, he said, and he'd put in a word for us. When were we next planning to go to England? Just give him an approximate date and he'd find a ship to take us. As with most of our guests, he was fascinated by Sally's back story and when she got to the bit about rescuing her mother's gems from the Standard Chartered Bank back in 1998 he revealed he dealt small-time in gems and could he take a look at those we still had? "Sure, but we've had them valued and they're worth very little". But he looked at them, commented knowledgeably about them and assessed their value significantly higher than we'd been told at the time – though not so high as to raise our suspicions and always with the caveat that he was no expert.

He added that he had some plans to buy stones while in Kandy and he arranged on his phone for a valuer to come up, partly to help him and partly to look at our little collection. What's more, he'd sorted for the guy to come with the captain of another Maersk ship due to dock the next day, Scott Morelli, another American who he'd been raving to online about Jungle Tide and who wanted to bring his wife Hannah and four year old daughter Sarah to stay a few days with us. And what's more still, having discovered our love of seafood and that being about the only thing that made us regret not living on the coast, he made more phone calls to his driver and arranged for him to pick up several kilos of lobster and assorted other denizens of the deep, pack them in ice in an Esky, and have the good sea captain bring them on up to us. He added that Scott was also a first-rate cook and loved nothing more than to rustle up a fine jambalaya. Our mouths watered at the prospect.

Through Martin he contacted a neighbour who had some land to sell and quickly struck a deal with her. All this dealing in land and gems, plus his desire to spend some time with Scott and his family, meant that he'd need to stay a little longer at Jungle Tide if we still had the room. We did. He said he'd spoken to Scott who would settle both bills up with us in US dollars if that was OK. Then Scott's problems started. His ship was due to dock early morning on 1st February and they were due here that afternoon. But then we heard that there was a backlog at the docks due to the road closures and congestion caused by rehearsals along Galle Face Green for Independence Day (National Day) on 4th February. Again, we knew from first-hand experience in previous years that the whole of Galle Face Green from the Galle Face Hotel up to Fort and the docks is taken over on 1st February for huge military rehearsals. Whether this has a knock-on effect on the operation of the Port of Colombo of course we didn't know, but it seemed plausible. Joe even told us the names of the two ships which had precedence over Scott's ship and was on his phone many times allegedly trying to arrange a launch to take Scott and his family off the ship and land them early as control of the vessel was now in the charge of the Colombo harbour pilot - another 'fact' which seemed plausible and may or may not have been true.

Eventually the ship was allowed to dock and we started receiving enthusiastic e-mails from Hannah looking forward to their visit. They were a day late but on their way, and could they stay an extra night at the end to make up for the night they'd missed? Certainly. Their expected arrival time came and went. Joe phoned and came back to say their driver had been stopped by the police for a minor traffic infringement but was being held for a while before they would be allowed to continue. Having experienced something similar with our own driver in Kandy only the previous week this again seemed entirely credible if frustrating. It's how the Sri Lankan police behave if you don't hand them a sufficiently large bribe. Then news came via Joe that little Sarah had had a massive allergic reaction to something she'd eaten and her face had swollen up. Hannah had decided to take her back to Colombo for hospital treatment. It was only then that we began to suspect all was not as it seemed, although Joe kept telling us what a stupid bitch Hannah was and she was panicking, but neither we, nor he, nor Scott could make her see sense. And we continued to believe him. At least we hadn't paid for the fish which would by now be pretty high. No-one was robbing us. But it was beginning to get fishy in every sense.

Not content with one set of victims Joe turned his attention to our other guests, a lovely couple from the Channel Islands who were thinking aloud about where to move on to from Jungle Tide. He recommended and then, using his credit card, booked them into a place near Habarana. Meanwhile he and Agna headed for the plush Kandalama hotel near Dambulla, planning to come back to Jungle Tide in a week or so to finalise the land deal. Later that day we took a phone call from our other guest Harry. "I'm afraid I've got some bad news" he said. "The place Joe recommended in Habarana is uninhabitable, half built, standing in a field with no staff on site. Can we come back to Jungle Tide?" "Sure, but we thought it had lots of good reviews. How come it's so bad?" "Well – are you sitting down? - the real bad news is that while we were trying to see how we could contact Joe on Facebook a message flashed up saying he's a con-man who uses various names and always has the same bogus story of working for Maersk, which he doesn't. Has he taken anything from you?"

A check of money, gems and other valuables and our on-line bank accounts quickly revealed that all was in place. We were still not sure whether the guy was genuine or not – after all, he'd paid us upfront for two nights and nothing had been stolen. And social media is full of lies and fake news. Moreover, if he'd ruined Harry's day, as he certainly seemed to have done, he hadn't personally profited by it as far as we could tell.

Agna was the next to get in touch. Had we seen Joe? He'd left saying he was coming back to the Kandalama but wasn't answering his phone and she hadn't seen him for hours. Meanwhile the Morellis had not arrived and hadn't been in contact since the morning. Early the next morning Joe's driver phoned from Colombo asking whether we knew where he was. He'd asked him to drive him from the Kandalama back to Colombo allegedly to meet up with Scott Morelli, had then got out and said he'd be right back, but had not reappeared. Needless to say Joe owed him a lot of money. Then Agna phoned again to say that Joe hadn't paid his bill at the Kandalama and they had also found he had absconded from the place

261

they'd stayed at in Mirissa without paying. Had he paid us? We told her he'd partly paid but owed us for three nights half board.

We e-mailed Hannah with our concerns and she, then Scott, replied that this was so out of character. They'd known Joe for more than ten years and he was a completely trustworthy guy. That was just too unbelievable and removed the final tiny slice of doubt we'd been harbouring that Joe was basically OK. Indeed we belatedly came to the obvious conclusion – that Scott and Hannah and little Sarah didn't exist and that it was Joe himself writing all those e-mails (sometimes from under our own noses out on the veranda).Captain Scott Morelli, eh? Captain Scott? Captain Corelli? Suddenly it all seemed to fit.

Oh well, we thought. We live and learn. What he'd paid us in cash pretty much covered the costs of the food he and Agna had had so we hadn't taken much of a blow financially. The Kandalama is big enough to shrug off the occasional bad debt. We did feel sorry for his driver. We felt sorry for our other guests but although Joe's activities had cost them money and grief he hadn't actually made any money from them. As for Agna, was she a victim or an accomplice? We still don't know. And the discussions about the gems had prompted us to get them properly valued sometime soon, while I had obtained some excellent material for this book. A score-draw, really.

We did feel concerned for our neighbour regarding the land deal and called Martin in to explain what had happened and to ask him to pass on the information to her that unfortunately she hadn't managed to sell the land. Martin's jaw dropped and he eventually found the words to explain to us that Joe had phoned him to say he had a short-term money problem and could Martin put Rs38,000/- into his bank account to pay for some gems he was buying? He would repay in cash as soon as he got back to Jungle Tide that evening. Martin, who is as honest as the day is long but way too trusting and hasn't the faintest clue about managing money, went off and borrowed the cash from his uncle with a promise of immediate repayment and put it into the account whose details Joe had texted to him. Joe had asked him "not to tell Madam as she will not like it." Too right!

That was just sickening. The other bits of the Psychopath Test, the bits we couldn't have spotted at the start, were now coming into play. Complete absence of empathy, lack of guilt or remorse. Until we heard Martin's story we were telling ourselves that we hadn't lost much money and that in a way we'd been rewarded for our slight financial loss by having a highly entertaining and knowledgeable guy with us for five days. We were pretty philosophical about it. Not any more. When we told the story to our friend Yvonne she said "I don't believe in violence but if I could get hold of that guy I'd tie him down in the long grass in a rainstorm and let the leeches at him." Amen to that.

A visit from the Excise

They turned up mid-morning, five of them. One in a khaki police uniform, four dressed in the unofficial uniform of black trousers and pale blue shirt that Sri Lankans who want to look important and official invariably adopt. Martin had let them in before we knew anything. "Can we help you?" we asked politely, assuming it was a visit in relation to the Joe Samarasinghe investigation (the Kandalama Hotel had reported the matter to the police and we had been mentioned among other victims). "Yes, please can you show us all the alcohol you have on the premises?" asked the guy in khaki. "Sorry, what's this all about?" "We are from Excise, we have to check on all hotels selling alcohol". "OK, there must be some mistake. We don't have an alcohol licence and we do not sell alcohol to our guests. Any alcohol is for our own use." "But this is a hotel, no? So we need to check you are not having too much alcohol on the premises." Stalling for time we asked if he had any ID. He pointed to an epaulette badge saying 'Excise': "This is my ID, you can see. Please show where you keep alcohol."

We explained again that all the alcohol was for our private use, that Jungle Tide was our home as well as being a guest house, and that aside from a couple of bottles in the fridge all was kept in our private study which was locked when we were not around. All of which was true but ignored by our visitors (the four in black and blue kept a morose and silent watch throughout). "Ah! This is more than ten litres of alcohol" said khaki man as he scanned our wine rack and a few bottles of beer and a bottle of gin standing next to it. "Ten litres is the maximum you can possess without a liquor licence."

I tried asking for chapter and verse on these regulations which no-one had brought to our attention in eight years of running the business or of buying wine online but that didn't go down well and things looked likely to turn nasty if I persisted. Sally took over, chatting amiably about her Sri Lankan heritage and I took the hint and shut up. But Khaki was not to be diverted by sweet talk and insisted that the law stated ten litres is the maximum amount of alcohol anyone can have even in a private residence. "We will have to confiscate the alcohol and you will have to appear in court in five weeks." "Hang on", I said. "Is that ten litres of beer, or wine, or arrack? These are very different, no?" This produced a "Shut up, Jerry" stage whisper from Sally and the bewildering response from Khaki that "all alcohol same, Sir. Beer, arrack, all same." He then appeared to be reconsidering, glanced at Martin, turned back to us and said: "But we cannot prosecute you as you are not Sri Lankan citizens. So we will prosecute this servant", indicating Martin. This was too much, even for Sally. "This is not his alcohol! He does not even drink any alcohol! This is not his house. You cannot prosecute him!" But Martin quickly interjected. "This all right Madam.

I go to court, pay fine, then you can pay the fine for me. Five thousand rupees, I think." We tried to dissuade him but he was adamant that this was the only way the guys were going to go away, and moreover they would leave us with ten litres of alcohol of our choice, plus any opened bottles.

So the 'deal' was struck and our visitors made off with several bottles of beer and some wine which they no doubt sold, leaving us with a bottle of gin and some bottles of wine. And Martin duly appeared in court a month later and was fined for possession of an illegal quantity of liquor. We paid his fine, his fares and his solicitor's fee. Meantime we had been to see a solicitor in Kandy. Ahamed Zain assured us that the Excise were acting beyond their powers and he would be willing to take a case against them on our behalf. But, he warned, although we should win in the end it would take a minimum of two years, the case would be repeatedly adjourned and we would be required to attend a reconvened hearing at a few days' notice even if we were out of the country at the time, and the legal costs would be prohibitive and probably not reclaimable even were we to win. Meanwhile we would make sworn enemies of the Excise and their police friends who could be relied on to harass us at every opportunity. The legal advice, in short, was crystal clear. Mr Zain gave us a photocopy of the relevant legislation which ran to some forty pages. When I got it home and read it there was of course not a single reference to either the stocking of alcohol in private homes or unlicensed guest houses or any limit on the amount of alcohol anyone could keep on their premises. The legislation is concerned entirely with companies which produce, distribute or sell alcohol, as one would expect.

Though it had its amusing aspects, the whole incident left a very nasty taste in our mouths. We had had first-hand experience of what we previously had only been told about –that the authorities in Sri Lanka make up the rules as they go along and are interested mainly in bribes. Indeed, we agreed later, if this were to happen to us again we would simply offer to pay the 'fine' direct to the Excise officer or police officer in question, since we assume that this was what he was after. Paying bribes sticks in the craw, but if you want to live in Sri Lanka it's a requirement every bit as much as having your visa stamped. The government claims to be cracking down on the culture of bribery and corruption. I'm not holding my breath.

What's yours?

The drinking culture in Sri Lanka is not one we in the west would recognise. The concept of social drinking is completely alien. Outside of the most westernised top echelons of society there are three stances people adopt towards alcohol. Many people are completely teetotal – far more than in the west. A larger proportion drink only rarely but when they do the object is to get absolutely slaughtered. Literally sometimes. Sally recalls in her youth seeing a man swig down an entire bottle of arrack and fall down dead. Martin – himself a teetotaller – showed utter amazement when he first saw us having an early evening G&T and putting the bottle back in the cupboard after one glass each. In Sri Lanka it is de rigueur to polish off a bottle once it has been uncorked. Then, finally and inevitably, there is a hard core of alcoholics as there is in pretty well every society. Women, other than a few top-enders, scarcely ever drink at all. But the burgher community has a reputation for serious drinking, a merry culture of regular alcohol abuse which is freely celebrated in various novels and memoirs. Railwaymen – who tend to be burghers – are particularly avid boozers.

Being seen buying alcohol in Sri Lanka compares roughly to being spotted going into an 'adult shop' on a British high street – or so I would surmise, not having frequented such shops. Honest. Outside of Colombo and the west coast the oddly-named 'wine stores' (they rarely sell wine and if they do you have the choice of their single bottle of red or their single bottle of white) keep their stocks behind metal grilles through which purchases and cash are passed through hand-sized holes. Fine (kind of) if you know exactly what you want to buy but if you wanted to inspect the many alternative arracks on offer it's a long process of fetching each one off the shelves for examination. Prices are rarely displayed. Wine stores all have fascia boards in the same shade of green, for reasons I've yet to discover. Is this colour of green representative of something evil in Buddhism maybe?

Kandy is the worst place in Sri Lanka to buy booze. There is only one place as far as I know where you can actually get up close, handle bottles and read labels and prices before deciding on a purchase, and that's some way out of town. There used to be another similar one near the Queens Hotel in the city centre but the monks said it was too near to the Temple of the Tooth and forced it to move into a dingy alley a couple of streets away. The Queens Hotel, which used to have two of the loveliest watering holes in town, can no longer serve alcohol to non-residents as it is across the road from the temple. Its colonial-style main bar serves non-alcoholic drinks only while the former 'Pub Royale' – a kind of sub-Wild West saloon – is now a dreary café but still looks exactly like a boozer. Thank goodness (or Bacchus) the glorious Royal Bar on King Street is still in business. The Buddhist establishment – nowhere more in evidence than in sacred Kandy – is easily offended by the thought of non-Buddhists doing their non-Buddhist things in public. For more than three weeks each year in the Perahera season, the entire city is out of bounds for alcohol sales or public consumption including in hotels and guest houses. That was one, albeit minor, reason why we chose to buy land outside of the Kandy city limits.

Once we managed to acquire some suitable fondue cheeses through some Dutch guests and, on a rare night when there were no guests or volunteers, we got out and de-cobwebbed the fondue set we'd brought from England. But we had no meths. We tried to explain to Martin what we wanted and to find out where we could get it, assuming it would be in one of the hardware stores in town. Eventually, after showing him a web page with a picture of a bottle of methylated spirit, a beam of understanding crossed his face, quickly replaced by a look of concern. "Ah! Wine spirit, Sir!" He told us of a shop in a back street where we could buy it but the look of concern only vanished when we explained we planned to burn it, not drink it. When we did eventually get hold of the stuff it was passed to us in a brown paper bag. Meths is sold only in two litre bottles – enough for about a thousand fondue meals – and the only people other than a handful of fondue-obsessed westerners who ever buy it are the local alkies.

Noni's house

Whether it's fair to regard builders, plumbers, carpenters and electricians as con-men is a moot point. In Sri Lanka as in the UK. They have certainly cost us a lot of unnecessary money but it's impossible to tell whether this is down to deliberate cheating or simple incompetence and lack of planning. Unreliable wi-fi, endless power outages, trees fouling cables, roof leaks, broken gutterings, water pipes that mysteriously become disengaged from one another, termites feasting on wardrobe bases, monkeys smashing roof tiles, road closures cutting us off from Kandy, locals stealing anything not nailed down, shoddily built step-ladders collapsing, volunteers puncturing submerged water pipes – lurching from one minor but unexpected problem to the next has become part of a costly way of life. But our little problems fade into nothingness compared to what happened to Noni, who works full time for us but lives in a nearby hamlet, not at Jungle Tide.

In May 2016 days of continuous torrential rain caused flooding and landslips across the hill country which made the international news agenda. Hundreds died and thousands were made homeless. Among the latter was Noni. Her cowshed and cow (our primary source of manure as well as her source of saleable milk) were swept away and her home damaged beyond repair. Noni is a widow with two children at school. She found temporary lodging with her sister's family but needed a permanent solution. So we decided to get involved.

Sally and I both had limited experience of crowd-funding when in the UK but were sceptical about the possibilities. We thought we'd give it a shot, anyway, so we launched a page on *Just Giving* with a target of £6,000, enough to build a decent quality modest home on a bit of land we could donate. And within a month the target had been exceeded. As well as people we knew dozens of former Jungle Tide guests whose names we only knew from e-mails and invoices chipped in, many of them very generously. To say we were moved is putting it mildly. Our builder Anton was also inspired: "Madam, I will build this house for only the cost of materials" he solemnly promised. "Also I will give fifty thousand rupees to your fund."
"Anton, are you sure?" "Yes, Madam and Sir. If these English people are giving money then we Sri Lanka people must also help. I will tell my people they must help you build Noni house."

269

So a chunk of our land became a building site, but first the requisite ceremonies had to be performed. The five corners of the new house site were marked out with stakes and lanterns of bamboo and palm leaves were placed at each apex with small candles. The auspicious hour was established by whatever mystical means are used for such calculations and the local astrologer was summoned to perform the ceremony. Obviously I didn't follow a word of it but just to be present in the half light of a rainy July morning with the leeches for company still felt like a huge privilege. At the end of the ceremony Anton handed his *mamoty* to Noni who raised it above her head and brought it down with great force to cut the first sod, then knelt in prayer. The symbolism, Anton explained later, was to hand over ownership of the site and the building project from the builders who had cleared the site to Noni, for whom his team would in a sense now be working.

No building project, large or small, goes smoothly. It's a law of nature. And inevitably, despite the generosity of our donors (some of whom also responded to a second appeal when the money ran out) it's cost us a lot. Taking the charitable view, Anton was guilty of massively over-promising on things he could not deliver or hadn't thought through, in particular the willingness of his crew to work unpaid. Less charitably, he used the project to obtain a lot of free timber from us and never had any intention of seeing it through to completion. He's now left the building trade and we no longer work with him. Which makes us sad. (Anton is not his real name).But the house was built and Noni and her children will live there rent free until the kids are grown up. At that point, we plan to give the house and land to Martin and Rani. They married late and have no children to support them when they get old. A house with a bit of garden including our productive clove trees and mulberries will make the difference for them between a comfortable life and one of poverty. They'll even have the room to take in paying lodgers if they want to. Knowing their generosity, though, they'll probably use it as free accommodation for some of Rani's inexhaustible supply of relatives.

At least the timber comes cheap. We have more than enough on site. Eucalyptus trees (locally called Turpentine trees on account of their flammability) grow two metres a year and need to be cut back frequently. Partly so we can maintain our wonderful views but also because their root systems, in what seems to be an evolutionary error, aren't designed to support such tall heavy tops. Tree surgery sessions at Jungle Tide are X-rated viewing as guys toting chainsaws but lacking any form of harness, goggles, headgear or gloves clamber up tree trunks and hang out precariously as they saw off great branches. They do use ropes, but only so the ground crew can pull the falling timber in the right direction to stop it crushing other plants, structures or bystanders. Trunks and large branches are planked up and used for a variety of purposes, mostly in the garden.

Dog days

Buddhists are forbidden to take life. But a poor village family can't afford to feed endless dogs as their bitch keeps on breeding. Living on subsistence wages they can't afford to get the creature spayed either. Aaiyo! What to do? Abandoning the puppies is OK with the Lord Buddha it seems. That way you're not taking life, even though the result of your actions is almost certain death for the puppies. In Sally's day it was common practice to put unwanted puppies live in sacks and leave them on the road for cars to run over. Then only the unsuspecting car driver gets a dent in his chances of attaining Nirvana as well as in his fender. Stray dogs act as though they own the roads. "These dogs, they all think they safe, Madam, because most drivers Buddhist people. But these dogs not safe because I am Christian man" was the wry comment of one of our drivers.

We were returning home from Kandy one afternoon when Sally noticed three tiny puppies in a roadside ditch about a kilometre from Jungle Tide. There seemed nothing we could do so we drove on. But back at the house one of our guests had seen them too, and she and Sally soon decided on a rescue mission. Confronted with doe-eyed vulnerability resistance is futile so I kept my reservations to myself. I'm not a dog person but had readily agreed that in Sri Lanka we'd need to have a few dogs both to deter unwanted human visitors and to keep the monkeys and wild pigs at bay. But I had expected to get there in a planned way, involving breeders, inoculations and having first bought the requisite doggy paraphernalia, not via a gut response to seeing some small abandoned creatures. Hard-hearted bastard that I am.

One of the puppies, all less than a month old, was already dead by the time the rescue party reached them. Sally and our guest brought the other two back and quickly engaged Rani in the conspiracy. After a month the puppies – both female and called Zoe and Bou – seemed to be thriving. Then the Kandy Mystery Puppy Disease struck. Our British dog-loving friends all said "Oh, you mean Parvo." No, we mean the Kandy Mystery Puppy Disease, almost always fatal and apparently unknown to veterinary medicine either as to its cause, its epidemiology or its cure. And confined to the Kandy area. So off to the vets in a tuk-tuk. An hour's journey down a bumpy road is not good for sick animals and the vets, while professional and stupidly inexpensive compared to their British counterparts, do have an obsession with heavy-duty vaccines as the solution to all animal problems. Zoe survived the trip to the vets and just about survived the trip back but didn't last the night.

Bou, though, was getting stronger and turning into a useful little dog. Short for Boudicca as her recklessness in the face of overwhelming odds (monkeys rather than Romans in her case) rivalled that of the famous Iceni warrior queen. But she too had to make the long and bumpy tuk-tuk journey to the vets in Peradeniya a few times to get her various planned injections. Not much fun as she suffered from chronic motion sickness. A rash of Latino mania had hit the Kandyan tuk-tuk community as drivers began to sport a variety of mystifying slogans: *NEW GENERATION FOR CARIBBEAN; BOB MARLEY LIVE ON; PIRATES OF THE CARIBBEAN; CARIBBEAN OF THE PIRATES; PIRATES OF THE CAR BEAN; CHEGUVRA WANT YOU RIBEL.* What??? It was a long while before I deciphered that one as 'Che Guevara Wants You to Rebel' Later I spotted a rival one displaying the slogan *THE VICTIMS OF CHE GUEVARA.* Did this mean war? And why do long-forgotten goings-on in Latin America seem to hold such fascination for Sri Lankan tuk-tuk drivers?

Then, at five months, Bou also succumbed to the KMPD. Even I was pretty upset and Sally and Rani were heartbroken. We still had Kuta, Martin's now elderly dog. Kuta has been around almost since Martin and Rani moved in, chosen as the then strongest of the various pie dogs that originally infested the place and the one most likely, if fed, to defend his and our territory. And so it proved until he got into one fight too many and almost died. I'll spare you the gory details but only Sally's insistence on Martin taking him to the vets saved his life and he still has a lopsided look. But he's OK, if a little arthritic and ancient of days.

We've since acquired two almost fully grown dogs, Toffee and Suki, from Sonia, an expat who rescues abandoned puppies, spends a fortune on getting them inoculated and stuffed full of healthy things and then gives them away to good homes when her long-suffering husband, with whom I'm inclined to identify, calls a halt to further acquisitions until a couple of humane disposals have taken place. Toffee and Suki are old enough to have survived the risk of the KMPD and, with Kuta, have formed a doggy team to defend Jungle Tide. Toffee is big, noisy and cowardly and probably has some Labrador in her bloodline. Suki is small, quick and brave and from her colouring seems to have had some Friesian cow in her ancestry. We have also acquired a tiny cat, which is of no more than ornamental and nuisance value.

Our hens, by contrast, are very useful indeed. Once our volunteers had finished constructing a dog- and mongoose-proof chicken run, feeder station and shed off went Martin to collect the hens from a contact of his. Martin has a contact for everything. He phoned HQ to check with Sally before bringing them to their new home from where they can gaze on their less fortunate cousins in the intensive chicken sheds next door. I only heard one end of the conversation: "Martin, are you sure all these are ladies? We don't want any boy chicken." Martin must have replied in the affirmative. "And these ladies, all injection have?" (Affirmative). "These all clean ladies, Martin?" (Affirmative). "Good, you bring these ladies to Jungle Tide."
I wondered whether we were opening a brothel as a side-line business, but no.

Eggs, fruit, vegetables, sustainable timber – Jungle Tide is becoming more self-sufficient almost by the day, though I am absolutely set against us prefixing anything with 'eco'. I'm not prepared to make the necessary compromises and I don't like telling lies. Besides, most tourist places prefixed with 'eco' are no more than an excuse for accommodating guests with more money than sense in infested mud huts and charging $200 a night for the privilege of being in touch with nature and local culture. Allegedly. But Sally ploughs on, not content with eggs and garden produce. She now makes most of our bread and has started making cheese – initially simple cottage cheese, then progressing to a mean Feta using milk from a neighbour's goat, and now trying her hand at Cheddar. By the time you read this, for all I know she may have mastered Stilton.

Here endeth the last lesson

So what of the future? After almost two years of residence and two decades of visits I'm still learning to live in Sri Lanka. I certainly haven't attempted the language (or languages – though I don't expect to learn much Tamil). Unlike Sally's Dad who as a would-be planter was required to pass exams in spoken Sinhala and Tamil and was fluent in both, as well as in Urdu. English is one of three official languages in Sri Lanka which is my defence against accusations of laziness, but truth be told I do feel guilty about my lack of effort in learning Sinhala. Must try harder. Sally used to speak Sinhala and a little Tamil as a child and is finding it all coming back to her, slowly. She was in a shoe shop the other day and asked the assistant whether they had a particular pair in black, size six. He called back in Sinhala to a colleague who replied in Sinhala that they only had brown in that size. "Only brown?" said Sally disappointedly. "You speak Sinhala!" exclaimed the assistant in surprise. "No, I don't" said Sal. "But you understand Sinhala. My *malli*, he speaking Sinhala and you understand!" "*Tikkak*" (a little) agreed Sal.

Tikkak is about as much as I know so far about my new home. Every day brings surprises. Every day challenges my assumptions. Every day a mixture of delights and disappointments. Serendip is not paradise. Some of the politics are more poisonous than the *tic polonga* (Russell's Viper). Our experience with the Excise in particular did jolt us into thinking whether Sri Lanka is the place we want to make our future. The jury's still out.

I came from one small island to live in another smaller one, in a world that is itself becoming more insular, less outgoing and welcoming by the day. I'd love to say I was immune, a genuine citizen of the world, but the truth is that most of my friends here are other expats rather than Sri Lankans, and almost all of them British or other Anglophones. We all have some Sri Lankan friends and a few have Sri Lankan partners. This is not any kind of exclusive, gated community such as you may find in the Algarve, say. But we are birds of a feather, nonetheless. We tend to like the same activities – walking, gardening, cooking – and similar books, music and films. Every January the Galle Literary Festival brings together top local and international writers. In 2016 it even had an offshoot in Kandy and for a pifflingly small sum I managed to sit next to and chat to Sebastian Faulks at lunch. Sadly they're not repeating the Kandy experiment though our daughter Jemima – the performance poet Jemima Foxtrot – was one of the artists appearing in the 2017 event in Galle and got to perform for and meet the Prime Minister, Ranil Wickremesinghe. The festival is rightly rated as one of the top literary events outside Europe and North America and Sri Lankans ought to feel proud of it, but very few attend. The audience mostly consisted of expats and foreign visitors.

What of England? I miss the seasonality more than anything other than people. And pints of bitter in country pubs in summertime. And berry fruits. And pies. We persuade our British and other European visitors to bring us out supplies of good cheese, decent coffee, salami and other things one can't get in Sri Lanka (or which are only available in Colombo at the price of a mortgage). But that doesn't extend to crocuses, draught beer or strawberries, and is a little on the risky side with pork pies. No doubt by the time we're due to come back to Jungle Tide from our first long return visit to the UK I'll be desperately missing *pol sambol, kirihodi,* (which is not as you may suppose a part of the Latin Mass but a delicious spicy soup) short eats, bananas that actually taste of something and unripe mangoes served up with salt and chilli. Not to mention the sunshine and warmth.

I love England and I love Sri Lanka. I don't have much time for the way either place is run and, as is doubtless the case the world over, the people in both countries are a mixture of good, bad and indifferent. The Brexit vote brought me up sharply, aside from what the ensuing fall in the pound did to our income. It was sobering to realise how petty and ignorant are so many people in the land of one's birth. But on reflection that's true of probably every country. Even Scandinavian ones – or so our many Scandinavian guests assure us.

Sally gets the last word. Inevitably. A couple of years before we left England we saw and hugely enjoyed the film *The Best Exotic Marigold Hotel.* "That's given me an idea for Jungle Tide" said my beloved. "When we get old, we can make it our personal care home. Martin and Rani can be our carers. Good idea?"

Acknowledgements

The custom, it seems, is to thank one's best beloved last of all but this book could not have happened without Sally's stories, ideas and continuous input at all stages of the writing. The great majority of self-published books clearly could have done with the attentions of an editor and doubtless this one is no exception. But believe me, it would have been even worse without Sally's critical and helpful reading. But most of all, I want to thank Sally for putting up with twenty five years of bad puns and puerile humour.

Huge thanks to Marion Rout for the cover artwork and ideas for design, abetted I understand by someone I've not met and know only as 'Eric the Tech' – thanks, Eric!

Thanks, too, to my daughter Jo for proof-reading several early chapters and teaching me the rudiments of that skill. Of course, any errors are mine.

Brenda Sedgwick and Lynfa Moses gave invaluable advice on self-publishing and I am also grateful to various people who read and made helpful comments on parts of the book at various stages: Harry Swift, Jo and Andy Wiggans, Rita Ward, Brian Batson and Meg Rossoff.

Jerry Smith
November 2017

Printed in Great Britain
by Amazon